WOMEN TORCH

The Story of the Woman's Christian Temperance Union

ELIZABETH PUTNAM GORDON

Heaven doth with us as we with torches do,
Not light them for themselves.

—SHAKESPEARE.

SECOND EDITION

NATIONAL WOMAN'S CHRISTIAN TEMPERANCE UNION
PUBLISHING HOUSE
Evanston, Illinois

"Hold high the torch! You did
 not light its glow;
'Twas given you from other
 hands you know.
'Tis only yours to keep it burn-
 ing bright,
Yours to pass on when you no
 more need light.
For there are little feet that
 you must guide,
And little forms go marching
 by your side;
Their eyes are watching every
 tear and smile,
And efforts that you think are
 not worth while
May sometimes be the very
 helps they need,
Actions to which their souls
 would give most heed,
So that in turn they'll lift it
 high and say,
'I watched my mother carry it
 this way.'"
　　　　—Nelle B. Bradley in
　　　　The Youth's Companion.

Hold High the Torch

Crusaders of Hillsboro, Ohio, December 1873.
Praying in Front of a Saloon.

Dedicated to the members of the Woman's Christian Temperance Union—a multitude of home-loving, heroic and progressive patriots. Their activities, for fifty years, have made possible a Golden History and a Golden Prophecy.

FOREWORD

A Bible seer must have included The Woman's Christian Temperance Union in his prophetic utterance when he declared, "The women that publish the tidings are a great host." For fifty years a multitude of American white ribbon women have proclaimed the gospel of total abstinence, purity, peace and prohibition and are now sending to the ends of the earth the glad tidings of national victory over the thraldom of the liquor traffic.

In writing "The Story of the Woman's Christian Temperance Union," the historian could include only such names and statistics as are needed to make the account graphic and helpful. Principles and facts are emphasized that the oncoming generation may catch the spirit of the marching mothers of the Crusade and realize the high historic points of the national and international growth of the Woman's Christian Temperance Union. One of the outstanding results of the education, agitation and organization of the Woman's Christian Temperance Union, from Crusade to Jubilee days, is the steady growth of public opinion in support of the fundamental principles of total abstinence for the individual and prohibition for the state and nation. Hence, it is essential to the history of the W. C. T. U. that high authorities in science, social economy, the church and the government should be cited. This is as joyous a feature of the story of fifty years as is the victorious culmination in the writing of the Eighteenth and Nineteenth Amendments.

The phenomenal history of fifty years cannot be compressed into one volume. A chronological summary given in the Appendix furnishes dates and data for handy reference. Fortunately the names of hundreds of noteworthy white ribboners who nobly and ably laid the foundations of the National W. C. T. U. are given in state histories, in state and national annual reports, *The Union Signal,* and in *The Brief History* prepared by Katharine Lent Stevenson. May we not reverently say that they are also recorded in "The Manuscript of God."

The book is published under the direction of a subcommittee of the National W. C. T. U. Jubilee Committee.

E. P. G.

Contents

ILLUSTRATIONS

CHAPTER I

The Woman's Crusade

IN the annals of history, December 17, 1917, is an epochal victory date. There was enacted that day in the Capital City of the United States one of the greatest moral, economic and legislative triumphs of the world. By a more than two-thirds vote the House of Representatives of the Sixty-fifth Congress passed a resolution submitting to the states a National Constitutional Prohibition Amendment— the Eighteenth. The Senate concurred. Ratification by three-fourths of the states occurred. On January 29, 1919, the Acting Secretary of State, Hon. Frank Lyon Polk, issued a proclamation declaring prohibition of the liquor traffic a part of the fundamental and organic law of the land. The law went into effect on January 16, 1920.

On that memorable day of decision, December 17, 1917, the friends and foes of prohibition crowded the galleries of the House of Representatives. Mother-hearted women and women masterly in leadership were there. From Maine to California, from the Great Lakes to the Gulf of Mexico, they had come. What had been their part in the setting of such a marvelous scene—a picture worthy to be etched on a Heavenly canvas? Who were these womanly women representative of all that is best in the home and church? They were the members of the Woman's Christian Temperance Union organized in every state and territory, an organization that for over forty years had been waging a peaceful war against the most relentless enemy of the home, the legalized liquor traffic.

"In the beginning," in the winter of 1873-1874, there were brave, home-loving Crusaders, the mothers and grand-mothers of these present-day white ribboners assembled December 17, 1917, in Washington, D. C. God heard the sorrowful, appealing cry of suffering women and children that went up from countless homes. He called to the defense of helpless humanity His last reserves—the mothers, wives, sisters and daughters. With mighty power the Cru-

1

sade swept over the land. How little the women realized
that it was the genesis of the Federal protection of the
home and the Federal emancipation of women. This revolt
of American womanhood against the legalized liquor traffic
was one of the greatest moral upheavals of the nineteenth
century.

In her Crusade classic, written in 1895, Frances E.
Willard gives this pen picture of the leader of the Crusade:

"Every whirlwind has its first leaf; for the laws of
motion oblige it to begin somewhere in particular. Other
leaves are gathered in so rapidly that it is usually impossible
to tell which one stirred first; but whichever that one was,
with it the whirlwind began. The 'Ohio Crusade' has
passed into history; the 'Ohio Crusaders' have won an in-
extinguishable fame. The 'Women of the West,' who led
the 'Whisky War,' as it is called through the British Empire,
gained for themselves, without intending it, the pioneer
place in that great Woman's Temperance Movement that
now belts the globe. The whirlwind of the Lord began in
the little town of Hillsboro, on the twenty-third of December, 1873. There the pentecost of God descended, and seventy women, without the slightest preconcerted plan, lifted
their hands as silent witnesses, when asked by the good
ministers and the famous lecturer, Dr. Dio Lewis, if they
were willing to go out from their homes and pray in the
places where their husbands, sons, and brothers were
tempted to their ruin. There the Crusade Psalm was read;
a rallying cry, 'Give to the Winds thy Fears,' was sung; and
the first silent, prayerful procession of wives and mothers
moved along Ohio streets. The gentle-hearted woman whom
they chose as their leader by spontaneous acclamation, was
one whose heart had been chastened by glorious discipline
and sorrow. Away back in 1836, she had accompanied her
father, then an Ohio delegate to the National Temperance
Convention held in Saratoga, New York, and when, at his
request, she went with him to the door of the hotel dining-
room, which afforded ample accommodation for all the
delegates in that rudimentary period of the movement, and

2

he asked her to enter with him, Elizabeth Thompson, who was a girl of but twenty years, naturally hesitated, saying to her stout-hearted sire: 'Why, father, I am afraid to go in. I looked through the door, and there were no women present, only men.' Upon this the governor exclaimed: 'Come right along with me; my daughter must never be afraid to be alone in a good cause!' And taking her by the arm, he introduced the first woman who ever entered a National Temperance Convention. Who shall say that in this scene— how much more worthy of a painter than most of the subjects that they choose!—we have not a prophecy of what was to transpire nearly forty years later in the town of that sweet girl's nativity? Ancestry counts for much, and it should never be forgotten, in our study of heredity, that the leader of the Crusade came of a long line of devout Christian ancestors, whose earlier history dated back to Virginia, that famous state which was the home of George Washington, and is known in history as the 'Mother of Presidents.'

"Hillsboro is the cradle, even as Washington Courthouse is the crown of the Crusade. So far as I can learn, the women of Hillsboro put forward no claim, nor did their leader. Perhaps, this was because there was no need for them to do so; and to my mind, the strongest confirmation of their deserved pre-eminence is the quiet, gentle, peacemaking spirit that they have shown from the beginning. For my part, I can testify that it has only been 'by the hardest' that her comrades have been able to induce Mrs. Thompson to come forward and gently take her place as 'leader of the first Praying Band.' On some notable occasions, this typical woman of the home, the church and school has stood forth as a historic figure. Who of us, whose lot has been cast as an officer or delegate to the National Convention since the beginning, can forget the genial, smiling presence and piquant words of that Crusade mother whom we all love so much? To hear her tell the story of the way in which the movement broke out in Hillsboro is an experience to be cherished for a lifetime. Her quaint, refined presence; her mild, motherly face, framed in its little cap;

3

her soft voice; her peculiar manner of utterance, combining remarkable originality with the utmost gentleness and good breeding; her inimitable humor; and, most characteristic of all, her deep, abiding faith in God and in humanity—all these have made an indelible impression, and helped, beyond what we can at all estimate, to form the character of the White Ribbon Movement. Naturally of a conservative disposition, Mrs. Thompson has, nevertheless, kept time to the company's music; she has taken every wave of the onrolling tide of impulse that we believe to be from God, as a strong swimmer breasts the incoming waves of the sea. It was no trifle for a woman with the traditions of 'Old Virginia' to accept our woman's suffrage resolution away back in 1877; and the beauty of it was, that her manner of announcing the faith that was within her lent so much of quiet strength to the decision of the Convention.

"It was my good fortune, as far back as 1876, to make a tour among the Crusaders of Ohio, visiting well-nigh forty of their towns and villages. I could write a volume on the history, experience, and inspiration of that memorable pilgrimage. It was one of the few times in my life that I ever went forth alone; and I was mothered in the homes of those devoted women with a tenderness that will never be forgotten. My own stipulation in making the trip was that I should go to Hillsboro, the home of Mrs. Thompson, and to Springfield, the home of Mother Stewart, in both of which we took sweet counsel together.

"Mrs. Thompson's home is the old family mansion where the governor spent all his days, and which he bequeathed to his beloved only daughter. It stands on a slight ascent and in a wooded grove, at the edge of a well-built town of four thousand inhabitants, and is as roomy and hospitable as heart could wish. Here I met Judge Thompson, the genial, witty lawyer, and the husband of our leader; Mrs. Marie Thompson Rives, the accomplished elder daughter; and Henry Thompson, the youth who brought the tidings to his mother that she was expected at the church on that memorable morning. I longed to see that lovely younger

4

daughter, who from her pocket Bible brought to her mother the Crusade Psalm that is the Magna Charta of the White Ribbon Movement; but she was gone, having been married to Herbert Tuttle, the distinguished professor in Cornell University, Ithaca, New York."

Mother Thompson's own account of her Crusade call is a valuable record. She tells of the lecture given by Dr. Dio Lewis of Boston, in Hillsboro, Ohio, December, 1873. She did not attend the meeting, but her sixteen-year-old son, much excited, ran home to tell the thrilling incidents of the evening. This is her story:

"My son related how Dr. Lewis told of his own mother and several of her good Christian friends uniting in prayer with and for the liquor-sellers of his native town, until they gave up their soul-destroying business, and then said: 'Ladies, you might do the same thing in Hillsboro if you had the same faith'; and turning to the ministers and temperance men who were upon the platform, he added: 'Suppose I ask the ladies of this audience to signify their opinions upon the subject.' They all bowed their consent, and fifty or more women stood up in token of approval. He then asked the gentlemen how many of them would stand as backers, should the ladies undertake the work, and sixty or seventy arose. 'And now, mother,' said my boy, 'they have got you into business, for you are on a committee to do some work at the Presbyterian Church in the morning at nine o'clock, and then the ladies want you to go with them to the saloons.'

"My husband seemed asleep as he rested upon the couch, while my son, in an undertone, had given me all the above facts, but as the last sentence was uttered, he raised himself upon his elbow, and said, 'What tomfoolery is that?' My son slipped out of the room quietly, and I betook myself to the task of consoling my husband with the promise that I should not be led into any foolish act by Dio Lewis or any association of human beings. But after he had relaxed into a milder mood, continuing to call the whole thing, as he understood it, 'tomfoolery,' I ventured to remind him that

5

the men had been in the 'tomfoolery' business a long time, and suggested that it might be God's will that the women should now take their part. Nothing further was said upon the subject that had created such interest the night before, until after breakfast, when we gathered in the family room. First my son approached me, and placing his hand gently upon my shoulder, in a very subdued tone said, 'Mother, are you not going over to the church this morning?' As I hesitated, and doubtless showed in my countenance the burden upon my spirit, he emphatically said, 'But, my dear mother, you know you have to go.' Then my daughter, who was sitting on a stool by my side, leaning over in a most tender manner, and looking up in my face, said, 'Don't you think you will go?' All this time my husband had been walking the floor, uttering not a word. He stopped, and placing his hand on the family Bible, that lay upon my work-table, said, emphatically, 'Children, you know where your mother goes to settle all vexed questions; let us leave her alone'; withdrawing as he spoke, and the dear children following him. I turned the key, and was in the act of kneeling before God and His Holy Word, to see what would be sent me, when I heard a gentle tap at my door; upon opening it I saw my dear daughter, with her little Bible open, and the tears coursing down her young cheeks, as she said, 'I opened to this, mother. It must be for you.'

"She immediately left the room, and I sat down to read the wonderful message of the great 'I am' contained in the one hundred forty-sixth Psalm. No longer doubting, I at once repaired to the Presbyterian Church, where quite a large assembly of earnest workers had gathered. I was at once unanimously chosen as the president, Mrs. (General) Joseph J. McDowell as vice-president, and Mrs. D. K. Fenner, secretary of the strange work that was to follow. Appeals were drawn up to druggists, saloon-keepers, and hotel proprietors. Then the Presbyterian minister (Rev. W. J. McSurely, D. D.), who had up to this time occupied the chair, called upon the chairman-elect to come forward to the 'post of honor,' but I could not; my limbs refused to

Annie Wittenmyer

Eliza Thompson

Mother Stewart

Zeralda Wallace

bear me. So Dr. McSurely remarked, as he looked around upon the gentlemen: 'Brethren, I see that the ladies will do nothing while we remain; let us adjourn, leaving this new work with God and the women.'

"As the last man closed the door after him, strength before unknown came to me, and without any hesitation or consultation, I walked forward to the minister's table, took the large Bible, and opening it, explained the incidents of the morning; then read the Psalm, and briefly (as my tears would allow) commented upon its new meaning to me. I then called upon Mrs. McDowell to lead in prayer—and such a prayer! It seemed as if the angel had brought down 'live coal' from off the altar and touched her lips—she who had never before heard her own voice in prayer! As we rose from our knees (for there were none sitting on that morning), I asked Mrs. Cowden (our Methodist minister's wife), to start the good old hymn, 'Give to the Winds Thy Fears,' and turning to the dear women, I said, 'As we all join in singing this hymn, let us form in line, two and two, the small women in front, leaving the tall ones to bring up the rear, and let us at once proceed to our sacred mission, trusting alone in the God of Jacob.'

"It was all done in less time than it takes to write it, every heart was throbbing, and every woman's countenance betrayed her solemn realization of the fact that she was going 'about her Father's business.' As this band of 'mysterious beings' first encountered the outside gaze, and as they passed from the door of the old church, and reached the street beyond the large churchyard, they were singing these prophetic words:

'Far, far above thy thought,
    His counsel shall appear,
When fully He the work hath wrought
    That caused thy needless fear.'

"On they marched, in solemn silence, up to Main street. After calling at all the drug-stores, four in number, their pledge being signed by all the dealers save one, they entered

7

saloons and hotels, on this and subsequent days, with varied success, until by continuous daily visitations, with persuasion, prayer, and song, and Scripture readings, the drinking places of the town were reduced from thirteen to one drug store, one hotel, and two saloons, and they sold 'very cautiously.' Prayer-meetings were held during the entire winter and spring, every morning (except Sunday), and mass-meetings in the evenings, at the Methodist Church one week and at the Presbyterian the next. This is, in brief, the story."

There were scores of prominent leaders whose names might well be mentioned, but Mother Stewart (Mrs. E. D.) of Ohio, was one of the outstanding Crusaders in the state and nation. Her personality and work were unique. In the south, as well as throughout the north, she thrilled her audiences as she pictured the adventures and power of the marvelous Crusade. Her fervent appeals awakened public sentiment for total abstinence and the closing of the saloons by law. She was the first American woman to carry the Crusade impulse across the sea; and her enthusiasm greatly helped in the formation of the British Women's Temperance Association.

At the fiftieth Crusade Anniversary Convention held September 7-14, 1923, in Columbus, Ohio, Anna A. Gordon entitled her presidential message, "The Marching Mothers of the Crusade."

"To Ohio's hallowed soil we have come," she said. "On the victorious battle-ground of the Crusade State we are to let the mighty memories of thousands of Crusade marching mothers have their complete, profound, pentecostal way with us. So shall we more adequately meet the challenge of the old crusade by the march of the new crusade—a 'March of Allegiance' to the polling booths of 1924.

"Fortunate are we of the National Woman's Christian Temperance Union to inherit the holy Crusade spirit kindled on thousands of Crusade altars by these women called of God. Their daring courage, their persistent faith, their superb attack on the strongholds of the liquor traffic forever will be the wonder-feature in the story of our great and victorious reform. The Crusade was an anguished protest of home-loving, cultured, ballotless women. It began in the winter of 1873 and, according to one chronicler, 'In fifty days it drove the liquor traffic, horse, foot and dragoons, out of two hundred fifty towns and villages, increased by one hundred per cent the attendance at church and decreased that at the criminal courts in almost like proportion.'

"At the height of their dauntless adventure, a sweet-voiced Quaker woman led her band to the chief saloon in an Ohio village. 'What business have you to come here?' roared the affrighted dealer. Going to the bar, she laid down her Bible and said, 'Thee knows I had five sons and twenty grandsons, and thee knows that many of them learned to drink right in this place, and one went forth from here maddened with wine and blew his brains out with a pistol ball; and can't thee let his mother lay her Bible on the counter whence her boy took up the glass, and read thee what God says: "Woe unto him that puttest the bottle to his neighbor's lips?"' '

"Like a prairie fire the Crusade swept across our continent. Frances E. Willard, as a young teacher, had an enthralling glimpse of it in Pittsburgh, when she knelt in front of a saloon with a praying band. Another prohibition hero, Henry W. Blair, termed this Christian uprising 'a great moral commotion, in which woman escaped and learned her power, never again to be caged.' Mrs. Annie Wittenmyer, first president of the National W. C. T. U., characterized it as a 'flash of heavenly light, a mighty spiritual swirl, a staggering blow that sent the rum-power reeling toward its fall.' Hundreds of dram-shops were closed, countless barrels of alcoholic drink gurgled into the gutters as church bells pealed forth the people's joy.

"One of the many attempts of the liquor trade to ridicule the marching mothers was made in January, 1874, at Canton, Ohio. A spectacular poster advertising the 'Great American Crusade Circus and Menagerie' was pasted on the doors of churches and the homes of Crusaders. Its chief decorative attraction was an American eagle gracefully carrying in his talons something strongly resembling our emblematic white ribbon. 'A partial list of animals' appeared with a brief description of each—a clue to the Crusader's name. Associated with the 'female rhinoceros,' 'laughing hyena,' 'northern gorilla,' 'American tiger,' and many others, we find 'The American deer—a very fine looking doe, better looking than the *majority* of the other animals that are allowed out of their cages—captured at *Ida* Island.' This Crusader of Canton, none other than our honored Ida Saxton McKinley, later became the beloved mistress of the White House.

"A few of the elect souls in Ohio and other states who forever wear the halo of the Crusade are: Mrs. Eliza J. Thompson, Mrs. M. G. Carpenter, 'Mother' Stewart, Mrs. H. C. McCabe, Mrs. W. A. Ingham, Mrs. Mattie McClellan Brown and Mrs. Abbie F. Leavitt of Ohio; Mrs. Jennie Fowler Willing, Mrs. E. E. Marcy and Mrs. Emily Huntington Miller of Illinois; Mrs. Annie Wittenmyer and Mrs. Dr. Gause of Pennsylvania; Mrs. Esther McNeil, Mrs. Mary C. Johnson and Miss Margaret Winslow of New York; Mrs. Mary A. Livermore and Mrs. Susan A. Gifford of Massachusetts; Mrs. Dorcas J. Spencer and Miss Emma Janes of California; Mrs. Hutchins Hills, Mrs. Fenner and Mrs. O. H. Wendell of New Hampshire.

"Forty-three years before the Ohio Crusade, in Auburn, New York, a saloon crusading band of women was led by Mrs. Delecta Barbour Lewis. This impressive incident occurring during the boyhood of her son, Dio, led him later in life, when a popular lyceum lecturer, publicly to urge this method upon the women in saloon-cursed communities. Fortunately for accurate history of the Crusade miracle, Dr. Lewis wrote in 1874 the vivid story of his early life and the winter of 1873.

" 'There was trouble at our house when I was a small boy. My father had forgotten everything but drink. There were five of us small people. Our mother, with her own hands provided for all. She earned and cooked our food, cut and made our clothes—in brief, was father, mother,

10

general provider, cook, housekeeper, and nurse. In addition to all this, she was the victim of abuse and violence. Often she would cry in the presence of her children, and sometimes, when she could bear it no longer, she would drag her weary limbs up into the garret. We knew what she went up there for, and sometimes we could hear her say, "O God, help me, help me! O Lord, how long, how long?" Then she would keep very still for a while. When she came down to us again, her cheeks were wet, but her face shone like an angel's. She taught us to pray. We grew up with a very large estimate of the power of prayer. The day was never so dark at home that mother could not go up into the garret and open the clouds. Today, more than forty years after those darkest times, I believe in my heart that woman's prayer is the most powerful agency on earth.

" 'Nineteen years ago, when I first began to speak in public, I prepared a lecture upon the potency of the prayers of women in grog-shops, which during those years I have delivered more than three hundred times. Lecturing before the lyceums of Ohio during December, 1873, I gave two evenings to the discussion of woman's prayer-meetings in saloons. In Hillsboro and Washington Court House, where this lecture was given, the women rose at once and declared they were ready. I saw the hour had struck. The world knows the story. I have not a doubt that the women of America will rid the country of dram-shops, if they can preserve the Christ-spirit in which they have begun, continue their combined movements against the enemy, give the politicians and wise men a wide berth, and keep themselves in the spirit of humble prayer before God.'

"Hatchets played a conspicuous part in the Crusade story. In the popular mind, today, Carry A. Nation of Kansas alone shares with George Washington pictorial hatchet history.

"It is happily true that in more than one of the early Crusades, hatchet brigades of devout praying women helped answer their own prayers for the utter destruction of their dread enemy—intoxicating liquor. One instance in proof must suffice. The date is fifteen years ahead of the general Crusade movement of 1874. The scene is Baraboo, Wisconsin, described by the narrator of the phenomenal story, Mrs. W. A. Hartwell, now of Milwaukee, as a 'most charming and lovely village looking as though made by a master artist, in a great workshop of beauty.' The arch enemy of the home entered its sylvan borders, and soon, to the consternation of the women, three groceries and two hotels established liquor bars. In vain the women prayed and pleaded with the business men of the town. Homes were ruined, and terrible crimes were committed by men under alcohol's influence. Then the mothers, wives and daughters 'struck.' Forty women of the influential circles of the home and church—women young and middle-aged—one fair morning in May, 1859, quietly marched down the main street of the village—doubtless appearing to the men as harmless as a flock of sheep. The fashionable outer garment of that period—the shawl—furnished a hiding place for the hatchets borrowed from home woodsheds. Hammers also were tucked away ready for use by these serene-faced but militant souls.

"The women, well versed in strategy by home experience, divided forces at each point visited, and they called at the widely separated groceries and hotels in successive and undisturbed regularity. At each point of attack, half the women engaged the proprietor of the building in conversation and heated argument, while the second group proceeded at once to the business in hand. Cellars were entered, kegs of beer rolled out, and barrels of whisky knocked in. As the liquor gurgled into the street, a crowd, suddenly gathered, sent up cheer after cheer of encouragement for the hatchet brigade and its effective efforts. Husbands and lovers, Mrs. Hartwell tells us, stood in the background, but never lifted their voices against this amazing spectacle. Mrs. Hartwell, just blossoming into young womanhood, ought to be believed when she tells us that lovers were there enjoying the bravery of their sweethearts. Some of the men with thoughtful mien were heard to remark, 'Wouldn't wonder if some day women will vote.'

"An exciting public meeting was held that night in the village church. No one uttered an adverse word about the forty brave women of Baraboo. Papers were numerously signed pledging the boycotting of liquor-selling groceries, and these groceries soon went out of the liquor business.

"No officer in Baraboo could be found by the enraged property losers to sign a warrant for the arrest of the women. Fifteen miles over the Baraboo bluffs the saloon men traveled and in the tiny hamlet of Sauk a man was persuaded to sign a warrant. The women were arrested and fined $500. Their attorney would not give bail and the women were committed to the Baraboo jail. Later, they were released, on a writ of habeas corpus, by a high-minded county judge who held them to bail for six weeks, saying at the expiration of that time he would announce his decision. The judge's decision that the defendants had not committed a crime and should be discharged, was rendered in a crowded courtroom. Turning to the attorney for the liquor men, the judge asked if he wished to hear the reasons on which this decision was based. Quickly came the illuminating and not unexpected reply—'No.'

"Today, the ballot is being vigorously used by the Christian women of this nation to annihilate the nullifiers of the Eighteenth Amendment—an amendment which the Crusaders and their hatchets helped to place in the Constitution of the United States. Would an application of the real hatchet to the illegal saloon, where one exists, speed to earlier victory the present-day struggle of the temperance forces?

"On December 14, 1873, at Fredonia, New York, Dr. Dio Lewis made his inspiring suggestion that women should enter upon a crusade against the direst foe of their homes. On that eventful date, cultured home women, two hundred and eight in number, with prayer and song marched two by two into the saloons and hotel barrooms of Fredonia, with Mrs. Esther McNeil as their devoted leader. What is more, they organized, the following day, under the name, Woman's Christian Temperance Union, and are justly proud of thus

13

antedating by nearly a year the name adopted at the organizing convention of the National W. C. T. U., November, 1874, in Cleveland, Ohio. Losing sight of this background of isolated instances of Crusade bands and of the fact that from Hillsboro and Washington Court House, Ohio, the Crusade fire that contagiously spread from point to point first blazed forth, we are justified in naming Ohio the Crusade State because of the large number of towns, cities and villages where the intrepid praying bands of women successfully carried on their holy warfare against the saloon.

"When Mrs. Judge Thompson and the seventy women who followed her, solemnly marched forth, two by two, from the Presbyterian Church at Hillsboro, Ohio, December 23, 1873, singing 'Give to the Winds Thy Fears,' God's hour had struck for the beginning of the end of the legalized liquor traffic in our liberty-loving republic."

Do not these Crusade stories picture some of the "greater things" that should come to pass? The inspired writers, Matthew, Mark, Luke and John, have given to all ages the story of Christ's gospel of "Peace on Earth, Good Will to Men." At Christmas time in America, in 1873, the echoes of that song reverberated down through the centuries, for to the women of the American Crusade came a Divine call—a compelling commission to carry to all nations a blessed interpretation and fulfillment of the joyful song of the angels.

Frances E. Willard

CHAPTER II

MOBILIZATION AND ORGANIZATION

IT was a victory-vision that initiated and invested with power the Woman's Christian Temperance Union. This God-given insight came to the Crusaders and their friends who attended at Chautauqua, New York, in August, 1874, the National Sunday School Assembly. At the suggestion of Mrs. Mattie McClellan Brown, a committee composed of women from all over the country sent out a call for a national delegated convention to meet in Cleveland, Ohio. This official invitation was signed by Mrs. Jennie Fowler Willing, chairman, and Mrs. Emily Huntington Miller, secretary. God's time had come for the deliverance of the pitiful victims of a pitiless liquor traffic. At Cleveland, Ohio, November 18, 19 and 20, 1874, the National Woman's Christian Temperance Union was organized with these officers: president, Mrs. Annie Wittenmyer of Pennsylvania; corresponding secretary, Miss Frances E. Willard of Illinois; recording secretary, Mrs. Mary C. Johnson of New York; treasurer, Mrs. W. A. Ingham of Ohio.

Frances E. Willard and Mrs. Mattie McClellan Brown presented a notable plan of work, Miss Willard writing this famous resolution: "Resolved, That, recognizing the fact that our cause is, and will be combated by mighty, determined and relentless forces, we will, trusting in Him who is the Prince of Peace, meet argument with argument, misjudgment with patience, denunciation with kindness, and all our difficulties and dangers with prayer."

The constitution was presented by Mrs. J. Ellen Foster of Iowa. The declaration of principles, including the pledge for total abstinence and the promise to work against the traffic in alcoholic liquors, written by Frances E. Willard, was a new Declaration of Independence—creating a higher level of thought for American manhood. These daughters of Puritan foremothers, inheriting the power to discern spiritual values, had a right to ask that, under the guarantees of the Federal Constitution, their homes should be protected from the iniquitous liquor traffic, living and thriving on the destruction of all most dear to them.

With ribaldry and sneers the liquor men had written and talked of the Woman's Crusade. To them it was merely an absurd, ephemeral movement that would be crushed quickly by the age-long appetite and avarice of men. What could ballot-less and money-less women do against a business entrenched in politics and in partnership with the government of the United States? This advanced step, however, this mobilization of American womanhood, this determined National W. C. T. U., brought dismay to the hearts of the brewers and distillers. Women of social prestige who joined this new organization met ridicule with reverence. Their Magna Charta was the word of God, "The way of the wicked shall be turned upside down." Their work was religious and patriotic. It was in the line of evolution and also of revolution. Their issue was the home, church and state versus the liquor traffic. This was made articulate in the W. C. T. U. national motto: "For God and Home and Native Land." In answer to the question so often asked in those history-making days—"What is the Woman's Christian Temperance Union?"—this was the comprehensive reply: "It is an organization of Christian women banded together for the protection of the home, the abolition of the liquor traffic and the triumph of Christ's Golden Rule in custom and in law; and it is the lineal descendant of the great Woman's Temperance Crusade of 1873-1874."

The reasons for joining the organization and signing the total abstinence pledge are given in this Declaration of Principles, written by Frances E. Willard:

"We believe in the coming of His Kingdom whose service is perfect freedom, because His laws, written in our members as well as in nature and in grace, are perfect, converting the soul.

"We believe in the gospel of the Golden Rule, and that each man's habits of life should be an example safe and beneficent for every other man to follow.

16

"We believe that God created both man and woman in His own image, and, therefore, we believe in one standard of purity for both men and women, and in the equal right of all to hold opinions and to express the same with equal freedom.

"We believe in a living wage; in an eight-hour day; in courts of conciliation and arbitration; in justice as opposed to greed of gain; in 'Peace on Earth and Good Will to Men.'

"We, therefore, formulate and for ourselves adopt the following pledge, asking our sisters and brothers of a common danger and a common hope, to make common cause with us, in working its reasonable and helpful precepts into the practice of everyday life:

" 'I hereby solemnly promise, God helping me, to abstain from all distilled, fermented and malt liquors, including wine, beer and cider, and to employ all proper means to discourage the use of and traffic in the same.'

"To confirm and enforce the rationale of this pledge, we declare our purpose to educate the young; to form a better public sentiment; to reform, so far as possible, by religious, ethical and scientific means, the drinking classes; to seek the transforming power of Divine grace for ourselves and all for whom we work, that they and we may wilfully transcend no law of pure and wholesome living; and finally we pledge ourselves to labor and to pray that all these principles, founded upon the gospel of Christ, may be worked out into the customs of society and the laws of the land."

Although formulated in 1874, this Christian Patriotic Declaration is still a maker of exalted public sentiment, the only change being in the pledge which, because of the national prohibition victory, now reads:

"I hereby solemnly promise, God helping me, to abstain from all distilled, fermented and malt liquors, including wine, beer, and cider, and to employ all proper means to secure the enforcement of the Eighteenth Amendment to the Federal Constitution."

During the administration of the first president, Mrs. Annie Wittenmyer, who had been prominent for years in church, journalistic and philanthropic work, twenty-three

17

states were organized as auxiliaries to the National W. C. T. U. and a National W. C. T. U. paper was founded. Mrs. Wittenmyer worked earnestly for the society. In all its earlier years, she also labored tirelessly in the lecture field, speaking sometimes six evenings in the week, besides traveling hundreds of miles. She attended all the large conventions, of which in 1875, forty-six were held. One of the notable acts which characterized her administration was the sending of a letter of inquiry to the International Medical Association, which met in Philadelphia in the summer of the Centennial year. This led to a hearing before a committee of celebrated physicians of Europe and our country, and resulted in the well-known "resolutions" expressive of the most important medical opinion against intoxicants on record, when the representative character of those who gave it is considered. Still another official act was the holding of the first "Woman's National Camp Meeting" at Ocean Grove, New Jersey, which, conducted wholly and addressed largely by women, commanded the earnest attention of the thousands present, and was equally remarkable for spiritual and intellectual power.

At the sixth annual convention of the organization held in Indianapolis, Indiana, in 1879, Miss Frances E. Willard of Evanston, Illinois, at the age of thirty-seven years, was elected president. Miss Willard was free to accept the national position, for she had resigned her educational responsibilities as Dean of Women and Professor of Belles Lettres in Northwestern University. The story of Frances Willard's career, as thrilling as romance, is admirably told by her biographer, Anna A. Gordon, in "The Life of Frances E. Willard," published by the National W. C. T. U. In the victory story of today, only the high points in the life of this notable educator, traveler. philanthropist, organizer, orator and seer will be touched upon. She was one of the greatest women of the nineteenth century.

"All history," says Emerson, "resolves itself into the biography of a few stout and earnest persons. Their success lay in the fact, not that they were born great, but that

God's thought for that century found in them an unobstructed channel so that the wonders, of which they were the visible conductors, seemed to the eye, their deed. That which to an outsider looked like will and immovableness was really willingness and self-annihilation." The greatest need of the world, as Elizabeth Barrett Browning has said, is—

> "God's light organized
> In some high soul crowned capable to lead
> The conscious people; conscious and advised;
> To plant the great Hereafter in the Now."

In the eons of history, as the thought of the world had been awakened by a Moses, a Columbus, a Luther, a Wesley, a Lincoln, so in the nineteenth century a new moral and spiritual atmosphere was created by Frances E. Willard. "My life a vow" was the spirit in which she faced her adventurous task.

The Woman's Christian Temperance Union today owes largely to Frances Willard the organization plans that are carried on in every state and territory of our country, and in fifty nations federated in the World's W. C. T. U. Gifted with a rare imagination, "that searchlight of the soul," Miss Willard had also a genius for constructive detail seldom equaled. With inherited pluck and a Willard's (Will Hard's) will she wrought out her world vision.

In 1876-7, on invitation from Mr. Dwight L. Moody, Miss Willard assisted him in Boston, for several months, in his gospel work. In undertaking this enterprise, she hoped that the temperance work might be united with the gospel work, and with it be brought to the front. The meetings for women, filling Berkeley and Park Street churches, and her words before the thousands gathered in the great Tabernacle, are memorable.

Mary A. Lathbury, in her introduction to Frances Willard's "Woman and Temperance," written in 1883, calls attention to one of Miss Willard's unfulfilled desires: "The deepest thought and desire of my life," said Miss Willard, "would have been met, if my dear old Mother Church had permitted me to be a minister. The wandering life of an evangelist or a reformer comes nearest to, but cannot fill, the ideal which I early cherished, but did not expect ever publicly to confess. While I heartily sympathize with the progressive movement which will ere long make ecclesiastically true our Master's words, 'There is neither male nor female in Christ Jesus'; while I steadfastly believe that there is no place too good for a woman to occupy, and nothing too sacred for her to do, I am not willing to go on record as a misanthropic complainer against the Church, which I prefer above my chief joy."

Years later, Miss Willard gives this account, so interesting to young women. of her first glimpse of Anna A. Gordon, then in her happy girlhood: "On my going to conduct the women's meetings for Mr. Moody in Boston, in 1877, there was no one to play the cabinet organ that was beside my desk on the platform. An earnest appeal was made, and after a painful pause and waiting, a slight figure in black, with a little music roll in her hand, came shyly along the aisle of Berkeley Street Church, and Anna Gordon gently whispered, 'As no one volunteers, I will do the best I can.' That very day she had taken her first lesson on the organ, meaning to become mistress of that instrument.

"She had just attended Mr. Moody's noon-meeting, in which the text had been 'Whatsoever He saith unto you. do it,' and had promised in her inmost heart that, by God's grace, she would try to do helpful things as the opportunity offered, and behold, the very first 'opportunity' was to come forward before twelve or fifteen hundred waiting women, and 'start the tune.' When I knew these things, I said in my heart, 'this is a rare, young spirit.'

"When I asked Anna Gordon if she could come and play for us every day, she said she would try, and I soon turned over my letters, messages, etc., to her faithful care. In the prompt and accurate execution of commissions, tactful meeting of people, skillful style in corresponding, I have not known her equal. As soon as the meetings were over, she had a lecture trip ready for me, extending all through New England.

"For fourteen years Anna was with us at Rest Cottage, and as my blessed mother grew older, she resigned into Anna's hands more and more of the care. The house became a charming place, as years passed by, and I was able to do more to make it the home I wanted it to be, chiefly for my mother's sake; then dear Mrs. Thorpe and Mrs. Ole Bull of Cambridge, Massachusetts, added that beautiful room, an enlargement of the 'Den,' and we 'set our house in order' with great particularity when we expected that beautiful woman, Lady Henry Somerset."

In 1881, the charming but conservative women of the "solid south" were enlisted in large numbers in the peaceful war of the Woman's Christian Temperance Union. On this first southern trip, accompanied by Anna Gordon and sponsored by Mrs. Sallie Chapin of Charleston, South Carolina, and Mrs. Georgia Hulse McLeod of Baltimore, Maryland, Frances Willard made the white ribbon "God's olive branch of peace." Her message, her faith and love, and her warm handclasp were mighty, cohesive forces. "It was the first ray of hope that had come into our lives since the Civil War." said one of Miss Willard's grateful, gentle hearers; and another, a cultured, forceful woman who later became prominent in National W. C. T. U. work, enthusiastically exclaimed to a friend: "The first time I heard Frances Willard I lay awake all night for sheer gladness. It was a wonderful revelation to me that such a woman could exist. I thanked God and took courage."

Bishop Stevens, who, as Colonel Stevens, commanded the battery that fired the first shot on Fort Sumter, introduced Frances Willard to a magnificent audience in Charleston, South Carolina, and thus fired the first moral shot at the greatest enemy that imperiled the southern homes. In his gracious speech, he said: "Our friend tells me there were three reasons why she was almost afraid to come with a public message to the south; first, because she was a woman; secondly, a northern woman, and last of all, a temperance woman. We warmly welcome her, for she brings us the magic initials, W. C. T. U. Shall we not interpret them to mean: We come to unite the north and the south and we come to upset the liquor traffic." An editor, hearing of this remark, said: "The W. C. T. U. is certainly a womanly organization, for the W. C. T. U. means 'Washing contracts taken unconditionally,' and the white ribbon women are in the forefront in washing the stains from the nation's flag."

The writer was with her sister and Miss Willard on this memorable trip and well recalls the delighted surprise and spontaneous response of the men and women in Frances Willard's many large audiences. In Nashville, Tennessee, a young man student said to her:

"Hundreds of people, many of them students, are here tonight, out of curiosity. They had never thought it possible for a woman to speak so superbly. We are naturally so conservative about women, but as Miss Willard stands before us tonight, she is the embodiment of the qualities she said women should possess, 'womanliness first—afterward what you will.' She seems to us so sisterly and so motherly, with a divine mind." Realizing, as Miss Willard did, the extreme prejudice of the south against women's public work and its great need of redemption from the liquor traffic, she humbly sought the wisdom that comes from God, and always knelt in prayer as she left her room to meet a public engagement. At the next national convention, held in Washington, D. C., when southern women for the first time met in counsel with their northern sisters, they enthusiastically said to their beloved leader and friend, "We have enlisted with you to wage a peaceful war for God and Home and Native Land."

A unique incident that occurred during one of Mrs. Sallie Chapin's organizing trips through the southern states shows the kindly spirit that in religious and temperance work existed between the white and colored races. When Mrs. Chapin had finished an address to negroes, one evening in a state not far from her own. a colored minister arose and said: "I don't care what state claims Mrs. Chapin; these Southern ladies were all raised in our laps. They are of us, and Mrs. Chapin was sent an angel from heaven, to talk to my poor, downtrodden race and to raise us to the skies. I ain't an educated man, but if I knew every language in the world, all put together, I would not know words enough to express our love and gratitude. We will, in a body, promise you, Mrs. Chapin, to work for prohibition, ma'am; we will follow you all over the world with our prayers, go where you will; you won't be able to get out of the reach of them. and we will, God helping us, meet you in Heaven."

In one year, 1882-1883, these pioneers traveled 30,000 miles, visited every state and territory in the nation, every capital city save one and completed an itinerary that, by the census of 1880, included every city of 10,000 or more inhabitants. They organized state and local unions. Always, Miss Willard averred, that without Anna Gordon's devotion, versatility and aid in speaking, she could not have carried out so successfully her program of organization. What wonderful trips they had in the twenty-one years of comradeship, and into how many families and churches they carried the thought that "only the Golden Rule of Christ can bring the Golden Age of man." How many hardships they happily endured! The principles of total abstinence for the individual, and prohibition for the state and nation, were from the first reiterated; also the plans for membership, and "dry" campaigns, for petition work, for woman suffrage. and for legislative and congressional hearings and bills. Frances Willard was a pioneer in all these lines. It was she who first suggested scientific temperance instruction in the public schools and quarterly temperance lessons in the Sunday schools. Always she emphasized the importance of work among young people and boys and girls. She initiated child welfare and social morality measures, reached out a welcoming hand to foreign-speaking people and endeavored to secure justice and better living conditions for women and children in industry.

On this nation-wide trip, unprecedented in the annals

of womankind, these pioneers were makers of American history. "Across the Continent," letters to *The Union Signal,* narrated racy and patriotic incidents, and providentially, no accidents. In her first travel notes to *The Union Signal* in March, 1883, Miss Willard writes, "As our train rolls over these Missouri plains, this line sings itself in my heart:

'No pent up Utica contracts our powers,
But lo! the whole broad continent is ours.'

"This seems to me the genius of our beloved W. C. T. U. and I gladly work on the circumference of its widening circle during these years of my prime, anticipating with not infrequent desire the future years when I hope to work nearer its center."

The travelers were royally dealt with by the St. Louis ladies and Miss Willard by her addresses added largely to the membership. She was delighted with a lecture by Professor William T. Harris, who by invitation of the notable author, Louisa May Alcott, then secretary of the Concord (Massachusetts) W. C. T. U., was writing a scientific temperance textbook.

As our white ribboners sped along over the continent, they were purifying the springs of human life. Like the torch-bearers, of whom the celebrated poet, Alfred Noyes, so brilliantly has written, Frances Willard was lighting many torches as she won the hearts of hundreds of women, saying to them, "Mother love works magic, but organized mother love works miracles."

En route from Sante Fe to Tucson, Frances Willard wrote: "At Trinidad, Colorado, we found Professor Henry E. Gordon (brother of Anna), a graduate of Amherst College and principal of the New West Commission Academy. He introduced me to a genuine cowboy, and I was indeed glad to rectify my opinion of a class much misunderstood by the east. He loves a free, outdoor life above all things— yet he is bound to make himself the heir of the ages as well, so he studies with Professor Gordon." Here a W. C. T. U. and a Band of Hope were organized. Continuing that jour-

ney, the travelers reached Santa Fe and were entertained in
the pleasant home of Mrs. William Breeden, wife of the
State's Attorney. A saloon on an advantageous corner was
called the health office; another the senate, and a third, the
little church. "Could ghastly travesty go further?" Miss
Willard wrote. "Whitin University," named for Mrs. John
C. Whitin of Massachusetts, who helped to set it literally
"on its feet" was visited, also the Presidio or old palace
where Gen. Lew Wallace finished writing that matchless
book, "Ben Hur." At Albuquerque, a thriving W. C. T. U.
was organized.

Pioneer traveling had its delightful surprises, as well
as its unsuspected dangers. Miss Willard possessed an unusual gift of racy humor and keen insight. No difficulty
could daunt her, and in her search for a new world of vital
morality she "sailed on and on," ever overcoming prejudice
and injustice; and as Anna Gordon's heritage was one of
joy, delight in music, poetry, scenery and little children, the
days of travel were never monotonous. Years after, in one
of her merriest moods, Miss Willard wrote thus of her
cherished traveling bag: "There isn't a particle of humbug
about it. All through these many years it has gone its way
in varied climates and has met adverse circumstances; it has
been evilly and despitefully treated, used as a footstool. a
writing desk, a pillow; it has patiently disgorged thousands
of letters, postals and documents, but it survives, and I deem
it the fittest of all survivals to me personally known." Often,
as she encountered new experiences, there came to Miss
Willard a keen remembrance of the happy years of overseas
travel. She was eager to see and know everybody and
everything—unchanged from the old days when a girl,
standing in the barn door of Forest Home, she said to her
sweet younger sister, Mary, "Shall we ever go anywhere,
know anything. or see anybody?" In Tucson, for ten years
the capital of Arizona, a W. C. T. U. was organized, and
early in May the travelers arrived at Los Angeles.

"We are at last in the land of enchantment," Miss
Willard wrote, "where heliotrope climbs all over the fronts

25

of the houses; where corn grows seventeen feet high, and one can have a bouquet of fresh roses and a strawberry short-cake on the table all the year round. We are with people as genial as the climate, and breathe an air that makes wine seem more than ever an unnecessary and absurd exhilara-tion. The dignified president, and the keen brained secretary of the California W. C. T. U., came from San Francisco, five hundred miles, to meet us. The big hearted Californians have given us a most generous reception. The mayor of Los Angeles, at our first meeting, welcomed us on behalf of the town, the clergy on behalf of the church, and the Good Templars for the grand lodge of the state. Blessings on them all!"

In San Jose, California's "garden city," Miss Willard's visit was the event of the season. It seemed a sort of poetic and practical justice that in the auditorium where a recent political convention had pledged, at the behest of whisky, the repeal of the Sunday law of the state, the foremost champion among women for temperance should protest in the name of the women of California; and protest she did, with cogency of argument, originality of illustration, and chasteness of rhetoric. Her keen satire, vehement censure, trenchant reasoning and impassioned appeals were accom-panied with a womanly grace and dignity that convinced the intellects and won the hearts of the people. One thousand dollars was received in collections at the meetings held in California, but Miss Willard generously left it all to the state W. C. T. U. to be used in strengthening the unions she had organized.

In addresses given later, in the east, Miss Willard was wont to draw lessons from an incident of her wonderful trip to the Yosemite Valley. As she rounded "Inspiration Point" with a party of holiday Methodists, the greatest vision of her life opened to her view. All her hopes had been realized. She said: "I have seen Niagara, but then the lips moved and comments passed, but before that wondrous Yosemite Valley view, where God had seemed to condense in such a wonderful degree His loveliness and beauty, one involun-

tarily paid the highest homage—the silence that is golden."
Then, with an expression of intense sympathy, she exclaimed, "Never before have I been so sorry for the people
who are blind." She often stated that the temperance reform was a moral Yosemite and marked the antitheses in
strikingly beautiful descriptions.

The California W. C. T. U., organized in its early years
as one state union, later was divided into two unions—
North and South. The tour of the state by Miss Willard
and Miss Gordon is a record of hospitable reception, in all
the chief cities of this commonwealth of the Pacific coast.
In San Francisco, Oakland, Berkeley, Stockton, Sacramento,
Grass Valley, and at other points in northern California,
friends entertained them, planned public meetings for adults
and for children, and gave the travelers a fine send-off as
they steamed up the coast to Oregon.

"Beautiful for situation, and a generation hence, the
joy of this noble republic, is Puget Sound," wrote Miss
Willard four months after leaving Boston. "Welcome,
Puget Sound, with its fathomless land-locked blue and the
imperial presence of such snow-clad mountains as are found
nowhere else, no, not in Switzerland. Here is the Pacific
cowed and conquered, purring like a tamed tiger at the seat
of these young cities. No one can appreciate the transformation save those who, like ourselves, have experienced
the untold miseries of the voyage between San Francisco
and Astoria, Oregon. We are happy to have been borne
hither on 'that tide in the affairs of men, which, taken at
the flood, leads on to fortune.' There is a boom on every
hand. Henry Villard has just been here, the magic railway
king of the Northern Pacific, a branch of which will visit
every leading town upon these lovely shores."

The new Northwest was a wonderland to the travelers.
As a girl, Frances Willard had been thrilled with the story
of the adventurous pioneer missionary, Marcus Whitman,
who saved for the United States the "Oregon Country,"
now the three states of Oregon, Washington and Idaho.
Miss Willard realized that she and the Woman's Christian

27

Temperance Union were beneficiaries of Mr. Whitman's genius. Early settlers told Miss Willard of his splendid missionary and temperance work with the Indians and of his heroic mid-winter horseback ride of 4,000 miles from the Valley of the Columbia to Washington, D. C., a ride for life or death rivaling in historic interest that of the renowned Paul Revere. Whitman, this martyred man of destiny, was imbued with an unselfish love of humanity and devotion to his country. His aim was to reach Congress before adjournment. After weeks of floundering through mountains, snowdrifts and dangerous ravines, encountering savage beasts or savage men, he reached Washington, D. C., March 3, 1843. Suffering with frozen limbs and clothed in torn fur garments and leather breeches, he stood, a tragic and dignified figure, before the President of the United States. His story was a complete refutation of the statements of senators and representatives, who, having no patriotic vision, had asserted: "The Rocky Mountains are an impassible barrier whose bases are skirted with deserts of irreclaimable land." "I will never vote one cent to place the Pacific Coast one inch nearer to Boston than it is now." "The people of the Pacific and those on the Atlantic can never live under the same government." So successful was Whitman's appeal that a treaty was consummated with Great Britain, and on August 5, 1845, the great Northwest came under the American flag.

> "Our Whitman rode to save
> New stars for freedom's banner.
> Three stars he added to that flag of fame,
> And won an empire and a deathless name."

As a Christian statesman, Miss Willard often said that a student of history is always an optimist. She well remembered the emigration of 1,000 people from the east that followed Whitman's visit to Washington, and in her imagination pictured the scene, as with 125 wagons, 1,000 head of cattle, sheep and horses, these venturesome people reached the top of the Rockies and viewed the Pacific slope. Entertained throughout her trip, in simple but delightful homes, Miss Willard realized that she was meeting with descendants of that memorable eastern emigration of 1843 who adventured, not for selfish trade, but for godly homes. Pondering on the tremendous difficulties overcome by Whitman in his journeys, and especially in his dealings with Congress, Miss Willard took courage for her seemingly insuperable task. In her heart of hearts, "a fire burned for a beacon light." Like Sacajawea, the Indian princess, who, at sixteen, with her baby on her back, led brave pioneers through trackless forests to this unclaimed country, so Frances Willard, possessing the brain and brawn of her distinguished pilgrim ancestors, resolved, with God's help, to point out to these privileged people living in the Valley of the Columbia, a still higher civilization, the only sure way of protection for their homes.

The fine temperance influence of these eastern-western pioneers is typified in the story of an Indian boy who had received instruction in one of their schools. In a village conference on the licensing of a saloon he was given a chance to speak and said: "One thing I must have put on paper—that you white men no more sell Indians rum. White man makes it heself; he must drink it heself." In the territory of Oregon, early in its history, a prohibitory law was passed, but later, through the efforts of unscrupulous liquor politicians, was repealed. A prominent minister met an emigrant family going west. On one of the wagons there hung a jug with the bottom knocked out. "What is that?" asked the doctor. "Why, it's my Taylor jug," said the man. "And what is a Taylor jug?" asked the doctor again. "I had a son in General Taylor's army in Mexico and the general always told him to carry his whisky jug with a hole in the bottom; and that's it. It is the best invention I ever met with for hard drinkers."

"I never knew nobler women than those of Oregon," wrote Miss Willard in June. "Portland was the storm center of a wonderful crusade in '74. We have grand audiences, over ninety delegates, and a delightful Band of

Hope meeting, in whose procession of children marched a dear old soldier, one hundred years old, carrying his banner side by side with the boy whose drum taps guided the long procession into the church. Anna Gordon organized a large Y. W. C. T. U., addressed the convention, and also spoke to the Band of Hope. The convention was one of deep spiritual power."

In Seattle, the beautiful town terminus of the Northern Pacific, the first general temperance convention ever called in Washington territory was held. Delegates came from twenty-five towns; seventy-nine gentlemen and one hundred and five ladies. A W. C. T. U. for the territory was organized and a Christian Voters' League that declared for "prohibition straight" and the "full ballot for women." The leading pastors and the mayors of the respective cities— Olympia, New Tacoma, Seattle and Port Townsend—were among those who gave God-speed to the messengers of the W. C. T. U.

As nature had divided the territory by the Cascade Mountains, it was thought best to have two, separate, state organizations. A two days' convention at Cheney resulted in the organization of a W. C. T. U. for eastern Washington, as the convention at Seattle gave a western division. Attendance at Cheney was good, representatives coming from Walla Walla, Colfax, Spokane Falls, Deep River, Medical Lake and elsewhere. "All hail, bright young stars of the new Northwest!" wrote Miss Willard.

In her official letter, Miss Willard tells of an interesting adventure that occurred in Lewiston, Idaho. Leaving the railroad at Texas Ferry, the travelers took the pleasant steamer, "John Gates," for an eighty-mile trip up the Snake River to Lewiston, the oldest town in Idaho. In their roomy stateroom, especially reserved and the best on the boat, they wrote letters, articles, and read with infinite zest the "Letters and Memorials of Jane Welsh Carlyle," prepared for publication by her unique husband. "A more breezy, zestful, pungently flavored book I have not whetted my literary appetite upon in many a year," wrote Frances Willard.

Esther Pugh, Lillian M. N. Stevens (standing),
Caroline B. Buell, Frances E. Willard, Mary A. Woodbridge.

"Jane Carlyle is as refreshing as Puget Sound's salt flavored air, Mount Hood's August zephyrs, or the cherries in an Oregon temperance woman's garden."

On reaching Lewiston, Miss Willard heard that the city authorities, taking advantage of a diphtheria scare that was abating, had forbidden all public meetings—just two days before the long-time advertised date on which Frances Willard was to speak. Leading citizens declared that this action had its animus in the liquor traffic. However, not to arouse antagonism, it was resolved to heed the admonition. In the parlors of a noble-hearted Presbyterian lady, the leading women of the city assembled, and after earnest waiting upon God, proceeded to organize the convention, adopt a constitution, and select the officers. When it was time for the travelers to return to the boat, the whole convention packed the coach.

Everywhere, the travelers were greeted with wonderful floral decorations—mottoes, arches, banks, pyramids, symbolic designs— and all in flowers. In New Tacoma, a beautiful arch was placed over the entrance to the Opera House with a motto, "God Speed Temperance," and nobody interfered with it. One of the features in all the meetings in the "New Northwest" was the amazing number of babies present. Indeed, no sight was so familiar as the young parents entering church, or hall, the father gently carrying his little one.

Bishop Hargraves, of the M. E. Church South, had it about right when he said, "Montana has barely enough valleys to slip in between its hills." Never was a territory more aptly named. For beauty of railway scenery, Frances Willard thought no country furnished anything superior to the panorama between Spokane Falls and Missoula, Montana, on the spick and span new Northern Pacific. At Spokane Falls, about this time, when a division of the railroad hands on this splendid Northern Pacific road was paid off, within fifteen days, $6,000 of their money was in the tills of the saloons. Learning this distressing fact, Miss

Willard emphasized in her addresses the economic value of prohibition.

The travelers left Missouli late in July, in a covered conveyance, for Helena and Deer Lodge—a distance of 182 miles—Rev. William Shannon, his wife and little girl thirteen months old, accompanying them. Mr. Shannon had sent the conveyance ahead the night before—eighteen miles beyond Missoula—as the railroad authorities had kindly permitted the party to ride on the construction train to that point, the western terminus of the great iron track. Here they clambered into the wagon behind the unmated steeds loaned from two separate establishments, packed away big box, little box, bandbox and bundle almost to the overflowing point, and set out, "overland."

With the morning they started on their third day's riding, passing the place where a few days previous the robbers sacked a stage and killed a horse. On the fourth day, they saw the logs beside the road from behind which, not twenty-four hours earlier, three masked men had pointed guns at the stage load, and afterward a private conveyance, making them stand and deliver. Perhaps, it was on the principle, "They that know nothing fear nothing"; anyhow, Miss Willard and her party went on their way rejoicing. They reached their destination without accident and took the scenic route—only five months old—across the continent. Two meetings were held on Sunday in Ogden, Utah, and the W. C. T. U. was reorganized. When the travelers reached the Mormon capital, a true-hearted band of women met them. The territorial W. C. T. U., which had disbanded, was reorganized.

During this epochal year, 1883. Miss Willard and Miss Gordon, with their shining torches, kindled the flame of truth in hundreds of homes, winning the hearts and memberships of a host of women. At the tenth annual meeting, held in Detroit, Michigan, Miss Willard etched on the receptive minds of her hearers, a vivid word-picture of this memorable nation-wide trip when, triumphantly, she said: "The Woman's Christian Temperance Union was never

32

weak, but it is a giant now! The Pacific Coast, the New Northwest, and the South, are all with us today. But yesterday, Mary A. Livermore of Massachusetts, sent to Sallie F. Chapin of South Carolina, our forces being assembled in both states, this telegraphic message: 'If your heart is as our heart, give us thy hand.' Back came the message from our gifted southern leader: 'For God and Home and Native Land, we'll give you both our heart and hand.' The W. C. T. U., headed by Mary A. Woodbridge, Mary T. Lathrap, Clara C. Hoffman, Lillian M. N. Stevens, Mary Allen West, Louise S. Rounds, and a host of others, cannot go forth in vain. In my thoughts I always liken our organization to Joan of Arc. Evermore she heard and heeded heavenly voices and God grant that we hear and heed them evermore."

Local organizations, veritable W. C. T. U. telegraph stations, multiplied. From town to town womanly women wearing the white ribbon agitated, educated and organized. As organizers, lecturers and evangelists each had the same live message. Inevitably, they created, almost unconsciously, an interdenominational and inter-organization fellowship and an intersectional spirit. They were the first organization of women to walk in this broad path. "Together," Edward Everett Hale said, "is one of the strongest words in the English language," and in co-operation with chivalrous men who were educational, church and business leaders, and pastors, astonishing temperance sentiment was created, even conservative public opinion favoring the protection of the home and children. The charm of many of the meetings held under the auspices of the W. C. T. U. was their homelikeness. This quality, already enriching religious work, was destined to come helpfully into government. These women believed, as Mrs. Harriet Beecher Stowe divinely put it, that, "Whatever ought to happen is going to happen."

The intrepid white ribbon leaders of the Pacific coast, second to none, lost no opportunity to present their ideals before civic officials and state and national legislators.

Miss Willard, seeing that women were being translated

33

from the passive to the active voice, said: "It seems to me our Heavenly Father trusts us just as fast and as far as He can. Brains clean from alcoholic fumes and brains unperturbed by the fever of this transition age, alone can carry the success of the co-operative forces by which we shall yet change the old proverb, 'each for himself and the devil take the hindmost,' to 'each for the other that there may be no hindmost for the devil to take.'

"The Woman's Christian Temperance Union is to my thought but a vast and growing net-work of telegraph lines, along which fly swift and blessed messages, transmitted by that divine spirit whose central battery is the heart of Christ. Slow, difficult and adventurous as is the work of building these lines, establishing the stations, enlisting and teaching the operators, one forgets the hardship in remembering what are the messages and whence they come throbbing over the wires with their sweet, 'Peace on Earth, Good Will to Men.'"

In ten years, the Crusade praying bands, intense, intrepid, inspired, had become not only in name but in reality, the National Woman's Christian Temperance Union—steadfast, patient, far-reaching in purpose and in plan.

Campaigning in Colorado, in 1924 (above).
Pioneering in Montana, in 1883.

CHAPTER III

THE FIGHT FOR A CLEAR BRAIN

IT was through her unusual power to perceive that every sociological, business, educational and legislative question has its temperance aspect, and her persuasive power to make others see this truth, that Frances Willard evolved her "Do Everything Policy"—in reality initiating the system of department work. In this unprecedented vision she was like Ruskin, who said, "One of the greatest things a human soul ever does in this world is to see something, and tell what it sees in a plain way."

Imbued with this power of seeing the truth, thousands of white ribbon women who understood the art of progressive planning and constructive conversation, invested their time in systematic work that helped to give all classes of society a new concept of human values. Because it was Christianity applied, the plan of the "Do Everything Policy" was eagerly followed. It was an evolution as inevitable as any traced by the biologist, or described by the historian. The fight for a clear brain was an inclusive, as well as a peaceful warfare. All temperance activities of men and women previous to the organization of the W. C. T. U., had been conducted in one straight line—contact with the drink maker and the drinker. A scientific age required study of this subject in its correlations; and Frances Willard's plan allied the W. C. T. U. with all other moral forces. This resulted in the gradual adoption of forty departments of work under the six general lines: Preventive, Educational, Evangelistic, Social and Legislative—besides the department of Organization; two important branches formed were the Young Woman's Branch and the Loyal Temperance Legion.

"Everything is not in the temperance reform, but the temperance reform should be in everything"—a statement giving the pith of the new policy, was a compelling ideal. As the white ribboners, praying, persuading, educating and electrifying, accelerated the pace of public opinion they saw on the banner lifted aloft by their leader, the winged watch-

35

word, "The fight for a clear brain is a fight for Christianity."

"A one-sided movement," Frances Willard often said, "makes one-sided advocates. Total abstinence is not the crucial virtue in life that excuses financial crookedness, defamation of character, or habits of impurity. We have known persons who (because they had never touched a drop of liquor) set themselves up as if they belonged to the royal line, but whose tongues were as corroding as alcohol itself and whose narrowness had no competitor save a straight line." In answering, years later, some who controverted her famous "Do Everything Policy" Miss Willard gave this enlightening reply: "When we began the delicate, difficult, and dangerous operation of dissecting out the alcohol nerve from the body politic, we did not realize the intricacy of the undertaking, nor the distances that must be traversed by the scalpel of investigation and research. More than twenty years have elapsed since the call to battle sounded its bugle-note among the homes and hearts of Hillsboro, Ohio. One thought, sentiment, and purpose animated those saintly praying bands, whose names will never die out from human history: 'Brothers, we beg of you not to drink and not to sell—' This was the single wailing note of these moral Paganinis, playing on one string. It caught the universal ear and set the key of that mighty orchestra, organized with so much toil and hardship, in which mingle the tender and exalted strain of the clanging cornets of science, the deep trombones of legislation, and the thunderous drums of politics and parties. Standing in the valley, we look up and think we see an isolated mountain; climbing to its top, we see that it is but one member of a range of mountains, many of them of well-nigh equal altitude."

The views of educated and thoughtful women of various church affiliations began to broaden. In their assemblies, for the first time questions concerning the home and motherhood, from a national, governmental and world-bettering standpoint were considered. The genius of Frances Willard was seen in the twofold aspect of her plan of activities— protection of the home and the awakening of womanhood.

"Woman," she said, "will bless and brighten every place she enters and she will enter every place upon the round earth."

In a convention address given during this period of agitation and education, the national president emphasized the necessity of bringing to the home, the church, and the electorate, the scientific and moral reasons for total abstinence. In her prelude, she said: "You who are here gathered from every quarter of this vast republic, are elected delegates, with a great constituency behind you. Your relationships are to the home that of protector; to the nation, that of purifier. What manner of persons ought we to be, who have come unto the kingdom for such a time as this? I look beyond this hushed and hallowed scene to the sweet homes where you are cherished, and to the sad homes which your faith and works have brightened. I look beyond the endless procession of light-hearted boys and girls, with shining faces and satchels on their arms obedient this morning to the sound of the school-going bell. I look beyond the radiant flag flying peacefully over this radiant land, and then I look at the two hundred and fifty thousand reeking and cavernous grogshops of America, while my heart bows with yours beneath the measureless meaning of it all, and our relation to the future's awful battle for the saving of the homes and the downfall of the liquor traffic." There was an enthusiastic response to this heroic, intimate appeal.

May we not liken the Woman's Christian Temperance Union to a life-giving tree, the various departments as branches and leaves, reaching out for the health and protection of all the people? It is a tree of God's own planting, of which poetically it may be said:

"The wind that blows can never hurt the tree God plants:
It bloweth East, it bloweth West, the tender leaves have
      little rest,
But every wind that blows is best; the tree God plants
Strikes deeper root, spreads wider boughs, grows higher still,
For God's good-will meets all its needs."

"Organized Mother-Love," as so aptly the W. C. T. U.

has been called, well knew the value of striking deeper root. Through two generations, the principles of the W. C. T. U. have gripped the hearts and minds of the boys and girls of America.

All over the country, throughout these campaigning years, numberless groups of young people sang Frances Willard's popular song, "Saloons Must Go." This sentiment-making chorus was like the shout of the triumphal host that marched around the walls of Jericho. Did the liquor traffic "list" to the warning in "the tread of many feet, from hill and farmhouse, school and street"? Little they realized that it was the children's crusade march—the march of victory; the march of total abstinence that in a generation gathered impetus and numbers until it helped break down the walls of the liquor traffic. How these children, grown to manhood and womanhood, rejoiced as the stars and stripes floated over a sober capitol and a sober nation. Verily, "work on the foundation is hidden and slow, but the firmer you make it, the higher you go." The children of every English-speaking people loved to sing the marching cadences of "Saloons Must Go" and its rendering by a thousand public school children was one joyful event of an evening mass meeting held in Toronto, Canada, in connection with a convention of the World's W. C. T. U. Frances Willard was deeply stirred when presented by a winsome child, with a beautiful bouquet of flowers. She told the eager boys and girls and the students who filled the galleries, of her belief that they would help establish for their homes and their country the highest and holiest habits of life.

With enthusiasm, they arose and repeated with her one of her own original watchwords, "Character is habit crystallized." How this popular song, "Saloons Must Go," came to be written is a little story of precious memory to Anna Gordon. Her widely used "Marching Songs for Young Crusaders"—a standard series—were active vote-makers and another number was desired. "You must write a song for this new book, Frank," Anna Gordon said to Miss

Mrs. Hannah J. Bailey Mrs. Anna S. Benjamin Mrs. Edith Smith Davis
Mrs. Adelia E. Carman   Mrs. J. K. Barney   Mrs. Sallie F. Chapin
Mrs. Emilie D. Martin Mrs. Mary H. Hunt Miss Elizabeth W. Greenwood

Willard when one day they were on the train going home from Chicago to Evanston. With her usual spontaneity, Frances Willard replied, as she tapped her foot rhythmically on the floor, "Shall it not be a march like this, Anna, and I'll call it 'Saloons Must Go.'" In less than half an hour, as the train reached Evanston, the copy for this soulful song was completed. One stanza just as it was written is given.

Mary T. Lathrap, the "Daniel Webster" of the W. C. T. U., who often had been thrilled as she heard this song, on one occasion enthusiastically exclaimed to a large audience, "If you put down your ear and listen, you will hear the tramp, tramp, tramp of ten thousand little feet, some of them in kid slippers, some of them in copper-toed shoes, and some of them, bless their dear little hearts, barefoot, and they have total abstinence pledges in their hands."

The ultimate goal of the white ribbon women was the protection of the homes and streets of every rural community and municipality. In the endeavor to secure safety for their loved ones, the women were learning the uses of strategy and common-sense, in the difficult operation of "dissecting out the alcohol nerve from the body politic." They knocked persistently at the door of the public school and Sunday school, and organized for the children-at-large the Loyal Temperance Legion. Here, they put into practice the scientific and moral teaching of the public and Sunday schools and into the lives of more than twenty million boys and girls there came the assurance that the privileges guaranteed under the Constitution—"life, liberty and the pursuit of happiness" would be theirs. Through the national leadership of the Loyal Temperance Legion for many years of Helen G. Rice of Boston, who had in Massachusetts the splendid backing of Mary A. Livermore, pledged Loyal Temperance Legion boys and girls held rallies, oratorical and musical contests—presenting the alcohol question from every conceivable standpoint. Mark Twain endorsed the viewpoint of the women who were building for a better citizenship when characteristically he said: "Training is everything. The peach was once a bitter almond, and the cauliflower is only a cabbage with a college education."

It was the dawn of the triumphant day of Federal Prohibition when the National W. C. T. U. secured in Congress and in all the states, beneficent laws requiring scientific temperance instruction in the public schools. Heroic scenes were enacted that might well be depicted in pageants. This mighty victory was naturally evolved from Frances Willard's initial plan given in 1874 at the first W. C. T. U. convention—"Teaching children in Sabbath Schools and public schools the ethics, chemistry and hygiene of total abstinence." Miss Willard inaugurated temperance instruction in juvenile unions, and in 1875 recommended that Miss Julia Coleman's "Temperance Catechism," and the temperance text-books, "The Bible Rule of Temperance" and "Alcohol and Tobacco," should be thoroughly taught to members of the juvenile unions.

In 1876, it was resolved that "the ruinous work done in our colleges and universities by intemperance should arouse our great fear and awaken our greatest efforts to secure such moral influence and such legislation as shall protect the gifted sons of this republic from this curse which makes all culture vain and all life a failure." The same year it was recommended "that our children in our public schools be taught the effect of alcohol on the system and Miss Willard asked that a manual of instruction and exercises should be published for the use of juvenile societies; also that a committee be appointed introducing temperance work into schools and colleges, saying that "three years of experience seem to indicate that the children of a country may be reached best through the schools." One of the resolutions passed was as follows: "That we recognize the relation of scientific truth to temperance and that we urge the teaching of God's natural laws respecting heredity and health as an essential part of temperance education."

At the W. C. T. U. convention of 1878, Mrs. Susan J. Steele of Appleton, Wisconsin, became chairman of the committee on colleges, seminaries and public schools. By

Miss Willard's special invitation, Mrs. Mary Hanchett Hunt of Boston, Massachusetts, attended the convention of 1879, and was appointed chairman of the standing committee of scientific temperance instruction. In 1880, at the convention held in Boston, Mrs. Hunt spoke of Sir Benjamin Ward Richardson's text-books as having been introduced into several of the states; also of the new primary book by Miss Julia Coleman of New York, of which she said, "This has been prepared with the utmost care and with reference to authenticity of statement and is, we feel, just what we want." In 1880, the designation of chairman having been changed to that of superintendent, Miss Willard nominated Mary Hanchett Hunt for superintendent of the department of Scientific Temperance Instruction, and she was elected unanimously. As Mary Hanchett, the natural sciences had been the specialty of the new superintendent, and in this department she taught with a success foretelling her life work. After her marriage, her interest in scientific studies continued. In 1873, when the Woman's Temperance Crusade swept over the country, reaching the east, Mrs. Hunt's thoughts were turned to the physiological or scientific side of the temperance question. These impressions were intensified by listening to lectures on "Alcohol and the Brain" given by Rev. Joseph Cook of Boston.

The seed-thought of teaching the children of all public school grades the value of total abstinence to a life, dropped into Mrs. Hunt's achieving soul, came to splendid fruition. "The Star of Hope of the Temperance Reform Stands over the Schoolhouse" was her watchword, as valiantly and nationally she battled for laws making mandatory, scientific temperance instruction in the public schools. In answer to Mrs. Hunt's cogent appeals, boards of education elected by beer- and whisky-drinking constituents said to her, "We must teach only what the law requires." Adequately backed by the National W. C. T. U., Mrs. Hunt proceeded to see that the law required in every state the teaching of scientific temperance. She made a careful study, in her travels, of the best and latest researches in England and France, as well

as in America, concerning the effect of alcoholic stimulants
upon the tissues of the body and the temper of the soul.
Her board of counselors was comprised of men of the highest distinction both in this country and abroad. The story of
this marvelous campaign and of Mary Hunt's great general-
ship, as well as the splendid co-operation of the W. C. T. U.,
is recounted in the libraries of all English-speaking nations.

It was Mrs. Hunt's custom to exhibit at each National
W. C. T. U. convention, a map of the United States, each
state being covered with a black cap. When a commonwealth secured a mandatory law requiring scientific temperance instruction in the schools, the black cap, amid
cheers, was removed. Before cutting the stitches from the
black cap covering Georgia, the last state to secure the law,
Mrs. Hunt said: "I stand in the presence of this map grateful for what God hath wrought. Its whitening fields, as cap
after cap has been taken from these states, speak of divine
purposes of mercy to us as a nation. My heart goes out to
the hundreds of thousands of women, the great rank and
file of the Woman's Christian Temperance Union, who have
stood by in carrying out every plan that led to the victory."
Mrs. Katharine Lent Stevenson of Boston said at this celebration: "We know that Frances Willard, the founder of
the World's W. C. T. U. and the greatest organizer of the
century, never showed her own powers of discerning leadership more clearly than when she nominated you, Mrs. Hunt,
in 1879, as chairman of the committee which afterwards became the department of Scientific Temperance Instruction.
We are glad to come in for our share, as individuals, in
your great victory, since 'we all belong' to the great organization which has helped to make it possible. We congratulate Georgia—the last state to pass the Scientific Temperance Instruction law."

The law in its provisions is far reaching. West Point
Academy, the Naval Academy, all the territories and the
District of Columbia are obliged, in any teaching supported
by Federal funds, to give a prescribed amount of instruction
upon the physiological effects of alcohol. It is believed gen-

erally by the allied temperance and religious forces that this temperance educational victory was the greatest factor in securing a Federal prohibitory law. It is still the strongest element in making public sentiment for the observance and enforcement of law. At Mrs. Hunt's request, in 1903, at the National W. C. T. U. convention held in Cincinnati, Ohio, the name of the Scientific Temperance Instruction department was changed to the Bureau of Scientific Temperance Investigation and Department of Scientific Temperance Instruction in Schools and Colleges. It is well to remember Mrs. Hunt's wise insistence that the children in the lower grades of the public schools should receive their full share of scientific temperance instruction—as a large number of them never reached the higher grades. In this extract from one of her addresses are seen the educational ideals and scientific facts that Mrs. Hunt gave to an oncoming generation:

"The slavery of alcohol and other narcotics is the worst of human bondages because it tends to become a willing bondage that enslaves the soul as well as the body of its victim, while it mortgages his children to the enslaver. It must be overthrown if our race is to move on, through generation after generation, up the heights of its utmost possibilities. The popular use of alcohol, usually begun in ignorance of its seductive power, is a menace to that capacity for self-government without which a republic must ultimately perish. A republic has no power with which it can compel majorities. As long as a majority of the people believe in alcohol, they will drink it, and they will vote for the manufacture and sale of alcoholic beverages. If we want the saloon closed, we must teach the majority, the law-making power, that alcohol is by nature an outlaw that should be banished from human habits and traffic. Compulsory scientific temperance instruction in the public schools is the one method that reaches the coming majorities.

"All history is the aggressive advance of the future upon the past, the field of collision being the present. Coming generations with clear brains and untainted blood are aggressively advancing on the alcoholic past of our inheritance, and are demanding of us a wise selection of weapons for this 'collision,' which is primarily a battle against ideas inciting to the drink habit that enslaves the drinker. It is the clash of the new teaching of modern science, that alcohol is a poison at war with human well-being, against the old notion that alcohol is a good creature of God for human sustenance. Here are the weapons for this warfare:

"1. Scientific investigation as to the character of alcohol and its effects on the human system.

"2. The widest diffusion of that truth.

"Education through the schools of all the people in the plastic period of childhood, before the appetite for alcohol is formed, in the physiological reasons for total abstinence from alcoholic drinks and other narcotics is the sane and sure method for the dethronement of alcohol. It is sane and sure because history has shown that in the ultimate contest truth is the strongest of all forces. God has so made the human mind that it cannot be forever inhospitable to truth which, sooner or later, overthrowing ancient error, sits enthroned in conscience, guiding human action.

"The child is born who will see the last legalized saloon, brewery and distillery of alcoholic drinks disappear from the land if we now do our part and get the truth to the people, to the majority, which is the law-making power. The day is surely coming when from the schoolhouses all over the land will come trained haters of alcohol to pour a whole Niagara of ballots upon the saloon."

After Mrs. Hunt's death in 1906, Mrs. Mary F. Lovell, Mrs. Hunt's department associate, was in charge of the important work until the National W. C. T. U. convention held in Hartford, in November, 1906, when Mrs. Edith Smith Davis of Milwaukee, Wisconsin, was elected national superintendent.

The Woman's Christian Temperance Union was most fortunate in securing another widely known leader of exceptional ability. Of distinguished English descent, college-bred and an author of reputation, Mrs. Davis easily obtained

44

a strong board of counselors which included men of recognized authority in science, medicine, philosophy and religion. Seeking to build on the enduring foundations already established by Mrs. Hunt and the W. C. T. U., Mrs. Davis toiled incessantly, and soon won for herself and her cause, friends and fame. In one of her first public utterances she said:

"Upon the broad basis of the past, we rest our hopes and our efforts for the greater work of the future. Law and gospel, fact and theory, science and sympathetic co-operation will all be blended in the great results which are yet to be achieved through this important line of work evolved and carried forward by the W. C. T. U. The latest statement of expert scientific investigation in relation to alcohol is that alcohol is a protoplasmic poison to all forms of organic life, and it is impossible to say what minimal amount can be taken and not be harmful to the tissues of the body. You tell me that Jeffries, the prize fighter, went down before Johnson. I tell you, no, Jeffries went down before alcohol. That is the history of every prize fighter from John L. Sullivan down to the present day. I look across the seas and I see those magnificent Olympic games over in Stockholm where the water-drinking American boys carried off trophy after trophy. I see Germany, England, France and Italy looking in amazement at the temperate Americans and I say, thank God for the truth which is being taught in colleges and the universities of the United States—that the athlete must leave alcohol and tobacco out of his life."

Through travel, Mrs. Davis came in close touch with the scientists of Europe as well as of the United States. She attended the meetings of the Congress Against Alcoholism in Stockholm and London; and in 1911, at The Hague, personally investigated the schools and temperance conditions in many a country of Europe. After years of experience, Mrs. Davis, in one of her fine forceful addresses, gave a most revealing incident: "Where there is no vision," she said, "the people perish. I have studied not only the children in the slums of New York, Chicago and St. Louis, but the little folk in the slums of Dublin, Glasgow, Edinburgh and London. I have looked into the white, pinched faces of children who have been robbed of their birthright by their own fathers and mothers; little ones who have come into this world crippled physically, mentally, morally and spiritually. General Booth in 'Darkest England,' wrote: "They are not born into this world; they are damned into it.' I want you to think for a minute of the children who have been robbed of that which can never be estimated in terms of dollars and cents. We know that alcohol, having a special affinity for the brain, puts to sleep the centers of inhibition and the boy taking it in any form is robbed of his self-control, while every animal passion is stimulated. We know that the child may be cursed before he is born by two dreadful venereal diseases and that back of both is alcoholism.

"Let me describe a scene which I witnessed in one of the most beautiful school buildings of St. Louis. As the teacher took a cluster of roses and pinned it to a curtain, she said: 'One.' Then she placed beside it another cluster of roses and said: 'One and one make how many?' And although some of the children had been with her for more than eight years, not a child in the room could tell how many one and one made. I asked the teacher if she could tell me the kinds of homes from which those children came. She replied: 'This is a very expensive private institution. We have a separate teacher and a separate attendant for each child. These children are from the richest, most beautiful homes in St. Louis and they are what they are through the drink habits of their fathers and their mothers.' "

Both Mrs. Hunt and Mrs. Davis specialized in the training of teachers—giving lectures in grade and high schools, and at summer institutes. Educators prized the scientific journals, charts, and carefully prepared experiments furnished by these leaders. On the death of Mrs. Davis, Mrs. Elizabeth O. Middleton of Kansas City, Missouri, was chosen national superintendent of the department. Ably and indefatigably she pushed the work along the lines so well established. Miss Cora Frances Stoddard of Boston,

Saloons Must Go.

1 Marching Song
for Loyal Temperance Legions
By Frances Willard

1. List to the tread of
many feet

From home & play ground
farm & street;

They talk like tongues
their words we know:

"Saloons, saloons, Saloons
must go."

First verse of "Saloons Must Go."
A facsimile of Frances E. Willard's original copy.

who had been made the head of the National Bureau of Scientific Temperance Investigation, became later the national superintendent in schools and colleges, while Mrs. Middleton continued to fill the important position of a department field worker. In a later chapter, the continued triumphs of this department will be given.

In this era, before the advent of the automobile, phonograph and moving picture, temperance mass meetings everywhere were popular, and large audiences assembled to hear the women speakers. Through the columns of the daily press, their speeches reached millions of readers and the W. C. T. U., this "tree" of God's own planting, rapidly "spread wider boughs" and grew "higher still." Frances Willard, always lecturing on the scientific phase of temperance, burned out her life for the childhood of the nation and of the world. Her creed, "My life a vow," was no conventional, impulsive statement. It really voiced, as did Mrs. Elizabeth Barrett Browning's "Cry of the Children," an impassioned, unflagging desire for the protection of the boys and girls. Many of Miss Willard's heartfelt utterances almost unconsciously were woven into the fabric of educational, social and civic life.

The states having a Temperance Day in the public schools are: Alabama, Tennessee, Kansas, New Mexico, Kentucky, Wisconsin, Pennsylvania, Maine, Mississippi, Oregon, North Dakota, Missouri, South Dakota, South Carolina, Nevada, Nebraska, Ohio, North Carolina, Minnesota, Georgia, Washington. In many of these commonwealths the special temperance day is named for Frances Willard.

It requires great valor to be a hero on the battle field, but often a higher type of courage is displayed on the moral and civic field. Captain Richmond Pearson Hobson, the acknowledged naval hero of the Spanish war, was acclaimed a still greater hero in the national peaceful war against King Alcohol. When Lieutenant Hobson bravely risked his life and under fire from the enemy sank the "Merrimac" in Santiago Harbor, he had the clear, electric brain of a young man who had never used alcoholic liquors. As the "Merrimac" went down Lieutenant Hobson with the seven sailors under his command, took to a raft and after several hours they were hailed by an enemy's launch, that of Admiral Cervera, the Spanish commander. The admiral, on learning the identity of Lieutenant Hobson, called out to him with fine Castilian courtesy, "Bravo, young man!" The captain and his men were taken on shore and made prisoners of war.

Tramping up and down in his narrow prison cell, he looked out between the bars and saw in the distance the Spanish flag flying from a Spanish blockhouse beyond San Juan hill. He could not help associating it with oppression and wondered what would happen when the United States flag that stands for universal liberty should arrive. One afternoon he heard the great guns as a battle was fought, and then he saw the Spanish flag fall and in its place appeared the stars and stripes. Later, all over the United States, the school children were given Captain Hobson's dynamic message. This is what the hero of the "Merrimac" said: "The drink traffic is a menace to liberty—liberty for which our flag stands. Every year, by the use of alcohol, the destroyer, millions of our people have their standards of citizenship lowered. We must eliminate this great agent, alcohol, that presses the standard down far below its proper level."

Soon after Dr. Lemuel H. Murlin became president of Boston University, he was asked to participate in a great temperance meeting held in Park Street Church, Boston, Massachusetts. After many prominent men had represented various societies, Dr. Murlin said that he appreciated the record of all that had been done through these various organizations. He thought, however, that the unprecedented, fundamental work accomplished through public schools, colleges, and homes by the National Woman's Christian Temperance Union had been the nation's most valuable temperance asset. Thoughtfully he said: "When I was a student in one of the leading Kansas universities, we were told that we were to have a temperance lecture—a lecture by a woman. We men didn't look forward to this with any enthusiasm. We had an electric thrill, however, when we saw before us Frances E. Willard, who was in the prime of life, a charming personality, as well as a magnetic speaker. The fact that we lived in a prohibition state had not made any vital impression upon most of us. Miss Willard, however, gave us a vision of the benefits of total abstinence and our opportunity to be patriots and enforce the prohibitory law in our own state; so helping the people of our entire nation to reach a higher civilization. From that time, my active influence was on the side of total abstinence and prohibition, and it was from a national standpoint. Kansas suffered from the importation of liquor from wet states, so I joined the forces that were working for Federal prohibition. Do you wonder that I honor the fundamental, far-reaching work of the Woman's Christian Temperance Union?" The W. C. T. U. honors Dr. Murlin.

The truth of the "vision" seen by Dr. Cheever of Salem, Massachusetts, early in the temperance reform was now becoming more widely known. Always Dr. Cheever will be greatly honored as a pioneer in the fearless defense of total abstinence and denunciation of the liquor traffic. As little girls, many who afterwards became active in the W. C. T. U. received their first impressions against alcoholic drink while they shivered with childish fear, as they were shown from the public platform pictures of "Deacon Giles' Distillery," in which little devils were hilariously running about manufacturing and dispensing alcoholic liquors. Here was depicted more of reality than vision.

It will be remembered that Dr. Cheever was prosecuted, convicted and for thirty days imprisoned in the Salem (Massachusetts) jail. Not long before his death, Dr. Cheever related this incident of strange fruitage from his early seed-sowing: "I had preached in Boston, and as I came down the aisle from the pulpit was accosted by a middle-aged, well-dressed stranger who introduced himself as Mr. Giles, the son of Deacon Giles, owner of the famous distillery. 'I stopped you, Dr. Cheever,' he said, 'to thank you for writing that "Dream." It was the means of making me think of the evil effects of distilling intoxicating liquors, and determined me to give up the wicked business. It also brought me to confess and renounce my sins and accept the offer of salvation through Jesus Christ.' "

The W. C. T. U., on the threshold of a new crusade, is emphasizing this authoritative and recent statement of one of the leading world scientists, Dr. C. W. Saleeby of London, England, vice-president of the National Temperance League and National Commercial Temperance League: "Sixteen years ago," Dr. Saleeby says, "I included alcohol as one of those substances I called racial poisons. Most injurious things do not poison the race. They hurt the individual and the injury ends there. Thus nature is doing her best ever to preserve the life of future generations. But certain agencies have this damnable quality—they destroy posterity in and through parenthood in the present generation. I call them *racial* poisons."

For many years Maine, Kansas and North Dakota were the only prohibition states. An incident often related by Lillian M. N. Stevens illustrates the inestimable benefit of total abstinence accruing even at that early period to the boys and girls of a prohibition state. A lively fourteen-year-old lad, who was president of a Loyal Temperance Legion in one of the smaller towns of Maine, accompanied his father to Boston and was a silent listener to the conversation between his "dad" and one of his Boston friends. They were sitting at a table enjoying their dinner when this refined gentleman in praising the state of Maine, said: "There is just one thing you need and that is a respectable saloon in a respectable place, so that a respectable man can get a drink." The men had forgotten entirely the presence of the boy. Suddenly he looked up with astonished gaze at the Boston friend and said earnestly: "Excuse me, sir! Don't you know that *respectable* men don't drink in the state of Maine?"

In the fight for a clear brain, no one was more highly

esteemed by the allied temperance forces, or more feared by the liquor men, than was Mrs. Lillian M. N. Stevens. From its earliest years, Mrs. Stevens was identified with the National W. C. T. U., attending as a delegate the National Convention held at Newark, New Jersey, in 1876, and assisting in all subsequent conventions. In 1880 she was chosen assistant recording secretary and a few years later recording secretary. A further record of Mrs. Stevens' devoted and brilliant W. C. T. U. service is given in the chapters on Legislative Achievement, the World's W. C. T. U., and the Eighteenth Amendment.

During the regime of local option, annual or biennial campaigns for license or no license were held, and children's choruses, drills and recitations were powerful, winning factors. Drinking men were grateful for the total abstinence instruction given their children. Mary A. Livermore, then president of the Massachusetts W. C. T. U:, as well as a popular lyceum lecturer, often told how she came to organize a Loyal Temperance Legion. In order to lure the men away from the saloons, the Boston W. C. T. U. established coffee houses. Many drinkers were reformed, but found it difficult to remain sober. One of these, the father of promising boys, seeing legalized saloons on nearly every corner tempting his sons, in desperation sought Mrs. Livermore and said: "We men are truly grateful for the help you are giving us, but, lady, we are badly damaged by the drink. We shall never be what we might have been. If you can do anything for anybody, we want you to save our boys."

Mary Livermore and all home-loving men and women ardently endorsed these eloquent words of Frances Willard regarding the danger to the brain and body of using, even moderately, alcoholic liquors: "The human brain with its fair, delicate, mystical filaments, is God's night-blooming cereus, its white radiance forever inclosed and shut away from sight within the close crypt of the skull, but exhaling its fragrance in poetry and revealing its deep, pure heart in science, philosophy and religion. The brain must think with

51

lightning speed, the hand must be steadfast as steel, the pulse must beat strong, yet true, if a great commercial nation is to hold its own with the forces of chemistry, electricity, and invention now on the field.

"We have the testimony of a great chemist, the late Dr. Nichols (for many years editor of the Journal of Chemistry, Boston) 'that the resources of that magical science are such that every useful purpose ever served by alcohol has been already superseded by chemicals already known to the laboratory and soon to be everyday articles of commerce.'

"What is it that the indifferent doctor, editor, public school teacher, and Sunday school teacher lacks? What is it? The arrest of thought. What people lack is imagination. Evil is wrought for want of thought more than for want of heart. Suppose that in this day of science the school should echo the mother's total abstinence teachings. Suppose that with the majesty of law and dignity of learning, the state should require and the teacher inculcate lessons like these. Then, indeed, it would be manly to let strong drink alone. Then it would be steadily wrought into the warp and woof of boyhood's character and habit to abstain from fleshly lusts that war against the soul. But all the way toward manhood that dramshop so seductive has been just across the street. The boy has found out that in municipal council room, legislative hall, and national Congress, the so-called guardians of the public weal have been the guardians of the liquor traffic. The logical outcome of total abstinence is total prohibition. In our day, this must come through ballots as a result of home, school and church training that will make those who vote conscientious on this subject."

In this period of W. C. T. U. history, white ribbon leaders, in their fight for a clear brain, considered the hygienic and temperance findings of the physiological laboratories, both in America and abroad, their greatest asset. Through the efforts of public and Sunday school teachers, the Young People's Branch of the W. C. T. U. and the Loyal Temperance Legion, these scientific facts formed a basis for public school essays, elocutionary medal contests, Sunday school temperance concerts, posters in shop windows, exhibits in booths on fair grounds, in articles given to the cosmopolitan press, and leaflets sent out as "leaves of healing."

The following were some of the scientific data and appeals that through W. C. T. U. publicity moulded public thought: "If we can safeguard the young to the utmost," said Sir Thomas Barlow, physician to King Edward VII, "and not only keep alcohol away from them, but make them realize from early years the terrible ills that it brings to body and soul, then there may be some chance of the next generation looking at the whole subject in its true light, and our children's children may realize that abstinence is not fanaticism or asceticism, but rational self-control in respect to something which is fraught with untold risks."

"The sale of drink is the sale of disease; the sale of drink is the sale of poverty; the sale of drink is the sale of insanity; the sale of drink is the sale of crime; the sale of drink is the sale of death." This was one of the greatest sayings of that great man, Sir Benjamin Ward Richardson —given to the world in 1892. "Drink causes more injury to humanity than war, pestilence and famine combined," was the forceful dictum of William E. Gladstone.

In America, in the less enlightened day of medical practice, a discerning physician declared: "When a patient is cold, we give him alcohol. When the patient has fever, we give him alcohol. When the patient is sick from any cause, we give him alcohol, and when he is well, he takes it himself. The use of alcohol has led to most of the vice and crime with which our country has been plagued."

Under the direction of Dr. J. H. Kellogg at the Battle Creek Sanitarium (Michigan), a great variety of experiments were made confirming and verifying the results obtained by European observers, and showing in the use of alcohol, the same physiological, psychological and pathological depression and anæsthesia leading up to final paralysis. Dr. Winfield S. Hall of Chicago, Illinois, declared that

53

laboratory tests had proved these facts: "Alcohol cannot be considered a food; alcohol decreases the efficiency of muscle, glands, and nervous system; alcohol is a narcotic in its drug action; alcohol given in minute quantities to lower animals seriously impairs fecundity. It leads to race suicide."

A number of important insurance companies aroused public opinion, proving that the longevity of the abstainer ranged from thirty to forty per cent greater than that of the moderate drinker.

A director of athletics made this authoritative statement: "I positively know from experience in fifteen Marathon races, both in this country and England, that alcohol used in any form in a race of this kind is a great detriment. Whisky nerves and beer-weakened muscles are spotted on the instant on the diamond." "Without the factor of right living, any measure of success on the diamond is impossible," said "Hurry-Up" Yost. Frederick Robertson defines true liberty thus: "People talk of liberty as if it means the liberty to do just what a man likes. I call that man free who is able to rule himself. I call him free who has learned the most blessed of all truths, that liberty consists in obedience to the power and to the will and to the law that his higher soul reverences and approves. He is not free because he does what he likes; but he is free because he does what he should, and there is no protest in his soul against that doing."

The stabilization of total abstinence sentiment was hastened by widely heralded current temperance events. The story of this period of agitation and education would not be complete without some record of the achievements of courageous men and women who, for conscience's sake, and the good of others, overcame avarice and prejudice.

One of the earliest Americans to work for total abstinence was General Neal Dow of Portland, Maine. The story of his life deserves to be recounted—from generation to generation: In 1836, Neal Dow, for the sake of a refined woman suffering from the drinking habits of her husband, visited in Portland a rum seller and endeavored to persuade him not to sell any more rum to this gentleman, in whom he was so interested. He was told the man was not in the saloon, but hearing voices, he opened the back door, found him and awakened his moral sense. Then General Dow appealed to the saloon-keeper, telling him that if he would refuse to sell liquor to the man, he would not go elsewhere to obtain it. The liquor dealer replied, angrily, that it was his business to sell rum and that he supported his family in this way and did not want any advice. Mr. Dow replied, "It is your business to sell rum, is it? You have a license to sell rum, have you? Heaven helping me, I'll change all that!" Then Mr. Dow began the battle. A friend helped him, and together for years they went all over the state creating public sentiment and holding meetings in school houses, town halls and churches. There were only a few railroads, so Mr. Dow took his carriage and sleigh and drove over the length and breadth of Maine. In 1851, after the prohibition law was enacted, Mr. Dow traveled through the state again. He found the jails and poorhouses nearly empty, though they had been crowded with inmates. Maine had been the poorest state in the Union. It became one of the most prosperous. General Dow lived to be ninety-three years of age. His birthday, March 20, is one of the Red Letter days of the W. C. T. U. When he was only twenty-three years of age, he was president of the fire company. According to their custom, they ordered liquors to be served on a social occasion, but rescinded their vote because of his earnest protest.

In 1885, an army general quite unknown to temperance circles, made on Commencement Day, a most significant total abstinence appeal to the graduating cadets at West Point, when, as a prerequisite to their promotion, he urged them to let alcoholic drinks severely alone. A big prohibition parade, aided by the W. C. T. U., caused a great stir in Chicago—more than a score of years ago. Headed by General Frederick Dent Grant, in uniform, and taking hours to pass in review, it brought consternation to the liquor men, who at nearly every corner stood before their saloons

—seven thousand licensed and many illegal places. The banners carried by boys and girls, men and women, voiced the protection of the home and the doom of drink. The appeal and warning sent by General Frederick Grant to the boys of the nation, in purport was this: "Tell the boys not to drink. Tell the boys I do not drink because I am afraid to drink." In his message he took the boys into his confidence by telling them incidents of his early life in the White House and at West Point where he was "treated" and feted because he was the President's son. Observing later, the harmful effect of wine and beer on himself and others, he ever after at social functions courteously declined the tempting glass and even the alluring "punch." The leadership of General Frederick Grank in the parade, wearing the full uniform of the United States Army, caused the brewers and distillers of Chicago to send the War Department at Washington an angry protest, that Secretary Dickinson wisely pronounced unworthy of consideration. General Grant, in reply to this protest, said, "It was most appropriate for a United States general to head a Law and Order parade; and that was the character of the one in which I so happily participated."

Andrew Carnegie, who, late in life, addressed a company of railway men, said, "A drinking man should have no place in a railway system; indeed, he should have no place anywhere." One of the compelling reasons why Andrew Carnegie did so much to multiply libraries all over the country is the fact that the free public library with the reading habit which it creates could be made at that time so powerful an offset to the ever curseful saloon.

John B. Gough, an orator of inimitable force, showed the inner urge of his life when he declared: "While I can talk against the drink, I'll talk; and when I can only whisper, I'll do that; and when I can't whisper any longer, faith, I'll make motions—they say I'm good at that." He talked right on against the drink evil until he lacked but six months of being seventy years of age, speaking nearly 9,000 times to at least nine millions of people, and traveling 450,000 miles to reach them. His last words, spoken with super-human earnestness to a great audience, were these: "Young man, keep your record clean." Mr. and Mrs. Gough, as personal friends of Frances Willard, ever co-operated with W. C. T. U. activities.

A brave pioneer in medical temperance was Dr. Nathan S. Davis, of Chicago. As a medical student, he did not question the statements of his professors who thought that in certain cases alcoholic liquors should be used. As a young practicing physician, however, he encountered occasionally patients who refused to take alcoholic liquor as a medicine, and was surprised to find that he was more successful with such patients than with others with similar diseases, who used alcoholic prescriptions. He was determined to find out the scientific truth, and obtained the control of a ward in a Chicago hospital, where he prescribed no alcoholic liquors—no matter what the disease. Before this occurred, Dr. Davis had written for the *Journal of the American Medical Association,* stating his belief that alcoholic liquors as medicines should be discontinued. There was scarcely a doctor who agreed with him, and he was called a fanatic. He continued his practice in the hospital ward for some years; and as he compared results with the patients in hospitals where alcoholic liquors were given, most favorable records were noted. These scientific findings, from time to time, were given in the national medical journal and Dr. Davis won a reputation for noteworthy scientific research. Later, he was elected president of the American Medical Association. In the Stock Yards district of Chicago is a community-center building on which is a handsome tablet, bearing this inscription: "To the memory of Dr. Nathan S. Davis, physician and philanthropist." It is interesting to know that in Evanston, where are located the headquarters of the National W. C. T. U., the principal street bears the distinguished name of "Davis."

A notable woman physician, Cordelia A. Greene, M. D., of Castile, New York, whom Frances Willard, when her patient, called "a chemical amalgam of saint and scientist," was a pre-eminent pioneer in promoting medical temperance. Few physicians in those early days followed her widely known example of not prescribing alcoholic liquors; but as she addressed her fellow practitioners in the meetings of the American, State and County Medical Associations, Doctor Greene bravely made known her temperance principles.

In 1889, Hon. John D. Long, Secretary of the Navy, gave an "arrest of thought" to ease-loving wine and beer drinkers when he prohibited the use of alcoholic liquor in the "mess" of the navy cadets and seamen. In the homes of these boys, fathers and mothers thanked God for such a brave official.

At an influential mass meeting held in Washington, D. C., in 1913, Hon. Seaborn Wright of Georgia said that southern statesmen were now heartily in favor of observing total abstinence in the business world and in the usages of society. "Frances Willard and those who have followed her have been most welcome in our southland," he courteously remarked. "Statesmen in the north, surprised at the rapidity with which southern states have become dry, often exclaim to me, 'Of course it is because of the negro that you have outlawed the liquor business!' 'Not so!' I answer, 'I want all our northern friends to realize that, while we believe the sober negro is the only desirable colored man, we did not fight the liquor traffic on his account alone. We saw, first of all, the direful need of saving from the alcohol habit our own youth. Knowing well, as I do, through my profession, the best people of the south, I do not hesitate to say that there is scarcely a family that has not been damaged by this accursed liquor business. Even many of our daughters are suffering because they have married young men who, because of drink, have ruined or debased their homes.'"

Judge Ben B. Lindsey, of Denver, another pathfinder in the temperance world, popularly called the "kid's judge," was warmly aided in his "probation" activities by the W. C. T. U., and many a white ribboner became a successful probation officer. The following stirring statements made by Judge Lindsey at a W. C. T. U. convention secured for the

Juvenile Court the support of all true friends and guardians of childhood. "About 100,000 boys," he said, "are brought to jail every year. It is an inspiring mission in life to have any part whatever in helping these boys and girls. The first commandment of the 'gang' is 'thou shalt not snitch'; 95 per cent of the boys we have tried to help have turned out well; it is because we have treated the boys 'on the square.' In the old days all we dealt with was the thing the boy did. Now, we go back of the deed and interest ourselves in the boy; and there is nothing in the world so valuable as a boy— except a girl." The Juvenile Court work is, after all. palliative. It was never the intention that it should be a cure-all. It affords much better methods of caring for the child who is a victim, by heredity and circumstance, of many evils than did the old jail and the criminal court system.

Students of temperance history recall the gratifying fact that General U. S. Grant, in traveling around the world, was an abstainer from alcoholics at the banquets of kings and the nobility; also that Mrs. Grant when Mistress of the White House banished intoxicants on New Year's Day, not only from her own table, but, through personal influence, largely from the cabinet circle.

Fashionable society gasped when the first lady of the land, Mrs. Lucy Webb Hayes, with the approval of the President, not only turned her own wine glass upside down but allowed no alcoholic liquors to be served at the White House social functions or diplomatic dinners. The social prestige of the Mistress of the White House was in no way diminished. The National W. C. T. U., through its president, Miss Frances Willard, presented to the White House a life-size oil painting of Mrs. Hayes. This gift, from the entire constituency of the W. C. T. U., represented their high appreciation of Mrs. Hayes' nobility and bravery. The artist was David Huntington of New York City, president of the National Academy of Design. The frame, carved under the superintendence of Ben Pitman by students of the Cincinnati Art School, was presented by ladies of that city. A photogravure of the picture, executed by

Barry, of Philadelphia, also was presented. In the spring of 1881, while Washington was in gala attire, in the presence of an immense evening audience, the picture, ten feet in height and seven in width, was unveiled by Dr. Frederick Merrick, a well-known professor in Ohio Wesleyan University.

As the portrait was disclosed, Frances Willard, who had joined in the appreciative applause, eloquently said: "Before we can at all estimate the significance to the temperance cause of the example of Mrs. Lucy Webb Hayes, we must turn away from the victories already gained and contemplate the mountains of difficulty that loom up ahead of our advancing hosts. There are three mighty realms of influence which the temperance reform, based as it is upon science, experience and the golden rule, has hardly yet invaded. The world of fine arts, of romance and of fashion still sneers at total abstinence. From the days of Homer and Virgil to those of Tennyson and Longfellow, the poets have been singing in tuneful cadences the praises of wine. From Praxiteles to Powers, the sculptors have delighted to idealize the coarse features of Bacchus. From the antique frescoes of Pompeii down to those of Meissonier, the choicest pigments of the painter have been lavished to furnish forth convivial feasts. Heroes have been men mighty to drink wine and heroines have found their prototype in Hebe, cup bearer to the gods. Now be it remembered that the poet, the artist and the novelist, mighty interpreters of nature and the soul, will always maintain their empire over the human heart so long as it is a willing captive to the love of beauty and the beauty of love, so that until we win an assured place for the temperance reform in these supremely influential realms of thought and expression, our success cannot be considered permanent. Until Genius, with her starry eyes, shall be gently persuaded to lay her choicest trophies at the feet of temperance, there will remain for us much territory to be possessed. This beautiful portrait, painted by the noblest master of his art in all the land is the

60

'avant courier' of many a trophy which our cause is yet to win.

"Think what it means to the total abstinence cause that the first lady of the republic, instead of cherishing intoxicating liquors as the emblem of hospitality and kindness and good will, banishes them from cellar, sideboard and table as the enemies of her home and of the guests to whom she would do honor. Wine has freely flowed in the houses inhabited by the world's rulers. It was left for a Christian queen of American society to be the first one who did not only hear but heeded the voice of God. It has been like a torch held up in the gloom, a beacon flaming grandly on the most dangerous headland of the republic's coast, and it shall grow and gather light and mount up to the zenith like another sun shedding its genial rays into the darkest heart and most desolate home."

During a later administration, Rose Elizabeth Cleveland, a sister of the president, was a valued white ribboner and never served liquor at her afternoon teas. On one occasion she publicly said: "Drink costs us millions of criminals, thousands of paupers, thousands of ruined women, and hundreds of thousands of men and women goaded by misery into suicide or madness."

In 1908, Mrs. Zillah Foster Stevens related at the National W. C. T. U. convention this remarkable story: "Until two years ago the International Sunday School Association that directly teaches twenty-six million children had no temperance department. It did do temperance work, but not in an organized way. In addition to the quarterly temperance lesson it has a temperance department now and this is its standard for action—Every officer, teacher and scholar in the Sunday school a total abstainer and a worker for the destruction of the liquor traffic and for the extinction of the cigaret habit. There is a little story at the bottom of the creation of that department and it tells why I say that the temperance department of the Sunday School Association is the big boy of the W. C. T. U.

"A few years ago one of our Sunday school officers

had a letter. It was from a mining town and the writer said, 'I was converted when I was eleven years old. I am a member of the Methodist church; we have ten saloons in this mining town and there is only this one Sunday school and there isn't a Christian woman in the place, not one, and I run the Sunday school and a young student comes over from the church Sundays and helps me, and I am the janitor and organist and a teacher in the Sunday school. The boys in our town are going into these ten saloons and I don't know what to do. Won't you please send me help for temperance work in the Sunday school?'

"So they looked through all their pigeon holes of the missionary work, primary work, cradle roll work and teachers' work and other work and what do you think? They wrote to the writer of that letter. They said, 'On temperance work we have nothing.' Think of it. And then this officer, when he found out he had nothing and being a man who wanted to get something right away, wrote me a letter telling me about that place and I said I would better go to see what kind of a person it was who was janitor, organist, teacher and was trying to do temperance work. So I took a day off and went over there and I got off right among the coal mines, and looking around supposed I would find a capable, self-assertive, vigorous woman. What do you think I found? A little girl in short dresses with her braided hair hanging nearly down to her shoe tops. She looked up at me in the most childish way and I said, 'I am hunting for such and such a person.' 'Why,' she said, 'here she is.' She looked like a flower. I said, 'How old are you?' She said, 'Fourteen.' And I said, 'How did you find out about temperance work anyhow?' 'Oh, I wear a white ribbon.' Well, I spent the day there and found that the child-janitor, organist, teacher, superintendent, Christian, head of the cradle roll and home department and so on was the single solitary influence between ten saloons and the boys in that town. And think of it! When she wrote to the International Sunday School headquarters they had to say, 'On temperance we have nothing.'

Lillian M. N. Stevens

"When it came state convention time I had that little girl there in a white dress and I told the folks about the mining town, the ten saloons and about the worker and I said, 'Would you like to see her?' They expected, of course, to see some great big, capable young woman. I called her out and she came trotting to the platform just like a little girl. When she faced a thousand people, she felt so little she didn't know what to do and she ran up to me and tucked her head down under my arm like a little girl of four years old. That convention went wild. They were on their feet all over the house and they said, 'We've got to have a temperance department.' And so the temperance department was created in the state of Illinois; other states fell into line and two years ago the International Sunday School Association, which plans the Sunday school work for the United States and Canada, Mexico, Hawaii, Japan, and Alaska—and I don't know where else—said, 'We will have an International Sunday School department and it stands for nothing less than total abstinence, the destruction of the liquor habit and the extinction of the cigaret habit.' They look to the white ribboners for help and now we have the quarterly Temperance Sunday; four times a year in the Sunday schools you will find temperance exercises." It is so apparent, is it not, that God called out the reserves!

William Jennings Bryan in one of his masterful total abstinence addresses made this statement: "God never made alcohol necessary to the human body, mind, or soul. The man who contracts the habit cannot lay it on to a necessity given him by the Creator. God never made a man strong enough to begin the use of intoxicating liquor with certainty that he would not become its slave. Every man who has fallen into a drunkard's grave has passed through a period of confidence and boasted that he could drink it when he wanted to and leave it alone when he wanted to; but he has overestimated his strength, and fallen a victim to a habit. Moreover, there is not a day between the cradle and the grave when it is safe for a man to commence the use of alcohol."

Archbishop Ireland wielded a strong influence against social drinking. He declared that "the great cause of social crime is drinking. When I hear of a family broken up, I ask the cause—it is drink. If I go to the gallows and ask its victim the cause, the answer is 'drink.' Then I ask myself in perfect wonderment, 'Why do not men put a stop to this thing?'"

In the latter part of the nineteenth century a young woman in high society dared the criticism of wine-drinking people. Her courageous act is thus described by a long-time friend of the W. C. T. U., that silver-tongued orator, Colonel George W. Bain: "For Christine Bradley, the eighteen-year-old daughter of a governor of Kentucky, to stand on the dock at Newport News, against the customs of centuries and facing the years of prejudice, baptize the battleship Kentucky with water, required as blood-born-bravery as coursed the veins of the Ensign who cut the wires in Cardenas Bay, or the Captain who sank the 'Merrimac' in the entrance of Santiago harbor. Because she dared to violate a long established custom by refusing to use what had blighted the hopes of many daughters, sent to drunkards' graves so many sons, and buried crafts and crews in watery graves, the Woman's Christian Temperance Union presented her with a handsome silver service."

It was Colonel Bain who was chosen to make the presentation speech, which he closed by saying—"Heaven bless Christine Bradley, who by her example said—

"I christen thee Kentucky,
  With water from the spring,
  Which enriched the blood of Lincoln,
  Whose praise the sailors sing.

"I christen thee Kentucky,
  With prayers of women true,
  That wine, the curse of sailors,
  May never curse your crew.

64

"I christen thee Kentucky,
And may this christening be
A lesson of safety ever
To sailors on the sea."

One of the bravest and most beloved workers in the fight for a clear brain throughout a long life, was Mrs. Mary T. Hill Willard, "Saint Courageous," the mother of Frances Willard. When an octogenarian, Mother Willard sent out from her home, Rest Cottage, Evanston, Illinois, to boys and girls everywhere, her own prophetic, appealing message. It reads (in part):

"The world will be what you make it,
        Little people;
It will be as you shape it,
        Little people;
Then be studious and brave,
And your country help to save,
        Little people.

"When we walk into the gray,
        Little people,
And you into the day,
        Little people,
We will beckon you along
With a very tender song,
        Little people."

After years of agitation, education and organization against the alcohol habit, how gratifying it has been to see total abstinence public sentiment rapidly awakening. At the National W. C. T. U. convention of 1915, the Spirit of Sobriety, garbed in the symbols of victory, suddenly appeared and announced triumphantly: "You are the friends who have made me articulate. In 1874 I was only a dream —a vision; today I am a living reality. Once I was hated; now I am beloved. When I tell you what total abstinence has accomplished, you will realize that I am the impersonation of that ideal of yours. Listen to my story:

"Total Abstinence is no longer a ridiculed fanaticism; it sits in regal state on the throne of empires and of kingdoms, and in republics sways, in ever increasing measure, the voting citizenship. It safeguards the soldier, the sailor, the aviator, and the crew of the submarine. It gives a clear brain to the railroad man, the athlete, the autoist, and the commercial, industrial and agricultural worker. It says, 'The first man to be taken off and the last man to be taken on is the man who drinks.'

"Total Abstinence framed 'Rule G,' enforced by every railroad of the country. 'Rule G' places a reliable man in charge of a transcontinental express train, or a safety block-signal worth ten million dollars.

"Total Abstinence declares whisky and brandy to be neither drugs nor medicine, but depressants. Law-breaking drug stores are taking notice that it requires a saloon license to sell these alcoholic liquors.

"Total Abstinence has caused many physicians and State Medical Societies to deal John Barleycorn solar plexus blows. He has led the National Society of Neurologists and Alienists to condemn unqualifiedly the use of alcoholic beverages, and to recommend that the various state legislatures take steps to eliminate such use.

"Total Abstinence has convinced captains of industry and labor organizations generally, that the 'Water Wagon' is the only 'universal safety device.'

"Total Abstinence declares that even moderate drinking is an untold risk. He teaches the young that rational self-control means absolutely no drinking of alcoholics. He gives to society an example safe and beneficent for each one to follow. Scientific and illuminating truths reveal the terrible ills that alcohol brings to body and soul; he impresses these truths on the young minds of millions of school children in every state, territory and the District of Columbia. Total Abstinence is the popular subject of thousands of essays written by boys and girls whose slogan is 'Where there's Drink there's Danger.'

"Total Abstinence controls the ruling of many life insurance societies, who affirm, 'We prefer total abstainers to those who imbibe even moderately.' 'The mortality is heavier among drinkers than non-drinkers.' 'We do not insure the lives of persons engaged in the sale or manufacture of intoxicating liquors.'

"Total Abstinence organized the National Abstainers' Union, under the Federated Council of Churches of Christ in America, which represents over seventeen and one-half million communicant members. He secured on the latest World's Temperance Sunday one million signatures to the temperance pledge. At the W. C. T. U., Young People's Branch and Loyal Temperance Legion meetings this year the number of pledge signers has been increased.

"To warring nations Total Abstinence utters the warning cry—'The nation that keeps sober is the nation that will win.'

"Total Abstinence has increased in ten years the sale of milk in New York City fifty per cent, and decreased the sale of beer. He dominated the New York City Health Department and caused it to declare an educational war on alcoholic drink. Commissioner Goldwater, when inaugurating this campaign said: 'The Health Board will fight the rich man's champagne as well as the poor man's beer.' By means of posters, illustrated lectures and moving pictures, the ravages of alcohol are being shown. The wise and fearless commissioner announces that 'it is as necessary to battle drink as to fight an epidemic.'

"Total Abstinence caused the state of Kansas to make liquor drinkers or cigarette smokers ineligible to office. This ruling applied to teachers and to the professional classes as well as to industrial workers and day laborers. Kansas leads the nation in refusing to employ brains muddled by alcohol.

"Total Abstinence holds a high place beside 'Truth,' as an ideal advocate, by the members of the Associated Advertising Clubs of the World.

"Total Abstinence has received the unqualified endorsement of many leading educators, who have reached the conclusion that alcohol is an unmitigated evil, and who assert 'that a man who takes alcohol in even a moderate degree is harming himself physically, mentally, morally and economically.'

"Total Abstinence laid its compelling hand on the youth of our country when the Associated College Newspaper Publishers in their convention a few weeks ago at Columbia University voted to bar liquor advertisements from their publications.

"Total Abstinence recently so controlled the state convention of Georgia bankers that in the interest of efficiency they resolved to exclude wine from their future banquets. Total Abstinence caused the Georgia Weekly Press Association and the Georgia police chiefs to take even stronger action; the Press Association renounced the use at their meetings of intoxicants of any kind, including near beer, and the police chiefs, realizing that 'the dignity of sobriety is becoming to an officer sworn to enforce the prohibitory law,' determined not to allow intoxicating beverages to be served at any of their entertainments.

"Total Abstinence was championed by genial 'Bob' Burdette, who said: 'No clause in the Declaration of Independence declares that a Sunday concert garden with five brass horns and one hundred kegs of beer is the inalienable right of a free people and the cornerstone of good government.'

"Total Abstinence has reared a generation of voters inimical to the traffic in alcoholic liquors. To the people of this Christian republic he is saying, I, Total Abstinence, will give to you health, wealth, efficiency and prosperity. To the oppressed millions who shall seek America's hospitable shores I will be a life-giver and a powerful protector."

CHAPTER IV

THE WORLD'S WOMAN'S CHRISTIAN TEMERANCE UNION

THE present-day "New Internationalism" was preceded by an epochal era of women's unselfish idealism and strategic action. History will record the World's Woman's Christian Temperance Union as a vital factor in securing this new inter-sphering of the nations. Frances Willard was the first leader of a temperance or philanthropic organization to send across the Pacific the spiritual cable of good-will and understanding. The story of the World's Woman's Christian Temperance Union is a story of heroism. A family of nations promoting peace, purity, prohibition, the enfranchisement of women and the establishment of courts of arbitration to banish war from the world, has been the beckoning goal.

Today, fifty nations are federated in the World's W. C. T. U., the new parliament of women, the new "Federation of the World." This international movement, organized in 1883, antedates the present internationalism by more than four decades. In unifying and forwarding the reforms which are of equal importance to all nations, the World's W. C. T. U. has secured unprecedented results. These victories presage the fulfilment of Matthew Arnold's prophetic dictum: "If ever the world sees a time when women shall come together purely and simply for the benefit and good of mankind, it will be a power such as the world has never known."

"For God and Home and Every Land" became the new watchword. "We are a world's republic of women—without distinction of race or color—who recognize no sectarianism in religion, no sectionalism in politics, no sex in citizenship," said Frances Willard. "Each of us is as much a part of the world's union as is any other woman; it is our great, growing, beautiful home. The white ribbon includes all reforms; whatever touches humanity, touches us."

The founding of the World's W. C. T. U. was the out-

come of Miss Willard's visit, in 1883, to the city of San
Francisco, California. It was Anna Gordon's high privilege
to accompany her. With sorrowful hearts the two visitors
walked through the streets of Chinatown—that one-time
vice and opium section of San Francisco. In the presence
of occidental avarice and oriental degradation, there came
to Miss Willard a distinct illumination, resulting in this
solemn decision: "But for the intervention of the sea, the
shores of China and the Far East would be part and parcel
of our fair land. We are one world of tempted humanity;
the mission of the white ribbon women is to organize the
motherhood of the world for the peace and purity, the protection and exaltation of its homes. We must sound forth
a clear call to our sisters across the seas, and to our brothers none the less. We must be no longer hedged about by
the artificial boundaries of state and nation. We must
utter, as women, what a great and good man long ago declared as his watchword, 'The whole world is my parish,
and to do good is my religion.'"

In 1884, the first clarion call for world prohibition,
world purity, and freedom from the opium trade was written by Frances Willard in her study at historic Rest Cottage,
Evanston, Illinois. This "Polyglot Petition" was addressed
to the "Honored Rulers, Representatives and Brothers," of
all governments. It reads: "We, your petitioners, although
belonging to the physically weaker sex, are strong of heart
to love our homes, our native land, and the world's family
of nations. We know that clear brains and pure hearts
make honest lives and happy homes, and that by these the
nations prosper and the time is brought nearer when the
world shall be at peace. We know that indulgence in alcohol and opium, and in other vices which disgrace our social
life, makes misery for all the world, and most of all for
us and for our children. We know that stimulants and
opiates are sold under legal guarantees which make the
governments partners in the traffic by accepting as revenue
a portion of the profits, and we know with shame that they

(*Reading down*)

Clara C. Hoffman	Louise S. Rounds	Elizabeth P. Hutchinson
Susanna M. D. Fry	Katherine Lent Stevenson	Mary Clement Leavitt
Helen M. Barker	Frances E. Beauchamp	Mary T. Lathrop

are often forced by treaty upon populations either ignorant or unwilling. We know that the law might do much now left undone to raise the moral tone of society and render vice difficult. We have no power to prevent these great iniquities, beneath which the whole world groans, but you have power to redeem the honor of the nations from an indefensible complicity. We, therefore, come to you with the united voices of representative women of every land, beseeching you to raise the standard of the law to that of Christian morals, to strip away the safeguards and sanctions of the State from the drink traffic and the opium trade, and to protect our homes by the total prohibition of these curses of civilization throughout all the territory over which your Government extends."

At once, opportunities to sign this appeal were given to individuals and organizations. The petition was translated into the languages of many nations. Almost every tongue used by the peoples of the world is represented in the signatures and endorsements. Frances Willard said, "In this far-reaching document there are columns of Chinese women's signatures that look like houses that Jack built. There is a list of Burmese signatures that looks like bunches of tangled worms. The thousands upon thousands from the spicy Isle of Ceylon are enough to make a shorthand man shudder; the incomprehensible but liquid vowels of the Hawaiian Kanaka jostle the proud names of English ladies of high degree; the Spanish of haughty senoras of Madrid make the same plea as the "her mark" of the converted woman of the Congo. There are Spanish names from Mexico and the South American republics, French from Martinique, Dutch from Natal and English from New Zealand, besides the great home petitions from the greater nations. The total, counting men's and women's signatures, endorsements, and attestations, aggregates seven and one-half million."

Mrs. Mary Bannister Willard first presented this proclamation to a convention for signatures, when she addressed the International Temperance Congress, held in 1885, in Antwerp, Belgium. The signatures in fifty languages, secured in many lands, were mounted on white muslin and during the first convention of the World's W. C. T. U., held in Boston, in 1891, the folds of the petition draped the walls of historic Faneuil Hall and Tremont Temple.

In 1895, Frances Willard and a committee representing the World's and National W. C. T. U., were received at the Executive Mansion by President Grover Cleveland, and formally presented to the United States government this history making petition.

During the same year, the great rolls were taken to London, and were the central feature of the World's W. C. T. U. convention. In Royal Albert Hall, where a monster demonstration meeting was held, the petition's countless folds encircled galleries and platform, resembling a huge white ribbon into which had been woven the symbolic badges of the great host of women who in every land are publishing the tidings of purity and total abstinence. A few weeks later, Miss Willard presented the petition to the government of Great Britain. Her Majesty, Queen Victoria, graciously received two richly bound illuminated volumes, containing the text of the petition and the protographed signatures of thousands of Her Majesty's subjects in Great Britain. The presentation of these elegant volumes was made possible through the generous kindness of Lady Henry Somerset.

In 1897, on the occasion of the fourth convention of the World's Woman's Christian Temperance Union, the petition adorned Massey Music Hall, Toronto, Canada. Miss Willard did not live to fulfil her earnest desire to present the petition to the Canadian government, and Mrs. Lillian M. N. Stevens, ably represented her at a great meeting held in Ottawa, presided over by Sir Wilfred Laurier. At the Panama-Pacific International Exposition, held in San Francisco in 1915, the famous petition was a part of a National W. C. T. U. Exhibit. The petition was taken to Columbus, Ohio, and was a notable feature of the World's and National W. C. T. U. exhibit at the Methodist Centenary celebration. This Polyglot Petition, great in its message, has become a priceless, revered and world-famed document.

In 1884, Mary Clement Leavitt, a true-hearted, gifted Boston teacher, became the first world-wide W. C. T. U. organizer. Through her untiring toil, the World's W. C. T. U. in foreign lands became a fact. Mrs. Leavitt adventured, at her own expense, and took the world for her inheritance. In eight years of constant journeying—this devoted woman expended but eight thousand dollars, of which all but one thousand, six hundred dollars was contributed by those for whom she labored. Local unions raised three thousand dollars, but Mrs. Leavitt drew on the treasury for only half that sum. She traveled 100,000 miles in forty-three different countries; crossed the equator eight times; held over 1,600 meetings; had the services of 229 different interpreters in 47 languages and formed 130 temperance societies, 86 of them W. C. T. U.'s, and 23 branches of the White Cross. For seven years she never saw a face with which she was familiar, and she went everywhere alone. She said "Always I found some touch of nature and of kinship, and was treated by all classes of men as kindly as if I had been their mother." Was not hers a glorious embassy?

When Mrs. Leavitt fared forth to Hawaii, to the Orient and then around the world, she carried with her an attested copy of the Polyglot Petition, often termed the Magna Charta of the home.

The self-sacrificing group of organizers, that through four decades have represented the World's W. C. T. U., are gratefully remembered. The organizers now (1924) in service abroad are Miss Flora E. Strout, who has just completed a five-year term in Burma, Malaya and Ceylon; Miss Hardynia K. Norville, South America; Miss Mary Campbell, India; Miss Christine Tinling, China; Mrs. Ren Yen Mei, China; Miss Olifia Johannsdottir, Iceland. Mrs. Ren Yen Mei of China retires from world service this year;

Miss Tinling returns to England. The death of Miss Johannsdottir, just announced, is a sad loss to the world.

Altruistic women who have been World's W. C. T. U. presidents, held high the torch. The story of their lives would fill all the pages of this book. Margaret Bright Lucas, England, sister of Hon. John Bright, served from 1884-1890; Frances E. Willard, U. S. A., 1891-1898; Lady Henry Somerset, England, 1900-1906; Rosalind, Countess of Carlisle, England, 1906-1921; Anna A. Gordon, U. S. A., was elected president at Philadelphia, Pennsylvania, in 1922. The other general officers now in active service are: Vicepresident, Miss Dagmar Prior, Denmark; honorary secretaries, Miss Agnes E. Slack, England, and Mrs. Blanche Read Johnston, Canada; honorary treasurer, Mrs. Ella A. Boole, U. S. A.

Women missionaries of various church denominations in many countries, have been able national and local W. C. T. U. officers, loyally co-operating with the program of the World's W. C. T. U. Without their invaluable aid the W. C. T. U. organizers would have failed to accomplish their constructive work. Today, church missionaries are the back-bone of "Foreign W. C. T. U. auxiliaries" that "stand by" as they push to the front the native W. C. T. U. organizations. To this date eleven conventions have been held: In 1891, in Boston; 1893, Chicago; 1895, London, England; 1897, Toronto, Canada; 1900, Edinburgh, Scotland; 1903, Geneva, Switzerland; 1906, Boston; 1910, Glasgow, Scotland; 1913, Brooklyn, New York; 1920, London, England; 1922, Philadelphia, Pennsylvania.

The first convention held in Boston, Massachusetts, in 1891, assembled in historic Faneuil Hall. This "cradle of liberty" in which a woman's meeting never before had been held, was "rocked by womanly women"—so said Frances Willard, who was most happy in initiating so appropriate a proceeding. Lady Henry Somerset, President of the British Women's Temperance Association, was the guest of honor. Welcomed and presented to the convention by Frances Willard, Lady Henry charmed her hearers. Glancing about the hall, at the statues and paintings of revolutionary heroes, she noted last of all, the gracefully entwined flags of Great Britain and the United States. "Someone asked me," she said, "if I did not consider it an insult to be asked to speak in a hall filled with mementoes of America's war against Great Britain. 'No,' I answered, 'I am glad to be here and join with you in a peaceful war against a greater enemy than ever you had in King George III; and that enemy is King Alcohol—one that imperils every home. Let us together work for his downfall and for the enthronement throughout the world of peace, purity and prohibition.' "

During Lady Henry's memorable visit to this country, she expressed great pleasure in meeting many notable Americans. One of the most delightful social events was the informal reception given to her, Frances Willard and Anna Gordon, at the home of the New England poet, John G. Whittier. Appreciating the democracy of soul of his aristocratic English guest, Mr. Whittier remarked to Lady Henry, "You, my friend from old England, are the daughter of one hundred Earls. Frances Willard is the daughter of the best blood of New England, and of the prairies, and I am only a singer for liberty; yet we are of one mind and soul in our ideals for the betterment of humanity." Frances Willard naively reminded her Quaker friend of the encouragement he gave her when years before he had written to her, "Thee is becoming quite a conspicuous figure out on thy prairies." At the request of Lady Henry, Mr. Whittier wrote, in the presence of his guests, these lines to be placed on Anne Whitney's bust of Frances Willard:

> "She knew the power of banded ill,
> But felt that love was stronger still;
> And organized for doing good,
> The world's united womanhood."

Honorable John D. Long, former Secretary of the Navy and governor of Massachusetts, acted as toastmaster at a banquet in connection with the World's W. C. T. U. convention held in Boston, Massachusetts, in 1906. He paid the organization the following gracious tribute: "The Woman's Christian Temperance Union is not a fad but one of the agencies of that universal reform in society and politics which was never under more vigorous impulse than it is today. The members represent the best and deepest convictions, not of a mere sect or special organization, but of all good men and women the world over, and to that extent certainly they deserve the cordial co-operation of all who love their fellowmen."

In 1913, in the absence of the president, the Countess of Carlisle, Mrs. Lillian M. N. Stevens, vice-president of the World's W. C. T. U., presided over the ninth World's convention held in Brooklyn, New York. Mrs. Stevens, though earnestly requested by the president to be a candidate for the highest office, refused this honor, and at her solicitation the countess, when cabled of her unanimous election, consented to remain as president. The convention hostess, Mrs. Ella A. Boole, president of the W. C. T. U. of New York state, was the resourceful coadjutor of Mrs. Stevens and Miss Gordon in promoting this convention, which proved to be the last before the great world war, and one of far-reaching influence. The severe strain of the tragic years that passed before delegates from thirty countries assembled in London in 1920, did not cause the women of the World's W. C. T. U. to break their ranks. The bond of fellowship, symbolized by the white ribbon, held.

At the international assembly, of 1920, in London, England, the first to meet after the signing of the world war armistice, the white ribboners of Germany sent a letter of greeting. The delegates were warmly received by civic and church leaders and a special service was held for them in Westminster Abbey. The proclamation sent out by Anna Gordon, November 11, 1918, the day the armistice was signed, gave to this convention the principles and plans needed for future work. It reads: "World democracy, world peace, world purity and world patriotism demand world prohibition. Representing the National Woman's Christian Temperance Union of the United States, a republic about to write prohibition in its constitutional law, we hereby call upon the peoples of all faiths and of all organizations in the world's family of nations, to clasp hands with the World's W. C. T. U. and to help bring to full fruition its hope and its heroic service of thirty-five years on behalf of a sober world. Science declares against alcohol. Health conservation and business prosperity demand total abstinence and prohibition. Together let us agitate, educate, organize and legislate, until the exalted vision of the founder of the World's W. C. T. U., Frances E. Willard, is realized; until the Gospel of the Golden Rule of Christ is worked out in the customs of society and in the laws of every land. At the close of the devastating world war, in the white heat of the limitless, unparalleled opportunities of a new internationalism, depending upon the help of God and of all who love humanity, we hereby proclaim the triumph of world prohibition." (Rest Cottage, Evanston, Illinois, U. S. A.)

It was the writer's privilege, in 1886, to attend as her first National W. C. T. U. convention, the annual gathering held in Minneapolis, Minnesota. Here she saw the gracious welcome extended to Mrs. Margaret Bright Lucas of England, the sister of John Bright, the great English Commoner. Frances Willard asked the delegates from all sections of the country to rise in groups—the east, the west, the north, the south—and give Mrs. Lucas a welcome salute. The great structure was cold, but the honored guest, when asked if she were not suffering from the chilly conditions, exclaimed: "No, indeed! Such a sight as this is enough to warm anybody's blood. I wish our English women would come to our help in such large numbers and be as enthusiastic as are these women before me!" Although over seventy years of age, Mrs. Lucas was traveling constantly, and organizing. The British Women's Temperance Association, founded in 1876 at Newcastle-on-Tyne, was the outcome of an inspiration caught by Mrs. Margaret Parker from "Mother" Stewart and other American Crusaders.

Rosalind, Countess of Carlisle, deeply regretted that it was impossible for her to attend any American World's W. C. T. U. conventions. However, she was personally and officially represented by members of her family—her husband, Lord Carlisle, and her gracious daughters, Lady Dorothy Henley and Lady Aurea Wace. Her eldest daughter is Lady Cecilia Roberts, whose husband for years was the champion of temperance legislation in the House of Commons. Another daughter, Lady Mary Murray, is the wife of Professor Gilbert Murray of Oxford University, a well-known author and dramatist, who has written and spoken most forcefully for the temperance cause. The Countess of Carlisle was president of the British Women's Temperance Association, as well as president of the World's W. C. T. U., to which position she was elected at the convention held in Boston, Massachusetts, in 1906. She was a great pioneer, a woman of large vision, great in her giving, great in her spiritual insight and outlook, great in her motherhood, and great in her passing from this life to the next. Years ago, when to be a total abstainer was to be considered a fanatic, Lord and Lady Carlisle banished from their hospitable board all alcoholic beverages, and the many distinguished men and women, some of England and America's most illustrious writers and artists, statesmen and men of affairs, who were royally entertained at Castle Howard, had their first object lesson of generous hospitality *sans alcohol*. The importance of the influence thus exerted may be measured by the high social standing of this couple in the hereditary nobility of Great Britain, and by their prominence among those who are constantly endeavoring to make the world a better place in which to live. As soon as the Earl of Carlisle succeeded to the title, the first move of these true patriots was to open their wine cellars and destroy all of the famous vintages, some of the finest in the kingdom. A storm of indignation arose, but Lord and Lady Carlisle went

The Lady Henry Somerset   Mrs. Margaret Bright Lucas
Rosalind, Countess of Carlisle

World's W. C. T. U. Petition to the governments of the world.

on their ways unheeding, and made their severance with the liquor traffic complete by closing all the public houses and retail liquor stores on the great estates belonging to the family. The countess was a platform speaker of great ability. Gladstone once said of her that she was one of the most valuable assets of the liberal party, and Professor Bunting, an editor of the *Contemporary Review,* characterized her as "the only woman in the world I should describe as a statesman."

During a memorable visit Lady Astor paid to this country, many white ribboners participated in the magnificent welcome accorded her. In one of her eloquent speeches, Lady Astor said: "This is a man and woman governed world. Together they make civilization based on Christianity a force—a civilization based on justice and mercy. I feel that men have a greater sense of justice and women of mercy. They must borrow our mercy, and we must use their justice. All legislation is better for a woman's point of view. Voting is not enough; woman must think for herself and speak 'out loud in meeting' so that the minds and imaginations of men will be stimulated by her fresher vision. American prohibition has been a big contribution to the spiritual regeneration of the world. It has shown itself not only a problem of social welfare but of clean politics as well. Let the men see that we desire a better, safer and cleaner world for our children and their children. By doing our bit, by facing unclean things with cleanliness, by facing wrong with right, by going fearlessly into all things that may be disagreeable, we will somehow make a better world."

In October, 1923, the big, beautiful American flag that on special occasions always flies from the elms in front of Rest Cottage, Evanston, Illinois, waved a welcome to honored English guests—Dame Margaret Lloyd George and her daughter, Miss Megan. Mrs. Lloyd George, who is a Dame of the British Empire, by a decoration conferred by King George V, an honor accorded to but few women, has for many years been conspicuously identified with the British Women's Temperance Association. She is an officer of the white ribbon organization in Wales and has devoted much of her time to speaking in its interests there and in England. When inspecting the beautifully engraved and illuminated book of testimonials presented to Frances Willard by her English friends and admirers while in Britain, in 1893, Dame Margaret's face lighted up as she remarked, "And I saw and heard Frances Willard that year in England." On her return to Great Britain, Dame Margaret made no attempt to conceal her favorable impression in regard to prohibition in the United States, which she considers a permanent policy of the republic.

Dame Margaret has a reputation all her own as a public speaker and a leader in moral reforms. When a slight illness made it impossible for her husband, the ex-Premier, to meet his engagement to speak to a great audience of Welsh people at Orchestra Hall, the first day of their stay in Chicago, Dame Margaret, on very short notice, stepped into the breach as his substitute and delivered an eloquent message from the women of Wales, taking as her theme "World Peace." She pleaded for a federation of all the English-speaking women of the world in the interests of international peace. "I am perfectly sure I voice the feeling of every woman in America, as well as of every woman in England, when I say we are sick of war. If the women of America, Wales and England would combine, I think the combination would be so powerful that no one would dare to speak of warring on any other nation."

The visits of these notable English leaders have helped to bind closely together the women of the two great English-speaking nations. Indeed, the entire membership of the World's W. C. T. U. forms a World's League of Friendship which cannot fail to promote international justice, purity, peace and prohibition. As America is the country in which the W. C. T. U. was first organized, it naturally followed that in the building of the World's Woman's Christian Temperance Union, the National W. C. T. U. of the United States should furnish the majority of organizers and workers. Beginning in 1897, Mrs. Helen M. Stoddard gave, in Mexico, three years of able, devoted service in pioneer, organizing and educational work. She was followed in 1900 by Mrs. Addie Northam Fields, who for several years systematically and successfully gave scientific temperance instruction in the public schools. She received the co-operation of the liberal educators. Other gifted leaders, who for brief periods have aided W. C. T. U. work in Mexico are Mrs. Ella Hoover Thacher, Mrs. Nelle Burger and Mrs. H. H. Faxon.

The Union Signal has recorded the achievements of the world-wide trips of organizers and resident missionaries: Dr. Kate C. Bushnell, Mrs. Elizabeth Wheeler Andrew and Miss Jessie Ackerman; also the admirable service in Japan of Mary Allen West, Clara Parrish Wright, Kara Smart Root, Ruth Frances Davis and Flora E. Strout, and the white ribbon seed sowing in South Africa of Rev. Alice Palmer. Cuba received a valuable W. C. T. U. uplift during the organizing visits of Mrs. Florence E. Atkins and Mrs. Elizabeth A. Perkins.

In 1907-1908, commissioned by the World's W. C. T. U., Katharine Lent Stevenson, a gifted national leader and president of the Massachusetts W. C. T. U., made a successful W. C. T. U. world survey. Mrs. Stevenson possessed insight as well as imagination, and she observed that "western civilization was imposing its vices upon the native races." She emphasized the need of "removing obstacles from the path of progress as a vital part of progress itself." "We must cast up a highway," she said, "so that the king's chariot can roll on to triumphant victory." Mrs. Stevenson's white ribbon songs have been translated into many languages, and she helped make true the refrain of her most triumphant composition, "We'll take the world for Christ's own kingdom, some glad day."

In the prohibition campaign in Newfoundland, in 1915,

Mrs. Emma H. Howland of Massachusetts, who was the gifted and successful representative of the World's W. C. T. U., heartily enjoyed joining with the devoted women of the Newfoundland W. C. T. U. in this victory song: "The rum curse has been doomed at last, Newfoundland, my New-foundland. And Satan's host are falling fast, Newfound-land, my Newfoundland. Our sons and daughters are the best, In all that's true they stand the test, We'll sing thy praises east and west, Newfoundland, my Newfoundland."

Mrs. Deborah Knox Livingston, in her tour of South Africa, in 1922, received ovations from officials, educators and temperance workers. Everywhere the response to Mrs. Livingston's marvelous message was most enthuiastic. As one journalist said, "Mrs. Livingston told the truth and pricked the bubble of the evils from prohibition very effec-tively."

In response to urgent appeals from New Zealand to aid its prohibition campaigns Mrs. Eva C. Wheeler, in 1920 and Mrs. Mary Harris Armor, in 1922, took the long jour-ney to the stalwart dominion in the southern seas. A mighty upward impulse was given. "New Zealand's Going Dry," the stirring, prophetic slogan Mrs. Armor set them singing, shouting, praying, will yet be triumphant. The United States tour of Mrs. Rachel Don, president, and Miss Chris-tine Henderson, corresponding secretary of New Zealand W. C. T. U., to see for themselves the benefits of the prohi-bition law will greatly aid future campaigns. Three times the electorate of New Zealand, by majority vote, has de-clared for the dry regime, and in 1925 it is confidently be-lieved the serious handicap of New Zealand's peculiar elec-tion laws will be overcome. If the majority vote alone could have determined a dry victory in the first, as well as in the latest campaign, New Zealand, as well as Iceland, would have antedated the United States of America in adopting the national prohibition policy.

In varying ways, American women have rendered serv-ice for foreign lands, some for a short time, others for many years. The lack of space forbids any comment on this heroic work, but this alphabetical list of names covering fifty years is most interesting:

Miss Jessie Ackerman, Mrs. Elizabeth Wheeler Andrew, Mrs. Mary Harris Armor, Mrs. Florence E. Atkins, Miss Muriel Ayres, Miss Julia Ames, Mrs. Ida A. T. Arms, Mrs. Harriet L. Ayres, Mrs. Layyah Barakat, Mrs. Frances J. Barnes, Mrs. J. K. Barney, Mrs. J. W. Bashford, Mrs. Ella A. Boole, Miss Adda Burch, Mrs. Suessa Blaine, Mrs. Nelle G. Burger, Dr. Kate C. Bushnell, Miss Alice E. Briggs, Mrs. Paul Barnhart, Mrs. Ella M. Barnes, Mrs. John W. Butler, Miss Mary J. Campbell, Dr. Mary M. Cutler, Mrs. Wilbur F. Crafts, Mrs. L. D. Carhart, Mrs. David Carter, Mrs. Anthony W. Chez, Mrs. Benjamin Chappell, Mrs. Mary F. W. Anderson Crawford, Miss Anna M. Cummings, Mrs. E. L. Calkins, Miss Grace A. Crooks, Mrs. Cornelia K. Carter, Miss L. C. Coombs, Mrs. S. W. Clemes, Miss Elizabeth C. Clarke, Edith Smith Davis, Julia Freeman Deane, Mary Owen Denyes, Fanny Root Danser, Margaret B. Denning, Miss Effa Dunmore, Miss Joan Davis, Mrs. C. L. Davenport, Margaret Dye Ellis, Mrs. Charlton Edholm, Ruth Schaffner Etnier, Mary Frost Ormsby Evans, Addie Northam Fields, Mrs. H. H. Faxon, Mrs. Dwight Furness, Mrs. M. J. Farnham, Miss Ellen Groenendyke, Miss Jennie M. Glassey, Mrs. A. W. Greenman, Mrs. Chauncey Goodrich, Miss Elma Grace Gowen, Miss Anna A. Gordon, Mrs. Alice Gordon Gulick, Elizabeth P. Gordon, Mary H. Hunt, Mrs. Jeannette G. Hauser, Mrs. Franklin E. Hoskins, Mrs. E. R. Hildreth, Mrs. Abbie B. Hillerman, Clara C. Hoffman, Helen L. Hood, Mrs. E. P. Herrick, Emma H. Howland, Jennie V. Hughes, Miss Lizzie Hewett, Mrs. John Howland, Dr. Rozetta S. Hall, Miss Isabella M. Hargrave, Mrs. May Pyne Berry Hawthorne, Mrs. Mary C. Johnson, Mrs. Lydia B. Johnson, Mrs. Octave Jacqmain, Mrs. Azuba Jones, Mrs. H. H. Jessup, Mrs. B. M. Jones, Miss Belle Kearney, Miss Elsie J. Keyser, Mary Clement Leavitt, Mrs. E. Spencer Large, Deborah Knox Livingston,

Miss Rosa E. Lee, Mrs. Lora LaMance, Miss Margaret
Leitch, Miss Mary Leitch, Mrs. W. E. Locke, Mrs. Mary
M. Love, Mrs. Caroline E. McDowell, Mrs. George B.
MacFarland, Mrs. G. D. Marsh, Mrs. Cornelia Moots,
Mrs. Florence Perrine Mansell, Hardynia K. Norville,
Josephine R. Nichols, Mrs. Thomas Nicholson, Mrs. Nor-
ton, Mrs. William Oldham, Rev. Alice R. Palmer, Miss
H. Frances Parmalee, Mrs. Matilda Patterson, Mrs. Eliza-
beth A. Perkins, Mrs. Maude B. Perkins, Mrs. Mary R.
Phillips, Mrs. F. B. Price, Miss Virginia L. Pride, Miss
Christine Penrod, Miss Mary N. Pearson, Mrs. F. D. Phin-
ney, Mrs. Alice Lewis Pearson, Miss Annie Robbins, Mrs.
Alys Smith Russell, Miss Helen G. Rumsey, Miss Mary
Robinson, Mrs. Bertha B. Roach, Mrs. Helen E. Rasmus-
sen, Miss Lelia Roberts, Miss Helen I. Root, Mrs. Kara
Smart Root, Mrs. Lillian M. N. Stevens, Mrs. Ruth Davis
Stevens, Miss Flora E. Strout, Mrs. Hannah Whitall Smith,
"Mother" Stewart, Miss Mary Campbell Smith, Mrs. Kath-
arine Lent Stevenson, Mrs. Clara A. Shrigley, Mrs. E. R.
Smart, Miss Ellen M. Stone, Mrs. Harriet P. Stone, Miss
Cora F. Stoddard, Mrs. Mary C. Stuckenberg, Miss M. A.
Spencer, Miss Amy Spalding, Miss Mary F. Swaney, Mrs.
Levi Salmans, Mrs. Kate Lunden Sunderlin, Mrs. Helen M.
Stoddard, Miss Christine I. Tinling, Mrs. Ella Hoover
Thacher, Dr. Mary Fowler Thompson, Miss Anna Y.
Thompson, Mrs. Merrit M. Thompson, Mrs. Henry Top-
ping, Mrs. Wilbur P. Thirkield, Miss Clara Belden Tingley,
Miss Bertha K. Tallon, Mrs. Anthony Te Paske, Mrs. Her-
bert Taylor, Rev. Mecca Varney, Mrs. Charles P. Vickery,
Miss Frances E. Willard, Miss Mary Allen West, Miss
Emily C. Wheeler, Miss Laura M. White, Mrs. Mary A.
Woodbridge, Mrs. Mary S. Whitney, Mrs. Mary B. Wil-
lard, Mrs. Jennie Fowler Willing, Mrs. Clara Parrish
Wright, Miss Nettie Wilbur, Miss M. H. Watts, Miss Anna
T. Webb, Miss Winifred S. Woods, Miss Sadie. L Weidner,
Mrs. Lenna Lowe Yost.

During fifty years of our organization, there has been

scarcely a National W. C. T. U. superintendent who has not helped in some measure abroad, and many missionaries of the various churches have been our strongest allies. The names, however, that follow include only the American W. C. T. U. women who have been or are World's W. C. T. U. superintendents or editors, or who have, in brief visits or through generous gifts, aided our international work:

Mrs. Martha M. Allen, Dr. Mary Wood-Allen, Mrs. Hannah J. Bailey, Mrs. Caroline B. Buell, Mrs. Summerfield Baldwin, Mrs. Helen L. Bullock, Dr. L. Pearl Boggs, Mrs. E. P. Bradley, Mrs. J. V. Brewer, Mrs. Wilbur F. Crafts, Mrs. Clara C. Chapin, Mrs. Adelia E. Carman, Mrs. M. B. Carse, Mrs. Joseph Cook, Mrs. Maude Carman Cathcart, Miss Julia Colman, Mrs. W. Jennings Demorest, Mrs. F. S. Evans, Miss Mary B. Ervin, Miss Eva Kilbreth Foster, Miss Elizabeth W. Greenwood, Mrs. Frances W. Graham, Mrs. Caroline F. Grow, Mrs. Evalyn Graham, Mrs. Anna P. George, Dr. Cordelia A. Greene, Dr. Mary T. Greene, Miss Lillian Herr, Mrs. Cornelia T. Hatcher, Mrs. Stella B. Irvine, Miss Ella G. Ives, Miss Lucia E. F. Kimball, Mrs. Gertrude Stevens Leavitt, Mrs. S. D. LaFetra, Mrs. Mary F. Lincoln, Mrs. Mary F. Lovell, Mrs. Mary T. Lathrap, Mrs. Sarah McClees, Mrs. Margaret C. Munns, Mrs. Emilie D. Martin, Mrs. Elizabeth O. Middleton, Mrs. S. L. Oberholtzer, Mrs. Frances P. Parks, Dr. Louise C. Purington, Mrs. Harriet S. Pritchard, Mrs. Esther T. Pritchard, Mrs. George Frederic Rooke, Miss Rebecca N. Rhoads, Miss Margaret A. Sudduth, Miss Jane A. Stewart, Mrs. Dorcas Spencer, Mrs. Ross Hayes Schachner, Miss Lella M. Sewall, Mrs. Mary D. Tomlinson, Mrs. Sarah Phillips Thomas, Mrs. Eva C. Wheeler, Mrs. Mary Sparks Wheeler, Mrs. Jennie Fowler Willing, Miss Margaret Whitechurch.

How the Jubilee dollars helped the World's W. C. T. U. is told by the National W. C. T. U. treasurer, Mrs. Margaret C. Munns: "As the oldest member of the family of the

World's W. C. T. U., the National W. C. T. U. of the United States would indeed be selfish if it did not give assistance to the countries struggling for freedom from the curse of alcohol. South America naturally appeals to its twin continent. The plea to help build headquarters in Argentina and Uruguay resulted in contributions of $26,000 and $15,000, respectively. Owing to favorable exchange conditions these gifts brought a substantial increase in amount. Native workers have been employed and altogether there has been spent in South America, to the end of the fiscal year, 1924, $59,980. Miss Muriel Ayres, who was sent by the National W. C. T. U., was compelled to return after about two years, on account of ill-health.

"China has had the advantage of three years' teaching of scientific temperance in her schools by Miss Christine Tinling. As China is depending in a peculiar way upon her young people for leadership, the influence of Miss Tinling's work cannot be overestimated. The same is true of Mrs. Frances Willard Wang Lu, a young Chinese woman of exceptional ability, educated in Northwestern University, Evanston, Illinois, who is organizing W. C. T. U.'s among the young women of China. Miss A. Amy Spalding of Indiana, is completing a two year's commission to aid the general W. C. T. U. work. Into the work in China, including maintenance of headquarters and translation of literature, has gone $24,800.00, up to the end of the 1924 fiscal year. Scholarships have been given in the Woman's Christian College to Miss Sumi Kananori of Japan, a grand-daughter of Madame Kaji Yajima; to Salometh Vincent of India, who studied at the Isabella Thoburn College; and to Miss Persis F. Stephens of India. At the Danforth Memorial Hospital in Kiukiang, China, a student is receiving the benefit of the Anna Gordon Scholarship established by the organized young people of the National W. C. T. U. This young woman is being trained as a nurse.

"Besides these countries, financial help has been given to Ceylon, Burma, France, Italy, Belgium, Malaysia, Sweden,

Finland, Mexico, Cuba, Germany, Austria and Denmark. The National W. C. T. U. participated in the campaigns of South Africa and New Zealand through the lecturing trips of Mrs. Deborah Knox Livingston and Mrs. Mary Harris Armor to those countries. The Cuba W. C. T. U. was reorganized by Mrs. Florence Atkins of Georgia. Consuelo Valdez, a bright young girl from the Philippines, was in this country a year preparing for leadership in her own land. Recently, she secured many new white ribbon members as she organized in the large cities in her country. She attended a girls' conference in a beautiful mountain city, speaking twice in the platform meeting, and giving a short study course on alcohol. Her class of one hundred members was very enthusiastic about the work presented.

"The World's W. C. T. U. has been given $18,000 for the aid of its great program. The world trips of Miss Gordon and Miss Deane to Europe and South America, which resulted in a great increase of interest in every country visited, and the trip made by Miss Gordon to Mexico, which resulted in the revival of the W. C. T. U. in Mexico, were made possible by the Jubilee Fund. Altogether there has been spent for World Prohibition up to the close of the 1924 fiscal year, $135,282. "It is easily seen that the National W. C. T. U. has added an incalculable sum to the legitimate endeavors of the organization and multiplied its influence in geometric progression."

Twenty-one republics of the Western Hemisphere, twenty of them south of the United States, are brought into friendly touch through activities centered in the Pan-American Building in Washington, D. C. Alcohol is the curse of all twenty nations that constitute Latin America. In Brazil, all of the United States, excluding Alaska, could be placed and have a margin of two hundred thousand square miles. Pan-Americanism, a Christian and a temperance international fellowship was strongly emphasized at the great Panama conference on Christian work where Miss Hardynia K. Norville, our white ribbon herald in South America, was our delegate.

The assembling in Washington in September, 1920, of the Fifteenth International Congress Against Alcoholism, was the oustanding event of that year. It was the first congress held outside of Europe. The leaders of our organization, national and international, were given a notable part on the program. The W. C. T. U. legislative representative at Washington, Mrs. Lenna Lowe Yost, was one of the hostesses and a member of an important committee. Mrs. Frances P. Parks, national corresponding secretary, made the W. C. T. U. exhibit a grand, educational success. The memorable pageant by Mrs. Suessa Blaine was of marked educational value.

Anna Gordon as superintendent of the Juvenile Division of the World's W. C. T. U., early rallied in many countries, enthusiastic and successful leaders. Children's choruses and demonstrations were lively features of white ribbon assemblies. She secured three hundred and fifty thousand names of children to the total abstinence pledge. The exhibit was an enjoyable feature of the W. C. T. U. booth at the Columbian Exposition in Chicago, in 1893. The names represented children from many countries who had contributed three thousand dollars for the erection of a fountain which later was presented to the city of Chicago, and now stands in Lincoln Park. It is one of the most inspiring works of art that any reform movement has produced. In popular language it is called "The Little Cold Water Girl" and represents the modern movement through which children have become a recognized factor as workers for the good of the world, being no longer content to be ministered unto with a cup of cold water, but ready gladly to offer it to others. The fountain is adapted to the use of man and to his four-footed neighbors. It was executed by Mr. George Wade, a noted London sculptor. The same figure in bronze has been unveiled, through W. C. T. U. contributions, in London, and a third replica is a memorial to Mrs. Lillian M. N. Stevens in Portland, Maine. The

Chicago fountain is named for Miss Willard, the one in London for Lady Henry Somerset.

Most of the children who contributed the money for the Willard Fountain earned their gifts, and no child was allowed to contribute more than a dime. The child's cup bears a facsimile of the badge of the Loyal Temperance Legion and a suitable inscription marks the fountain as childhood's gift. The countries of United States, England, Canada, Norway, Australia, Spain, Japan, Africa, India, France, China and Ireland, are represented in the pledge cards and gifts, and from unknown sources more than eight thousand cards were received.

A trip to a large city in Wales occurred during a visit to England of Frances Willard and Anna Gordon. One of the delightful incidents of that occasion never will be forgotten. Lady Henry Somerset had arranged a great meeting of men and women to welcome the visitors and many representatives of temperance organizations came to the platform to bring greetings. Last of all there came toddling down the aisle a little boy dressed in white carrying, with difficulty, a huge bouquet of beautiful white flowers. Lady Henry, in motherly fashion, stooped down and helped the child walk up the lofty, platform steps. Standing him on the high desk in front of the audience, Lady Henry exclaimed, amid the cheers and tears of happy fathers and mothers, "This is the reason we are organized. We believe in formation rather than reformation."

At this time, Anna Gordon was happy to organize in Reigate, England, among the girls in a Home, founded in honor of her father, by Lady Henry Somerset, a Young Woman's Christian Temperance Union. One night, in lively fashion these girls, who had come from the poorest sections of London, serenaded Frances Willard and their "Y" leaders, singing enthusiastically a white ribbon song. This led to their participation in the exercises, at a great evening rally in Royal Albert Hall, London, under the auspices of the British Women's Temperance Association.

An action song was announced on the program, but few of the audience were prepared for the touching and pathetic object-lesson now given. To the melody of the "Battle Song of the Y's," a group of little children, ragged, dirty and unkempt, from the East London slums, came upon the front of the platform. They looked about with amazement upon the sea of faces, the distant lights and the warm coloring, touching curiously with their grimy hands the dresses of those seated near them. Led by the "Sisters of the Poor"—the young girls from Reigate—they sang the affecting words of Mary T. Lathrap:

"There's a shadow on the home, many hearts are sad today,
It hushes e'en the laughter of the children at their play.
At its coming want and sorrow across the threshold creep,
And amid their broken idols the mourning mothers weep."

As the sounds ceased, across the great auditorium came children's voices in the words of the bright chorus:

"We are coming to the rescue, we are coming in our youth!
The homes we build tomorrow shall be guarded by the truth;
We are coming, coming to the battle of purity and right;
And for a winsome token we wear the ribbon white."

And a troop of well-clad children came down the aisle bearing the white ribbon. They swarmed upon the platform, encircling with the "winsome token" the sad little group there gathered.

In the forceful address given by the commander of the Salvation Army, Evangeline Booth, at the latest convention of the World's W. C. T. U. in Philadelphia, she made this heartfelt, throbbing appeal for the children: "Let the children speak—the little children, the wronged children, the crippled children, the abused children, the blind children, the imbecile children, the nameless children, the starved children, the deserted children, the beaten children, the dead children! O my God, this army of little children! Let their weak voices, faint with oppression, cold and hunger, be heard! Let their little faces pinched by want of gladness, be heeded! Let their challenge, though made by small forms—too mighty for estimate—be reckoned with! Let their writing upon the wall of the nation, although by tiny fingers, as stupendous as eternity, be correctly interpreted and read, that the awful robbery of the lawful heritage of their little bodies, minds, and souls may be justly laid at the brazen gate of Alcohol!"

Dr. Charles Mayo, the famous surgeon, recently said: "Protection of the health of children is today the world's greatest need. The lives of countless little children are sacrificed because of lack of proper care. Education and health must be coupled. Education helps from the neck up, while health makes for the whole man. Health and education are inseparable."

Miss Agnes E. Slack of London, the gifted, honorary secretary of the World's W. C. T. U., for many years, has organized progressive white ribbon groups in countries on the continent and has helped place the W. C. T. U. on the map of Europe. In those nations that are still struggling to overcome organized opposition, literally millions are standing for total abstinence and the abolition of the drink trade. How cheering it is to note that all India is awakening to the drink menace and India's one native woman ruler, Her Highness, Nawad Sultan Jahan, Begum of Bhopal, has proclaimed prohibition for her people. Her Highness sensibly considers the welfare of her subjects vastly more important than a revenue from the liquor traffic. India's daughters are taking their rightful places in the new life which is surging through the land. Five young women of high class have accepted the positions of organizing secretaries for the India W. C. T. U. Burma's government has placed scientific temperance teaching in the curricula of all government and government-aided schools. A talented native organizer is establishing W. C. T. U.'s among her own people. The president of the Palestine W. C. T. U. is one of ten women forming an advisory council to the British administration. This council stands for prohibition and has asked for a scientific temperance school law. The British high commissioner, a Jew, favors prohibition as does also the English bishop of Jerusalem, a convert since his visit to the United States.

A number of the countries are fortunate in having as chief executives those who favor the outlawing of the liquor traffic. Lined up with President Coolidge of the United States are President Hainisch of Austria and President Masaryk of Czecho-Slovakia. The mother of President Hainisch for many years has been an ardent W. C. T. U. worker and is now the honorary president of the white ribbon society of the Austrian republic.

The young people of Germany, including many university students, are breaking away from the drink traditions of their country, as they recognize in the drink habit one of its great handicaps. The Egyptian W. C. T. U. has secured the signatures of six thousand Egyptian women to a petition asking Parliament for the abolition of the manufacture and sale of liquor. At a great rally in Cairo called to proclaim this petition, Dr. Morton Howell, United States Minister, presided, and His Highness Prince Mohammed Ali was a sympathetic platform guest. Practically all the new republics of Europe, including Esthonia, Latvia and Lithuania—new members of our World's W. C. T. U. family—are enacting laws against the beverage alcohol traffic. The Latvian Parliament has adopted a law on the teaching of hygiene in the schools with special reference to the danger of alcohol.

For some years South Africa has been trying to secure a local option law. In 1923, the measure lacked only a few votes of passing the Parliament. The wife of Premier Jan Smuts is said to be a friend of the dry movement. For the protection of the native races—which outnumber the white five to one—the necessity for prohibition of the drink traffic is apparent. For four decades educational temperance work has been carried on among the young people and children of China. Thousands have been reached in the schools and colleges of Central China. Military leaders and government officials have given their approval and aid to W. C. T. U. work. The Parliament of Japan has enacted a law forbidding the sale of liquor to minors. This is the tenth country to pass such a beneficent measure. Sweden, Norway, Denmark, Finland and Iceland form a sturdy quintet of Scandinavian countries determined to outlaw beverage alcohol. In Brussels, Belgium, scientific temperance instruction has been introduced into schools. Emile Vandervelde, the Socialist deputy, has stated in the Chamber of Deputies that he will move for the enactment of a dry law for Belgium similar to the prohibition law in operation in the United States. The announcement was made in the course of a debate on a proposed measure for increasing the duty on alcohol for consumption. The Italian Medical Congress has endorsed a government program for restricted consumption of alcohol. Premier Mussolini, while not favoring prohibition for Italy, has said, "Wine and spirit drinking must no longer corrupt and debauch the Italian race."

The December, 1923, election in England was a victory for the opponents of the drink trade. The new premier, Ramsay MacDonald, is a pronounced dry. He says: "Everyone admits that the drink problem is pressing from a moral and economic point of view. The trade has become a menace to the public and to the country. It corrupts politics." The labor party declared that "it would place the drink traffic under popular control." The liberal party went further and stated that "the excessive consumption of alcoholic drink is one of the main causes of unemployment, disease and poverty; and the right of the citizens of a locality to decide for themselves the drink facilities in their own area should no longer be withheld."

Commissioned by the National W. C. T. U. to make a World's W. C. T. U. survey, Miss Gordon, accompanied by Miss Julia Freeman Deane, the gifted editor of *The Union Signal,* at the close of the London Convention, in 1920, visited many European countries, stabilizing the work already organized, encouraging the leaders and securing others who would specially aid in scientific temperance work in the schools. Miss Dean's journalistic assistance was invaluable. In 1921 these flaming heralds of Christian democracy and the protection of the home, traveled 20,000 miles to visit Peru, Chile, Argentina, Uruguay and Brazil. Their visit to Panama was given publicity by "Sancocho" whose "News in Rhyme" is a feature of the *Panama Star and Herald*. From his fourteen humorous verses one is quoted:

> "And Mistress Anna Gordon
> Is coming down this way,
> And says the whole world will be dry
> At an early future day."

In her report of this survey Miss Gordan said, "With admiration and hope the leading men and women of our twin continent have watched North America's deliverance from the legalized liquor traffic. Educators, legislators, leaders in social life, students, and thousands of public school children gave to the representatives of the W. C. T. U. a wonderfully enthusiastic welcome. Crowded assemblies in dignified University Halls testified to the determined purpose of South America to emulate the temperance triumph of the United States. In charming fiestas, and nature pageants in handsome theaters, boys and girls proclaimed the personal and public benefit of *aqua pura*. Prohibition is a live issue in Chile, Argentina, Brazil, Paraguay and Uruguay. Senor Alessandri, when President of the Republic of Chile, backed an extremely active campaign to make the republic dry, studying with keen interest the development in California and elsewhere, of food uses of the grape. The Uruguyan republic co-operated with the anti-alcohol league of women federated to the World's W. C. T. U.

"Tell us how you did it," was the universal appeal. During their three months' trip, tens of thousands heard from platform and press the wonder-story of the progress and prosperity that prohibition has brought to the sister republic—the United States of America. Miss Hardynia K.

(Above) Miss A. Amy Spalding; (in centre) Miss Christine I. Tinling; Madame Kaji Yajima, Miss Hardynia K. Norville; (below) Miss Flora E. Strout, Mrs. Frances Willard Wang Liu.

Norville, the World's W. C. T. U. representative, assisted
for two years by Muriel Ayres of New York, is loyally supported by government officials, women of the highest social
circles, leading educators, Bishop and Mrs. Oldham, and
many other Americans and British missionaries and friends.

In the early spring of 1922, Miss Gordon made a survey
of the work in Old Mexico. This trip was a part of the
world-survey made possible by the Jubilee Fund of the
National W. C. T. U. On her return to the United States,
Miss Gordon prophesied that in a new and significant sense
her countrymen would learn to say, "Our Mexico," as they,
in fellowship, shall exclaim, "Our United States." Miss
Gordon was greatly pleased at the eager response by Mexican
adults, young people, and children to the white ribbon appeal. After a few weeks of visitation and co-operation, she
reported the National W. C. T. U. of Mexico "well equipped
with officers, with a national organizer and superintendents
of the most essential departments." Senorita Ernestina Alva-
rado, the newly elected young president, has studied in the
United States and is deeply interested in social welfare work.
Mrs. Dwight Furness, who was elected to the vice-presi-
dency, but was then in the United States, promised assistance through correspondence. Miss Gordon was gratified to
find that the program of Christian education in Mexico has
a large place for scientific temperance instruction. She
saw the fruit of four years of unstinted devotion to anti-
alcohol propaganda given largely in the schools by Mrs.
Addie Northam Fields.

One day a young nobleman on horseback rode impa-
tiently up and down the streets of a village in Cornwall.
He was seeking for a public house, where he could get a
glass of that concerning which our Shakespeare said, "Alas!
that man should put an enemy in his mouth to steal away
his brain!" but his search was vain, and coming upon a
white-haired peasant on his way home after a day of toil,
the young man said, with rising anger, "Why is it that I
cannot get a glass of liquor in this wretched little village?"

95

The old man recognized to whom he was to speak, and taking off his cap, made his humble obeisance as he replied. "My lord, about a hundred years ago a man named John Wesley came to these parts" and the old man walked on. "A hundrel years!" and he was living still. In 1974, the children and children's children of white ribboners living in a sober world, will be saying, "Our homes are safeguarded today because one hundred years ago, under the leadership of Frances Willard, the white ribbon women of the world united against the greatest enemy the home ever has known."

The president of the World's W. C. T. U. is also one of the three presidents of the World League Against Alcoholism. At the convention of this organization held in Toronto, in 1923, immediately after the World's convention of the W. C. T. U. in Philadelphia, Pennsylvania, Anna Gordon said, "My soul is thrilled by the significance of this gathering. I thank God that the World's Woman's Christian Temperance Union is a part of this great World League Against Alcoholism. I am glad our World's W. C. T. U. convention, with representatives from twenty-five countries and over five hundred delegates, each one representing one thousand dues-paying members, sent greetings to this convention. There must be co-operation if we want to gain a dry victory, and co-operation if we want to hold a dry victory. Tonight we can rejoice that the leading dry forces in this and other lands have determined to get together on a policy and a program to help bring about a condition in the world that will make it brighter for women, happier for humanity, and safer for little children."

The method of transportation is one of the problems in arranging for a World's W. C. T. U. convention. Civilization continues to pass important milestones. Arrangements for a World's W. C. T. U. convention will yet be made by providing the necessary number of airships for the journey. Lieutenant A. E. Reed, who heroically commanded the magical ship of the air that first completed an ocean flight, says that no drinking of intoxicants before or during the flight across the Atlantic was allowed. "Safety First" demands that airships shall be kept high and dry. One of the leading magazines is responsible for a witty and pathetic incident about the appearance in a country town of the first airplane. Near the edge of the crowd stood a black mammy and Uncle George, a little old darky with a fringe of white whiskers around his gentle, wrinkled face. As the plane appeared in the distant sky, Aunt Amelia rocked her huge body back and forth in true camp meeting style and beating her hands in time to the swaying, cried. "Thank the Lord; thank the Lord." Uncle George gazed up in silence until the wonder came very near. Then, raising his hands devoutly, he exclaimed: "I'se ninety years old and dat's the onliest piece of God's furniture I eber seen."

For the last four decades, the W. C. T. U. women of the Orient have been listening intently and hopefully to the message of international good-will. It was November 7, 1921, and the attention of all the world was centered on the Conference for the Limitation of Armaments, then assembling at the White House in Washington, D. C. Everyone welcomed Madame Kaji Yajima, the Frances E. Willard of Japan, who in her ninetieth year, traveled 8,000 miles to present to the President of the United States, a peace petition from her countrywomen.

It was Anna Gordon's happy privilege, representing the World's W. C. T. U., to present Madame Yajima to President Harding. Standing beside them were leaders of the major women's organizations of the country—a remarkably significant group. With a serene smile, and charming naturalness, this venerable gentlewoman whom the Mikado had decorated for her patriotic and humanitarian service, said to the President, as she placed in his welcoming hands the precious petition inscribed on Japanese rice paper:

"Mr. President, as a Christian woman of Japan I have come to America to pray for the success of the coming Conference for the Limation of Armaments. I perceive the invitation which you sent to the Japanese Government is

97

based on the Christian faith, and I wish to see the Christian foundation for the Conference reinforced by prayer. I am happy to recall the passage of the Scripture that you selected at your inauguration. Truly God has shown you 'what is good.' The delegates from Japan do not adhere to any of the Christian creeds, but they love honor and justice. I wish to pray particularly for the close and hearty co-operation between Japan's delegates and the other delegates who are Christians like yourself. I wish also to pray for the delegates of all countries represented at the Conference. Our languages may differ, but I believe God will hear when we pray with all our hearts and with all our souls. Moreover, while prayers may be offered anywhere, I believe it will mean infinitely more if those with one purpose gather together at one place to pray for the one thing they crave. I have brought with me a resolution signed by more than ten thousand peace-loving women of Japan, who thus express their earnest desire that the Conference may succeed. These signatures really representing all the women of Japan were obtained in the two weeks preceding my departure, and I have the honor to present to you, Mr. President, this peace resolution embodying the aspiration of Japanese womanhood. May the blessing of God be with you as you labor under His guidance for the peace of the world; may the coming Conference prove a glorious event in history and usher in the dawn of a new era, wherein there shall be no more wars but peace and good-will shall prevail among all the nations of the earth!"

President Harding combined the gracious urbanity of a Christian gentleman with the dignity of an executive who represents one hundred and twelve million people of a great republic, as he said: "Madame Yajima, I am so happy to have you here. I feel a reverence for you. I think it is wonderful that during so long a life you have retained your interest in the affairs of the world and that you still radiate the spirit of youth. I think you are a dear, sweet, interesting old lady."

The most distinguished of the many receptions tendered Madame Yajima, her accomplished secretary, Azuma Moriya, and her missionary friend and able interpreter, Mrs. Henry Topping, was the one given by Prince Tokugawa of Japan, the distinguished delegate to the Conference, who represented the Shoguns, the most ancient royal family of Nippon. With charming oriental courtesy and dignity, the prince welcomed his guests, and especially Madame Yajima, as he said: "Even in these days of remarkable things, I think you will agree with me that the effort which Mrs. Yajima has made to prove once more the common kinship of our common humanity is worthy of highest praise. There is no world movement at the present time which is more significant than the interest which the women of all lands are now taking in every great question which concerns the uplift of the human race. In all that affects the status of woman and her elevation to that plane which is rightfully hers in the scale of civilization, you women of America have been the leaders and the pioneers. In your struggles for right and justice, in your devotion to the cause of peace and temperance, in your support of education and moral purity, you have been an inspiration to your sisters of other lands. The people of Japan are grateful for the honors which you have so freely showered upon the head of Mrs. Yajima, and I want to assure you that they see in your great kindness to her a certain omen of those closer and more cordial relations which are destined to grow up between the peoples of America and Japan."

Fearing nothing, not even an anticipated "hold-up" in the western Pullman car, Madame Yajima made friends for peace and white ribbon principles, prophesying that within ten years Japan would have prohibition. This poetic tribute by a mid-west metropolitan daily, found its way into many hearts and homes:

> "From cherry blossom land she comes,
>   A little woman quaint and old,
>   Risking her all that she may bring

A gift of spirit sweet and bold:
'One hundred thousand women hearts
    Petitioning for Peace!'

"No gifts she asks nor favor craves,
    Nor mandate brings for war to cease,
From where 'hearts mobilized' await
    She comes—a human dove of peace
'One hundred thousand women hearts
    Petitioning for Peace!'

"In this vast land can we do less
    Than 'mobilize our hearts,' as they,
The little women of Japan?
    And kneel with them and bravely pray?
An Army of the Spirit, thus
    Petitioning for Peace!"

Madame Yajima brought to Rest Cottage, in Evanston, Illinois, now World's W. C. T. U. Headquarters, as a gift to Anna Gordon a *sake* bowl presented to her by the Mikado. With the rare gift is shown a picture of a large empty *sake* bowl, in the temple of *Amanda Ike* in Osaka. Over it is a firmly shut lock; and the key is thrown away. It is a temperance pledge—the *ema,* or votive offering of a poor drunkard, who has tried to break away from his bad habit and now, in desperation, is seeking the help of the gods. Others addicted to drink have joined with him in his prayer. Each one of these men has chewed a "paper prayer" and thrown it at the locked *sake* bowl, a customary religious act. A typical *ema* is one that shows the kneeling worshiper gratefully offering two jugs of sacred wine— because of "desire fulfilled." The National W. C. T. U. of Japan is seeking to increase the *emas* depicting locked *sake* bowls—instead of the picture of jugs containing sacred wine.

The world is going dry! Yes, the religious world, the educational world, the business world, the social world, "are awakening out of slumber deep and long, and the race is beginning to understand that right can conquer wrong."

The fetters forged by alcoholic drink and its attendant evils will surely break. An international soul, as well as an international mind, has decreed the utter destruction of the legalized liquor traffic. The World's W. C. T. U. rejoices that this victory, so sure to come, shall be acclaimed one of the greatest triumphs of Christianity.

Bartholdi's statue of liberty has a woman's form and depicts his mother's face. It symbolizes "Liberty According to Law."

> "Not like the brazen giant of Greek fame
> With brawny limbs astride from land to land;
> Here, at our sea-washed sunset gates shall stand
> A mighty woman, with a torch whose flame is
>   the imprisoned lightning
> And her name, 'Mother of Exiles.'"

CHAPTER V

LEGISLATIVE ACHIEVEMENTS

BELIEVING, as Browning says, that "All's love, but all's law," white ribboners, though voteless, early resolved to make love legislatively articulate.

Protection of the home was the ultimate objective. The Federal government, in its partnership with the liquor traffic, did not exemplify love. Women, children and homes were exploited, while legal protection was extended to breweries, liquor men, distilleries and saloons. The liquor traffic, like a deadly cancer, was eating out the life of the people. National W. C. T. U. petitions to the national parties, asking them to embody in their platform resolutions against the manufacture and sale of alcoholic liquors, were rejected. The legalized liquor traffic, a great, financial, political monopoly, held the balance of power.

In 1875, a huge petition collected by the local and state Woman's Christian Temperance Union, asking for the prohibition of the liquor traffic, was sent to Congress. It was presented by United States Senator Henry W. Blair of New Hampshire, a fearless, heaven-sent statesman. A few years before his death, in an address to white ribboners, he recalled with pride this notable occasion, and said: "That first petition of the National W. C. T. U. was as big as a barrel. It was mounted on a large framework, rolled down the aisle and left in front of the Speaker."

In 1876, Senator Blair introduced the first bill for a prohibition amendment to the United States Constitution. Frances Willard was Senator Blair's inspiration, and from that early period the National W. C. T. U. followed this Constitutional Prohibition gleam.

The creation of a national legislative department made activities in this line more definite, systematic and effective. "Just where they were" in the home, school, professional and business life, thousands of women hopefully and untiringly worked for the outlawing of the liquor traffic. From 1874 to 1895, the able national leaders of the "Legal" de-

(Below) Part of National W. C. T. U. Legislative Headquarters, Washington, D. C.: Mrs. Lena Lowe Yost placing a W. C. T. U. Allegiance Enrollment Card in one of the filing cases.
(Above) Mrs. Margaret Dye Ellis.

partment were Mrs. Annie Wittenmyer, Mrs. Mary A. Woodbridge, Mrs. J. Ellen Foster, Mrs. Ada M. Bittenbender, Mrs. Catherine Waugh McCulloch, Mrs. Frances Belford, and Mrs. Mary Towne Burt.

In 1895, with the appointment of Mrs. Margaret Dye Ellis of New Jersey as National W. C. T. U. superintendent, National W. C. T. U. headquarters were opened at Washington, D. C., and for twenty-four years, until 1919, Mrs. Ellis was the national Legislative superintendent, and during the sessions of Congress, the resident Legislative representative. Throughout the years, she contributed to *The Union Signal* an edifying, weekly Washington Letter.

The story of this quarter of a century, covering the legislative activities of Mrs. Ellis, is coincident with the lives of Frances Willard, Lillian Stevens, Anna Gordon, Mary Lathrap, Clara Hoffman, Louise Rounds, Katharine Lent Stevenson, Mary T. Burt, Mrs. Silena M. Holman, and many other well-known leaders. It is a living picture of the American woman's indomitable, ballotless struggle for home protection.

Students of American history, as well as white ribboners, will be interested in some of the incidents of that period when temperance work was most unpopular and woman's entrance into the arena of politics was considered not only a regrettable delusion, but an unwarranted intrusion. With a deep realization and heartfelt appreciation of the co-operation she received from the general officers of the National W. C. T. U. and the rank and file, Mrs. Ellis has told reminiscently some of her adventures which today read like a romance. They are illustrative of the nationwide constructive legislative activities accomplished during this quarter century.

It was in 1873 in Alameda, California, a little town across the bay from San Francisco, that the Crusade fire reached Mrs. Ellis. Her home cares kept her busy, her husband and three little girls claiming all her attention. Aroused by the Crusade news from Ohio, the Alameda women of all denominations came together for prayer. What should they do? In a few days, they courageously determined to visit the saloons and talk with the saloon-keepers. In her inimitable way, Mrs. Ellis tells the dramatic story:

"This was a difficult proposition; none of us felt equal to visiting saloons. I was only thirty-two and inexperienced. But we were made to realize that we were holding back that for which we had prayed. The town was districted and certain women were assigned the task of carrying an importunate message to the saloon-keepers. Mrs. Hill, who later became very prominent in temperance work in California, and I, were given the main street. Immediately she said, 'Tomorrow morning, I'll be here and we shall go together.'

"I slept very little that night. When at ten o'clock, Mrs. Hill failed to arrive, I was glad, for I confess to having been a coward. About a quarter past ten, she came full of apologies for having kept me waiting. As we walked down the street that beautiful, sunshiny morning, I felt as though enveloped in a fog. Mrs. Hill talked all the way, but I never knew what she said. When we came to the first saloon, there were three steps leading up to the swing-door. Mrs. Hill went right ahead, pushed open the door, and passed in. She had not noticed that I was not directly behind her; but as I stood looking at those steps, it seemed to me that I could die rather than go through that door. Finally, I had courage to enter. The proprietor, a German, was alone and came forward to greet us, 'Good morning, ladies!' he said; 'how can I serve you?' 'Good morning, sir!' she replied; 'Mrs. Ellis has something to say to you.' And I didn't have a thing to say—I scarcely knew my own name. He saw my confusion and his attitude changed in a minute. In his sarcastic way he said, 'Oh, yes! I suppose you are here on the same errand those women over in the states are at'—for Californians spoke of everything east of the Rockies as 'over in the states.'

"Instantly my fear left me, for all a woman needs to help her carry a question of principle is opposition. I looked the saloon-keeper right in the eye as I said: 'Yes, sir, that is exactly why we are here—to urge upon you the closing of your saloon.' He said, 'Now, ladies, look at this from my standpoint. I am a German; I came to America to make money. I found that by the law of the state I could open what I call a beer-garden—what you call a saloon. But in order to do this, my application for a license had to have the names of twelve respectable men.' Then, looking at us most earnestly, he said, 'Do you ladies belong to that church up the street that has a cupola? I got three good names from that church; the one that has a steeple and bell—I had two names from there. Out of the different churches, I got nine names. Now, ladies, I paid my money; I got my names; I have kept the law, and I have received my seal of the state.' Hereupon, he pointed to his license, framed and hanging behind the bar. 'If your husbands want a different state of things, let them make laws that we foreigners must abide by and not let their wives come talking to us. You better stay home and take care of your children and not come to law-abiding saloons and ask them to close up. Let your husbands do the talking at the polls.'

"I saw it from his point of view and, putting my hand across the bar, I said, 'Shake hands! I never was in a saloon until this morning and I have never talked with a saloon-keeper.' That night I did some talking with my husband and I asked him why he had not explained to me about the license system. With great surprise he said, 'Why, Mother, I supposed you knew all about it!' 'How should I know? You were brought up in the prohibition state of Maine, but I was brought up in New York City where Tammany rules.' During the year and a half that I remained in Alameda, I had a young people's class every Thursday and that saloon-keeper's little daughter was a constant attendant. I won a friend in that man, but the saloon went on."

Frances Willard often saw possibilities in women of which they were quite unconscious. No other leader in the nineteenth century awakened and developed so many

105

women. When Mrs. Ellis said, in reply to Miss Willard's presidential request that she undertake the legislative work in Washington, "I am unequal to the task," Frances Willard exclaimed, "Margaret, I will not listen to any refusal. You take that place and mother the work, doing your best." Mrs. Ellis related this incident reminiscently and said, "I did it for twenty-four years. When I see Frances again, as I probably shall soon, I shall say, 'Frances, I wrought my best. When I was perplexed, but not dismayed, I have stood in front of your beautiful statue under the dome of the National Capitol and talked to you, and I seemed to hear you say, 'Go right on, Margaret, you are doing well.'"

Upon Mrs. Ellis' arrival in Washington, D .C., in 1895, having been elected National W. C. T. U. Superintendent of Legislation and appointed National W. C. T. U. Legislative Representative, she was accompanied to the Capitol by an uncle from California. As she approached the awe-inspiring building, her uncle said reassuringly, "Now, Maggie, don't feel that you are in the way when you enter. Your father, your grandfather and your great grandfather were American citizens, and your husband is a patriotic voter. These uniformed men and the elected Senators and Representatives are here to serve the people, and women as well as men are the people, so don't be afraid to ask for what you want and stick to it until you get it."

To her astonishment, Mrs. Ellis observed that at almost every table in the Capitol restaurants, beer and wine were being served. This was contrary to law, for although the government at that time permitted the issuing of licenses for the sale of liquor in the District of Columbia, no permit could be granted for the sale of liquor in the government buildings. Soon after, a bill was introduced in the House prohibiting the sale of liquor in any Capitol building. As Mrs. Ellis interviewed the Senators and Representatives, she found the subject most unpopular. W. C. T. U. women in sections from which the men came responded to Mrs. Ellis' appeal and Senators and Representatives soon heard from their constituents at home. For some years, these members of Congress were bombarded by letters and telegrams. Finally, in 1903, the bill prohibiting the sale of liquor in the two Capitol restaurants was placed as a rider to the immigration bill that had to pass and great was the joy of the temperance forces when the temperance rider passed the House, and later, the Senate. It met some opposition in the Senate, which was overruled by the speech of Senator Berry of Arkansas, an ex-confederate general who during the Civil War had lost a leg from a Yankee bullet. He earnestly addressed the president of the Senate, assuring him that for years he had been receiving letters and petitions from his God-fearing constituency in favor of this bill, and in closing his speech, he exclaimed, "Sir, my vote will be for the cleansing of our nation's Capitol from the sale of alcoholic drinks." Instantly, a half dozen Senators were on their feet in support of the measure, and the victory came. At once, an order directing that all alcoholic liquors be removed from the Capitol was issued to the lessees of the two restaurants. The order was obeyed. It was like an up-to-date moving picture show to see men carry out scores of wine cases and kegs of beer and load them on trucks. As the liquor disappeared down the street, Mrs. Ellis, looking up at the dear old flag surmounting the dome, said, "Praise God! May liquor never come back to our nation's Capitol!" In a brief time every one saw the beneficial effects of this action. It had not been an unusual thing, during hearings, for members of committees to visit the drinking places downstairs. Occasionally, during the regular sessions, a member of Congress was seen with his head buried in his arms, taking an alcoholic nap. Later, Speaker Joe Cannon was urged to use his influence for the repeal of the law. Drawlingly, in characteristic manner, he replied, "The-law-works-very-well! We think we will let it s-t-a-n-d!"

The rider to the immigration bill included prohibition of liquor at ports of entry and immigrant stations. It had been difficult for a mother to get a drink of milk for her child or a cup of coffee for herself, while beer was thrust upon them; but when the law was enforced, pails of milk and coffee and tea in large quantities were served to all the men and women arriving from other lands.

In the early days, petitions from voting constituents were extensively used, but later it was found that letters or telegrams had more weight; still, as educators, petitions were unsurpassed. As soon as a person had signed a petition, the sentiment became reflexive. He became more interested in the passage of a bill. Members of the W. C. T. U. were indefatigable in securing names and sending them to W. C. T. U. headquarters in Washington, where they were classified and then sent to Senators and Representatives. Thousands upon thousands of names for various measures were received. Every morning Mr. Ellis carried to the Capitol postoffice, petitions for the Senate and House, each one having been sealed and stamped. One day, he was accosted by a young clerk in the House postoffice, who questioned him rather officiously in regard to the petitions, saying, "They are no good. Men will put them right in the waste basket." "I should be most glad to get some of them," replied Mr. Ellis, "and if you find one for me, I will pay you a dollar." Even though the request was repeated day after day, and the promised reward reached the sum of $5.00, no petition was ever returned and the young clerk finally obsequiously acknowledged that it was only a bluff. It was heartbreaking to read many pathetic letters accompanying the petitions, sometimes coming from women over eighty years of age, who had walked miles on the prairies in mud or snow to get the names of men because they had a vote.

The first bill in the passing of which the national representative had a part was on raising the "age of consent" for the District from ten to sixteen years. There were hearings before the House Judiciary Committee, and Mrs. Ellis, with fear and trembling, went to the Capitol to speak for the voiceless girls. Sixteen members of the W. C. T. U. met in the ladies' parlor. They closed the door and held a brief prayer-meeting—the first of its kind in that historic building; then they crossed the corridor to the committee room where eighteen men were smoking, chatting, and writing. The chairman admonished the women not to overstep the time, and allowed them fifteen minutes. Mrs. Ellis and Mrs. Margaret B. Platt, president of the District of Columbia W. C. T. U., were the speakers. Their heartfelt appeals were made in twelve minutes. Later, the bill became a law, changing the age of consent from ten to sixteen.

The salutary influence of the National W. C. T. U. in foreign diplomatic affairs is illustrated by this incident:

During the administration of President McKinley, in 1897, a letter from Mrs. Isabel Strong, the stepdaughter of Robert Louis Stevenson—a letter written at Samoa, South Sea Islands—was received by the National W. C. T. U. representative in Washington, D. C. Mrs. Isabel Strong stated that the natives, a simple and kindly class, were the victims of the illegal sale of liquor. It appeared that the American consul located at Samoa was responsible for this infringement of law. As a result of the use of intoxicants, the people, formerly so friendly, became savage. Murders were frequent and whole families became addicted to drink. Mrs. Ellis was implored to do something to prevent the wholesale destruction of the people. She arranged to have Mrs. Strong's letter read before the United States Senate Foreign Relations Committee in Congress, and it was also brought to the attention of the President. The liquor selling consul was recalled, and a rule was established prohibiting any person representing the United States Government from selling liquor in a foreign country.

The description of one day's activities at the Washington W. C. T. U. headquarters is typical of many. After speaking at a hearing, the W. C. T. U. legislative representative hurried, by telephone request, to Saint Elizabeths, the Federal Insane Aslyum, and by her persuasion liberated the daughter of a W. C. T. U. mother who had been illegally incarcerated. After luncheon, she dictated letters, attended an executive meeting of the District of Columbia W. C. T. U., and an evening reception at the White House gave her splendid opportunity to make friends for the cause. It was no unusual thing, she recalls, to spend from one to three hours in an ante-room for an interview with the President, the chief of a department, or a Senator. "Many a spiritual blessing have I received," said Mrs. Ellis, "as I realized that it was not necessary to wait even one moment to have a personal audience with the King of Kings and the Lord of Lords."

Early in her W. C. T. U. service at Washington, an unexpected social affair gave the legislative representative an introduction to the American Anti-Saloon League. A committee of the leaders was in conference at the residence of Hon. Hiram Price, president of the Anti-Saloon League of the District. The topic for discussion was the desirability of opening legislative headquarters in Washington. Already, the W. C. T. U. had made a place for itself along Congressional lines, and with a desire to arrange for co-operative activities, Mrs. Ellis called at the residence of Mr. Price. She was most cordially greeted and Mr. Price, a widower, exclaimed: "You have come at the psychological moment. Lunch is about to be served, and I would be most grateful if you would kindly preside at the head of my table." Mrs. Ellis gladly accepted the invitation, as it gave her an opportunity to meet personally the members of the committee. In a formal conference that followed, she stated to the assembled gentlemen that the W. C. T. U. already was an acknowledged factor in Congressional circles, and in the political life of Washington, and she felt sure that the two organizations would work together most harmoniously.

It was in 1898 that a gentleman who had just returned from Manila handed Mrs. Ellis a little book, saying, "Here is some good work for the W. C. T. U." The publication contained the picture of a sixteen-year-old Filipino girl. Underneath was her autograph, "Marie—." The pages contained certifications by surgeons of the American army, who declared that on a certain day Marie— was found to be free from venereal disease. Marie was one of many girls who paid fifty cents for a fortnightly examination, and if they were found to be diseased, they paid two dollars and were taken to the hospital to be "cured." Then they were allowed to pursue their so-called profession. Mrs. Ellis took the book to Senator Gallinger of New Hampshire and said to him, "You are a physician and a father, and I am a mother, and these girls should be protected." He looked the book over and said, "I should like to borrow this for a few days, as there are one hundred men or more under this Capitol dome who would take an oath that no such condition exists in connection with our army in the Philippines. I should like to present this documentary evidence."

At the next interview, it was decided that the women were the best ones to undertake the task of enlightening the public. In consultation with Mrs. Lillian M. N. Stevens, president of the National W. C. T. U., who arrived at this time in Washington, the plan for an informing campaign was carried out. A few pages of the certificates signed by army surgeons were printed, the leaflet containing also the girl's picture. Thousands of these circulars were sent to white ribbon women, cabinet officers, and their wives, and to influential friends, with a request that letters and telegrams be sent to President Roosevelt protesting against such an un-American condition. The circular stated that American women are splendidly protected by their country's flag, and the women of the United States demand that women in our new possessions, Hawaii and the Philippines, should have equal safeguarding. One morning, weeks after, Mrs. Ellis was called to the Insular Division and the chief of the division said, "Madam, can you tell who has been sending out the circular letters about the Filipino girls and our army?" "Yes," Mrs. Ellis replied, "representing the W. C. T. U., I have done it." "You!" was his response. "Well, let me tell you, madame, that for three weeks I have had to have an extra corps of secretaries and I have writer's cramp signing my name. Perhaps you can tell me also how many women there are in the W. C. T. U.?" "About half a million," she replied. "I thought you were a million," answered the chief. "These letters, if piled up, would reach above my head, and I am six-feet-two. Mrs. Ellis, can't you call off your women?" "It isn't an easy matter to stop women who are as deeply interested as ours are," answered his visitor. "How much longer will they need to keep up this agitation?" "Madame," he replied, "you will be glad to know that the order for the suppression of registered prostitution was issued yesterday by President Roosevelt." The order contained these great words, "The only real, efficient way to control diseases due to immorality is to diminish the vice which is the cause of these diseases." In recounting this victory, Mrs. Ellis said, "I have been singing the doxology ever since. We sent out fourteen thousand circulars, and if every one brought a letter, it did the business. Now, I am working to secure a new clause in the Chinese exclusion bill that will keep girls from coming to this country to personate Chinese village life and then be sold here as prostitutes. Ninety-two who came for the Omaha Exposition were sold and no one could find them. I have been to see the Chinese Minister, Secretary of the Treasury Shaw, and several others. Secretary Shaw said with great earnestness, 'Tell your women the Chinese girls shall be protected.'"

During the extended agitation connected with the removal of the canteen from the army, Mrs. Ellis was approached by a seemingly intelligent woman who inquired, "Why do you work so hard to take away from the soldier the canteen which holds his drinking water?" Mrs. Ellis, amazed at her point of view, exclaimed, "Do you not know that the canteen we are fighting is a liquor saloon in the Army Post Exchange?" The canteen, or post exchange, started in the barracks in Vancouver, Washington territory, as a saloonless recreation room and store for the men of the regiment. A few years later, beer and other alcoholic drinks were sold. The result was most disastrous, and the W. C. T. U., in union with other temperance organizations, attacked the army saloon through a bill introduced in both houses of Congress. This bill was bitterly assailed by army people and members of the German and American Alliance.

112

Never was there a more persistent and powerful battle waged against the liquor traffic so firmly intrenched in the army and navy. While the temperance forces had a host of friends in both, still many officers of the highest ranks were opposed to any change. During one session, over forty thousand petitions in favor of this measure passed through the Washington W. C. T. U. headquarters. This number increased to hundreds of thousands before the bill became a law. For years the struggle continued. Avalanches of letters and telegrams kept pouring in on Congress until, in 1901, the allied temperance forces won the victory. The National W. C. T. U. at once began working for recreation buildings at army posts, and a half million dollars was appropriated by the Federal government for the building and maintenance of post exchanges. Later, an additional appropriation of $3,500,000.00 was made by Congress for the erection and equipment of gymnasiums, bowling alleys, reading and writing rooms.

The national legislative superintendent, in visiting the city of Portland, Maine, rejoiced that the man with an appetite for alcoholics was not met at every corner by a saloon and pictures of men holding out glasses of beer. Rev. Smith Baker of Portland, at the time of an election in Maine, said to a great audience, "I have lived in licensed Massachusetts and in prohibition Maine, and I say that the law of Maine does prohibit. Portland is one of the finest cities in the country. Scores of children who walk up and down these streets never see anything of a saloon or a drunkard. That does not mean that there are no people who drink, but it does mean that the children know that the law prohibits the selling of liquor. I would rather have my right hand cut off than have liquor come to Maine and to the city of Portland."

The superiority of the prohibition law of Maine to the license law of Massachusetts was impressed also upon the writer, when she was present at a liquor spilling in the basement of the city hall of Portland. A small but notable group gathered to witness this legalized destruction of alcoholic liquor. Through an aperture in the cement floor, jug after jug of whisky and beer and bottles of wine were broken and their contents gurgled into the Atlantic Ocean. Neal Dow, Frances Willard, Mrs. Lillian M. N. Stevens, Anna Gordon, and others participated in this unusual ceremony. To one accustomed to seeing in Boston, saloons on every corner and wagons of beer and other liquors rattling over the historic streets of the "hub," it was amazing to note how small was the amount of liquor that in three months' time had been confiscated.

This touching incident tells how one little Kansas woman saved the day for state constitutional prohibition. For fifteen years, Kansas had been blessed with a process of education by means of a local option law. In cities of the second class, women had an equal voice with men in voting on the liquor question. They were in a campaign to secure a prohibitory constitutional amendment. The bill for submission had passed the Senate, the day came when it was up in the House. Temperance people and liquor men were all out. There had been a long, stormy debate. It was midnight, and the roll was to be called. Men who were keeping tally saw that there was danger of losing the temperance victory—by just one vote. At that critical moment, a gentle and modest woman, with all eyes following her, left the throng and went down the aisle of the house where woman never trod before—straight to her husband, a party leader, and whispered to him, "My darling, for my sake, for the sake of our sweet home, for Kansas' sake, and God's, I beseech you, change your vote." Almost instantly, the man arose and in a deep voice said, "Mr. Speaker, before the clerk reads the result, I wish to change my vote from 'No' to 'Aye'."

In a local option campaign, occurring in one of the more newly organized states, a speaker for the liquor men closed his harangue with this assertion: "We shall win! We have the drinking men on our side, we have the saloons on our side, and we have the money on our side—and money is a power and don't you forget it!" In the same hall the next evening, referring to the dictum of the liquor man, Frances Willard made this unforgettable, eloquent statement: "We shall win! We have the women on our side, we have the sober men on our side, we have the churches on our side, and we have God on our side—and God is a power and don't you forget it!"

Still another little story recounts the home side of the many campaigns: A Kentuckian who had overcome the drink habit, was the husband of an earnest white ribboner. On the first election day after his reformation, his wife said to him, "Dear John, you know I never said a word about your politics before, but if I've been a comfort to you, do please go today and vote against the saloon for my sake and that of our little ones." John didn't answer. At the polls he met some of his old cronies and they handed him a ballot for "license." John didn't answer them, but secured a clean ballot. He took the license ballot and tore it to bits. Then, holding the temperance ballot aloft, he said, "Boys, I've always joined with *you* before, but by the grace of God, here goes a vote for *Sally and the children!*"

Scientific facts taught in the public schools, and on Temperance Sunday in the Sunday schools, made known to the people that alcoholic drink endangered the public health and the public morals. The home forces rejoiced when the Supreme Court rendered the following decision: "No legislature can bargain away the public health or the public morals; the people themselves cannot do it, much less their servants. Government is organized with a view to their preservation and cannot divest itself of the power to provide for them."

When the merging of Indian territory with Oklahoma was proposed, there was consternation on the part of the temperance people who feared if the two were joined, liquor would be introduced in the Indian territory where, by treaty, it had been prohibited. That precipitated another great struggle which proved of long duration. "It is surprising," said Mrs. Ellis, "how good men in both houses championed liquor." Senator Gallinger introduced a reso-

lution prohibiting the sale for twenty-one years in that part
of the state of Oklahoma known as Indian territory, but the
decision was finally left to the voters. The brewers bitterly
fought constitutional prohibition for Oklahoma on the
ground that they had made heavy investments there and
with prohibition would sustain heavy losses. They seemed
to forget that no man has an inherent right to engage in the
liquor traffic and that all money invested in the business is
put into it at the investor's risk.

"Old Glory is to have another star for the state of
Oklahoma!" So announced Mrs. Ellis in 1906, in her "Letter from Washington." "The last legislative act to admit
Oklahoma and Indian territory as a single state of the Union
was taken in the House, June 14, 1906, and received at once
the signature of the President. During the last six years,
one of the most notable battles of history has been waged
over statehood. We rejoice over the clause which insures
for twenty-one years prohibition in that section of the state
formerly Indian territory and that the liquor men driven
from local option counties in contiguous states are for it."
"It is recorded," said Lillian M. N. Stevens at the next
national convention, "that the first public prayer offered in
Oklahoma was by a woman, a white ribboner, and the only
woman present at the organization of the territory into a
commonwealth. All hail to the new great state which enters
upon its statehood life constitutionally free from the blight-
ing, blasting curse of the legalized liquor traffic!"

Mrs. Katharine B. Patterson, of New Mexico, wrote
Mrs. Ellis asking her to help influence the constitutional
convention in New Mexico, as it was made up largely of
liquor men. Mrs. Ellis went to Senator Blair for advice.
Following instructions from the national legislative superintendent, Mrs. Patterson had a large number of circular letters printed in Spanish and they were sent out under letter-
postage. Later, on investigation, it was found that eight
hundred were sent to the dead letter office. "It was the
W. C. T. U. that really got prohibition into the constitution," says Mrs. Ellis.

116

The New Mexico constitution had been written by the corporate interests (coal and railway) mainly, and was made practically unamendable. The Flood amendment was a provision attached by Congress for the people to vote upon, whereby the constitution could be amended by a majority vote. Without that, there could have been no hope for state constitutional prohibition. A great fight was made against the Flood amendment by certain interests; but it passed by a big majority, and instead of putting prohibition back, constitutional prohibition was carried in New Mexico by the largest majority vote of any state—in proportion to population.

Mrs. Katharine B. Patterson, who with the help of her sister, Mrs. Minnie Byrd, gave herself freely and indefatigably to the campaign against seemingly insurmountable obstacles, stated in an address at the next National W. C. T. U. convention: "New Mexico and Arizona owe to Mrs. Ellis, our courageous national superintendent of legislation, who sent out hundreds of letters and showed splendid strategy, to ex-Senator Blair (whom the New Mexico ring politician hates next to Senator Owen) and to Hon. Mr. Nicholson, national Anti-Saloon superintendent, a debt, the greatness of which nothing but the centuries can reveal."

It was on the steamship "Celtic," on her trip to Glasgow to attend the World's W. C. T. U. convention, in 1910, that Mrs. Ellis had a most interesting, incognito interview with one of the ship's officers. While she was taking an evening constitutional on the deck she thought she observed land in the hazy distance. An officer of the ship approaching her, she said, "Is that land I see?" "Yes, ma'am," and he proceeded to explain the points of interest the ship was approaching. "May I ask the position you occupy on this great ship?" was Mrs. Ellis' next question. With manly dignity he replied, "Ma'am, I am chief engineer on this vessel. I am responsible for your life and the lives of all these hundreds of passengers." Mrs. Ellis said, "I have heard that grog is no longer provided for the sea men. How do they get along without it?" "Why, they are infinitely better off," the officer replied. "At one time in an emergency we gave additional drinks to the seamen, but soon found that when the reaction came, the men at the engines were not able to cope with their arduous tasks." "What do you use in place of grog?" Mrs. Ellis asked. "Oatmeal water, and it satisfies and nourishes," replied the engineer. "How do you prepare it?" was the next question. "Pour a quart of uncooked oatmeal into a pail of cold water. The men stir it and drink it from their dippers. Too much cold water alone would have an unfavorable physical effect. The men in charge of the engines stand intense heat far, far better with this drink than they did with the grog."

In 1910, Mrs. Ellis was a delegate to the World's W. C. T. U. convention in Glasgow, Scotland. In 1911, during President Taft's administration, an invitation came from Wilhelmina, Queen of the Netherlands, to have American delegates sent to the International Congress Against Alcoholism, to be held at The Hague. Twelve delegates were appointed by the Department of State, including two ladies, Mrs. Margaret Dye Ellis and Mrs. Edith Smith Davis. The presiding officers of the Congress were the Secretary of State, the Attorney General, and the other officials of the Holland government, and the American delegates were tendered a reception by the American consul at his residence, a three-story building two hundred years old, in the erection of which no nails or screws had been used.

While the congress was in session, the state of Maine voted, after a strenuous campaign, on the retention in the constitution of the prohibition amendment. The first word reaching one of the largely attended sessions of the congress in The Hague was that prohibition in Maine had been defeated and the "Pine Tree State" had gone back on its record. The congress, including men from countries all over the world, received with consternation and tears the disappointing word. The next evening, however, one of the speakers was interrupted by a commotion. All eyes were fixed in wonderment upon a group of men standing in the door. Suddenly, with great enthusiasm, a gentleman came forward waving a cablegram and shouting, "Maine is all right—prohibition has triumphed!" "Who signed that message?" one of the American men shouted, and when he heard the answer, "Lillian M. N. Stevens," he exclaimed: "Then it is authentic, for Mrs. Stevens is not only president of the Maine W. C. T. U., but also of the National Woman's Christian Temperance Union of the United States." A joyous demonstration followed.

Why did Europeans as well as Americans attach so much significance to the name of Lillian M. N. Stevens? Let a brief outline of the background of Mrs. Stevens' legislative achievements reply. In 1894, the National W. C. T. U. created the office of vice-president-at-large. Mrs. Stevens, on the nomination of Frances E. Willard, was the first to be elected to that office. On Miss Willard's decease, February 17, 1898, Mrs. Stevens directed the national organization, and at the national convention held in the autumn of that year, was elected president. Mrs. Stevens was an extremely clever presiding officer, and her ability as an organizer, a speaker and a writer on the prohibition question was of a superior quality.

In 1900, Mrs. Stevens was chosen vice-president-at-large of the World's W. C. T. U. and presided over the International Conventions at Geneva, Switzerland, in 1903; Boston, Massachusetts, 1906; Glasgow, Scotland, 1910; and Brooklyn, New York, 1913. While interested in the different phases of the "Do Everything Policy" of the W. C. T. U., Mrs. Stevens was best known in her work for prohibition. For many years she was Neal Dow's chief coadjutor as they carried out plan after plan. In 1884, the Maine Woman's Christian Temperance Union, under the leadership of Mrs. Stevens, bore a large share of the burden of the campaign for state constitutional prohibition. Up to that date prohibition in Maine was only statutory, but as a result of an earnest and comprehensive campaign, prohibition was written into the constitution of the state by a vote of three to one.

Increasing temperance legislation throughout the country alarmed the liquor forces, who saw what it would mean if they could bring about the resubmission and repeal of Maine's prohibitory law. In 1911, the insurgency-tariff wave which had struck many sections of our country swept into office in Maine men who were in favor of resubmission, some of them strong advocates of a license law. Without doubt the turning point of national prohibition in the United States came with the victorious settlement of the resubmission question in Maine.

Mrs. Stevens' last public address was given in Portland on the occasion of a day of prayer for National Constitutional Prohibition. Its topic was "Why We Expect to Succeed." The address closed with these words: "Some glad day the states in which today is entrenched the liquor system, will rejoice that it has been abolished. Science, philanthropy, reform, religion, and the business world are testifying against the liquor traffic. In the light of all this we can see prohibition looming up all the way from Mt. Kineo in the east to Mt. Shasta in the west, from the pine forests in the north to the palmetto groves in the south. We verily believe that the amendment for national constitutional prohibition is destined to prevail and that by 1920 the United States flag will float over a nation redeemed from the home-destroying, heart-breaking curse of the liquor traffic."

Soon after the passing on of Mrs. Stevens, April 6, 1914, an unusual tribute was paid her at a great state meeting. Hon. Charles S. Hichborn in presenting a resolution of appreciation, said: "For the first time in our history the state flag is half-masted for a woman. It is the silent tribute of a great people to a great life. It is the symbol of a great grief at the passing of a great soul. It seems fitting, too, that this convention give expression to the following sentiment: In the midst of our deliberations we pause to pay the tribute of sincere respect to the memory of that woman whose name has become a household word wherever men and women are interested in the cause of temperance and righteousness. The great leader is dead, but the cause

120

still lives. All nations will pay homage to her virtues, and generations yet unborn will venerate the heroic character of Maine's illustrious daughter, Lillian M. N. Stevens."

On February 8, 1913, the Interstate Commerce bill for the protection of prohibition territory passed the House of Representatives. Accompanied by a group of white ribboners, Mrs. Ellis spent the day at the Capitol. The votes stood 239 in favor of the bill to 62 opposed. Monday, February 10, the bill came up in the Senate for final action. And the bill passed. It was sent to the White House for the signature of President Taft, who kept the bill until February 28, when it was returned to the Senate with his veto. Senator Gallinger, who was in the chair, brought the veto message to the attention of the Senate. In less than an hour the Senate passed it over President Taft's veto, sixty-three in favor, to twenty-one opposed. In the House, on the following day, after a prolonged discussion, the same favorable action was taken and the Interstate Commerce bill became a law.

The W. C. T. U. was a notable factor in securing this victory. Women, as well as men, filled the galleries. Representatives of the liquor traffic were present in force, and it was interesting to note the consternation on their faces as the tally of the votes was being taken. One man, who had been desperately prominent, was seen to wring his hands as the clerk read the overwhelming result in favor of the bill. Mrs. Ellis, as she listened to the speeches, recalled the fact that for years the W. C. T. U. women had splendidly responded to every appeal from the national legislative superintendent. Faithfully and systematically they had sent letters, telegrams and petitions to Senators and Congressmen. The men had heard from home. Enthusiastic W. C. T. U. leaders throughout the years had traveled long distances to attend and speak at the hearings. To one of these the W. C. T. U. of Georgia sent a delegation of forty, headed by Mrs. Mary Harris Armor.

At another hearing, a German member of the committee declared that Frances Willard in her last days repudiated prohibition. At the close of his testimony, Miss Anna Gordon, in a spirit of righteous indignation, addressed the chairman, saying, "I was Miss Willard's private secretary for twenty-one years. Everything she wrote passed through my hands. I was made executor of her private papers. I know her every thought, and up to the time of her death she supremely believed in prohibition."

In 1917, prohibition won in Porto Rico. It was the bottle and the cocoanut in contest. Porto Ricans were the first Latin people to declare against the traffic in alcoholic liquors and it was the first election in which the natives voted as American citizens. As seventy per cent of the registered voters were illiterate, the cocoanut was used as a symbol on each ballot by the drys and the bottle by the wets.

Several important hearings before the House Committee on Territories concerning prohibition in Hawaii and Alaska occurred in January, 1917. In her "Washington Letter," January 18, 1917, Mrs. Ellis said: "Miss Gordon, representing the National W. C. T. U., appeared before the House committee, the Hawaiian prohibition bill being under discussion. In urging a favorable report from the committee, Miss Gordon commended the work of our organization in Hawaii under the leadership of Mrs. J. M. Whitney, president of the Hawaiian W. C. T. U. Rev. John D. Wadman of Honolulu made a fine presentation of the subject and we are hoping and praying that the Hawaiian bill will pass both houses before their adjournment. The next day, a hearing on Alaska was held before the same committee. On November 7, 1916, Alaska voted dry, but being a territory, a bill has to be passed by Congress making prohibition legal. The W. C. T. U. was represented at this hearing by Miss Anna Gordon, Mrs. Ella Boole, Mrs. Cornelia Jewett Hatcher and Mrs. Lenna Lowe Yost. Judge Wickersham, delegate from Alaska, introduced his measure and spoke warmly in its favor. He then presented Senator Sutherland, a member of the Alaskan territorial legislature, and Mr. Herron, editor of the *Anchorage Times*, who urged the passage of the bill. Mrs. Hatcher, being thoroughly conversant with the situation, made a convincing presentation of the case, and Mrs. Boole spoke forcefully from personal observation made during a recent trip to Alaska."

At the National W. C. T. U. convention held in 1918, Mrs. Ellis made her twenty-third, and final annual report. She said in part: "I am deeply impressed with the advance of temperance sentiment during these last twelve months. No such year for temperance ever before dawned. Temperance sentiment has grown by leaps and bounds. To be sure, the war and its attendant demands for both army and navy have been responsible in some measure for this unprecedented advance. But whatever the underlying cause, we thank God for the marvelous result, and praise Him for the removal of obstacles that to human insight seemed insurmountable. We began the year's work at Washington, D. C., most auspiciously, by having the presence and enthusiasm of over nine hundred earnest white ribboners in attendance at the annual convention of the National W. C. T. U. The dear old Capitol building was the mecca toward which all hearts turned, and many remained over to attend the discussion, and be present when the vote for national constitutional prohibition was taken in the House, December 17.

"Among the very noticeable hindrances to temperance legislation in Congress has been that of the German-American Alliance, which in all possible ways has striven to circumvent and prevent the efforts of the temperance forces at the nation's capital. At the many hearings for the various temperance measures presented, members of the Alliance would appear in force, always declaring their intense loyalty to the government, but determined by all odds to have open saloons, and the sale of liquors unhindered.

"During this year of investigations, the German-American Alliance came in for its share of publicity. A sub-committee of Senators, not all 'dry' men, but loyal Americans, turned the light on the doings of the Alliance, and the disclosures of bribe and intrigue brought to light are far in advance of anything dreamed of. Back of the Alliance stood the U. S. Brewers' Association, who financed the organization, that they might successfully fight all temperance legislation proposed by Congress. It has been divulged that the brewers have paid in over $700,000 alone to defeat constitutional prohibition. The report of the sub-committee to the full Judiciary Committee was so convincing, and later so reported to the Senate, that a vote of that body ordered a repeal of the Federal charter granted them when organized, since which time the Alliance claims to have disbanded. Another committee of U. S. Senators are, at the present time, investigating the Brewers' Association, and so far have brought to light stubborn facts as to the loyalty of the organization. It has been found that since we entered into the war, the brewers have paid thousands of dollars to push German propaganda. They have bought daily newspapers published in different parts of the country, to fight prohibition. A list of persons engaged in business, and business concerns, who have aided temperance in any positive way, was shown the committee as those who especially came under the ban of the brewers, and would be punished accordingly. The investigation, which is still under way, bids fair to reveal a condition of things that will startle the country, both as to their disloyalty, and their defiance of law.

"Prohibition for Alaska, Porto Rico, and Hawaii, received due amount of attention. It seems impossible to convey in such a report as this, an idea of the amount of effort or the methods employed for measures such as these. The handling of petitions, the sending on of letters from home, the many interviews, over and over again, the many hearings, the disappointments, the obstacles to meet with cheerful face—the ways of doing legislative work are numberless—but when victory comes, the heights are reached, the long, hard road is forgotten, and we go on our way rejoicing, ready for the next hard piece of work.

"November 21, 1918, Congress closed the longest single session in its history to date, and surely one of the most important. When it adjourned, it had been in continuous session for three hundred and fifty-four days, only eleven days less than a full year. They have only eleven days' recess, as the Sixty-fifth Congress meets in its last session, Monday, December 2.

"When I began my work in Washington, there were just three states which had a prohibition law—Maine, Kansas, and North Dakota. Now there are twenty-eight, beside the District of Columbia, Alaska, Hawaii, Porto Rico, the Canal Zone, and the Virgin Islands. When I gave myself to the temperance cause, I enlisted for the war. When the final vote was taken in Congress and when forty-five states ratified the amendment and placed it in the Constitution, I rejoiced that it had been my privilege to work for forty years and so aid in bringing that wonderful victory.

"There passes before me like a panorama the many bills in which we have been interested. One of the pleasures connected with my service has been the unanimity of sentiment and feeling of brotherly kindness exhibited by the members of the different men's temperance organizations located in Washington, D. C., all working along the same lines for the same cause. What shall I say of the District W. C. T. U. presidents and the splendid rank and file of the Woman's Christian Temperance Union who were never too weary to carry out the plans of their representative, and always ready to do a little more. God bless them, every one! The W. C. T. U. was an open door for me into a closer walk with God. Through my association with white ribbon women, I was led out into a broader vision—national and international. I shall always thank God for what the Woman's Christian Temperance Union has done for me and for mine.

"Mrs. Lenna Lowe Yost, my associate for the past two years, has been a constant source of helpfulness. Her enthusiasm and good judgment have helped solve and smooth many knotty problems. I relinquish my position as representative of the National W. C. T. U. at Washington, D. C., to her, as one fully qualified to carry the work forward to complete victory. We have been greatly helped, and honored, in having our loved leader, Miss Anna Gordon, with

125

us at Washington headquarters weeks at a time. She is a veritable tower of strength, and her presence has been invaluable. That the work may continue to grow and expand until the whole world shall be freed from the power and dominion of alcohol, is my earnest prayer."

In 1918, Mrs. Ellis was succeeded by Mrs. Lenna Lowe Yost, of West Virginia. Possessing the ardor of young womanhood, exceptional acumen and expert experience, Mrs. Yost commenced her activities as legislative superintendent and legislative representative, at National headquarters in Washington, D. C. Mrs. Yost's unusual ability in legislative activities had been demonstrated when as president of the West Virginia W. C. T. U. she led in campaigns for state and national prohibition. She began her training in the practical school of politics early in her married life, going personally to each session of the state legislature to appeal for prohibition, woman suffrage, child labor laws, and many measures relating to the health and welfare of women in industry. At this time her husband, Ellis A. Yost, was a member of the legislature, and is highly esteemed as the father of the state prohibition act, known as the Yost law.

The devotion of her own and kindred organizations to Mrs. Yost, and to the principles for which she stood and worked, were unswerving. Judge McWhorter, one of West Virginia's prominent jurists, and chairman of the Ratification Federation for the state prohibition amendment, in a review of the campaign, in a public address, referred to Mrs. Yost as its Joan of Arc. Twelve years later, the same characterization was used by an associate in legislative activities in Washington, D. C., in reference to her work at the nation's capital.

Mrs. Yost's supreme fitness for the strategic position she occupies in the nation's capital city, at once was evident. Her attractive personality and cogent reasoning never failed to disarm the prejudices of the Senators and Representatives. From the first, Mrs. Yost has wisely co-operated with all the allied temperance forces. She represents the National W. C. T. U. on the Woman's Joint Congressional Committee, a remarkable committee representative of twenty-one national organizations of women. It acts as a clearing house for all the constituent organizations. It designates itself as "the outcome of a movement on the part of the great national organizations of women to pool their resources and co-operate for the support of Federal legislation which affects the interests of women in particular and makes for good government in general." Mrs. Yost is the vice-chairman and treasurer, and was the active chairman of the sub-committee that directed the campaign for the Maternity and Infancy Law now administered by the Children's Bureau. This sub-committee during the last few months of the campaign held more than one hundred sessions. The work of receiving reports and checking up on 531 members of Congress—the combined membership of the House and Senate—was the task. In the last week of the contest, interviews at the rate of fifty a day were held. This sub-committee interested the constituency back home and secured a co-operation that brought success.

During these later years, the growth of the legislative work had necessitated the removal of National W. C. T. U. headquarters from the building owned by the District W. C. T. U. to the Hotel Driscoll located near the Capitol, and Senate and House offices. Anyone who has viewed by night the artistic construction of the Capitol, illuminated by powerful electric lights, will appreciate this description given by Mrs. Ellis: "Nothing can equal the spectacle of the white edifice floating, as it were, above the city, the incomparable dome of perfect proportions shining in its purity against the sky; ethereal, yet tangible, it is a token of the stability of the government."

The two rooms in the Bliss Building, near the Capitol, that now constitute our Legislative headquarters, with Mrs. Yost in charge, are indeed a hive of industry. Rows upon rows of cards in the files of Allegiance to the Constitution enrollment are indexed by congressional districts and are silent witnesses to the strength of the dry sentiment in the country; for every card bears the name of a dues-paying member of the W. C. T. U. Not only the name, but the address of each one belonging to the W. C. T. U. is registered. The white cards of the women members are reinforced by blue cards bearing the names of men, honorary members. Frequent consultations with the commander-in-chief of the W. C. T. U. forces are necessary, so during sessions of Congress the national president must spend a part of her time at Legislative headquarters. The annual meetings of the National Temperance Council and the National Legislative Conference call several general officers to the capital city. Twenty-seven organizations interested in prohibition progress and legislation are represented in these meetings. Another important file at the Washington, D. C., headquarters, which, since 1918, the national legislative superintendent assiduously has kept up-to-date, is one giving the name and voting record of each member of Congress. The vote "Aye" or "No" on all prohibition measures for the last seven years can be ascertained. No member can escape his record.

Since women became voters, letters of inquiry from women leaders in forty-eight states have kept the headquarters force busy. Women keenly alive to the responsibility of the ballot want to know the standing of Congressmen seeking re-election. "What has he done to promote prohibition, the welfare of children, and measures of special importance to women and the protecting of the home?" are some of the questions asked. Evenings are spent looking up records. "On the whole," says Mrs. Yost, "there is a gradual increase in the number in the House and Senate who can be depended on not only to vote right, but actively to assist in promoting a pending bill for the better enforcement of prohibition law. In the first session of the Sixty-eighth Congress a goodly number who always have voted wet, gave active assistance in procuring the passage of additional prohibition law enforcement measures. Men and women holding responsible positions write the legislative superintendent that they highly value 'The Washington

Letter, that appears weekly in *The Union Signal* because the news given is condensed, interesting and accurate.' "

For the benefit of a host of inquirers, Mrs. Yost published, at the earliest opportunity, a pamphlet entitled "Twenty Years of Prohibition Legislation by the United States Congress." In an interview, Mrs. Yost said most earnestly, "I was amazed to find such a splendid record of Federal legislation. It was a great revelation—even to me. It reads like a romance! During a period of twenty-three years, there were only three years in which prohibition legislation has not been enacted. There has been a gradual growth of prohibition sentiment."

This pamphlet, giving a review of Federal legislation during twenty years against the legalized liquor traffic, includes the following laws:

"In 1901, saloons in the army prohibited; in 1902, prohibition in certain Pacific ocean islands; beginning with 1903, recreation buildings provided for army as substitutes for saloons; in 1903, saloons prohibited in the nation's Capitol building; in 1903, prohibition at immigrant stations; in 1904, beer halls suppressed in state and territorial soldiers' homes; in 1906, suppression of canteens in national soldiers' homes; in 1906, prohibition for the Indian sections of Oklahoma; in 1906, large appropriations for the suppression of the traffic among Indians; in 1906, internal revenue amendments to assist in prosecutions of anti-liquor laws; in 1906, prohibition in Arizona and New Mexico enabling acts; in 1907, prohibition zones created; in 1908, use of mails for carrying intoxicating liquors prohibited; in 1908, an appropriation by the Congress of $6,000.00, and a code of laws adopted to aid in the suppression and regulation of the liquor traffic among the natives of Alaska; in 1909, Mississippi River jurisdiction; in 1911 and 1913, appropriations for international congresses against alcoholism; in 1913, famous interstate shipping law; in 1914, penalty for intemperance in the army; in 1917, voting code for Alaska; in 1917, prohibition for Porto Rico; in 1917, prohibition for the nation's capital; in 1917, anti-advertising and bone dry law; on April 6, 1917, prohibition as war legislation; in May, 1917, President authorized to establish zones; September 10, 1917, Congress prohibits use of foods for malt and vinous liquors; in 1917, war prohibition for Hawaii; November 21, 1918, war prohibition for the nation, became effective July 1, 1919. In 1917, submission of the prohibition amendment. In the midst of war legislation the Senate of the United States received from its Judiciary Committee a favorable report recommending passage of the resolution providing for National Constitutional Prohibition and by a vote of 65 to 20 it was passed August 1, 1917. The House adopted the resolution with amendments December 17, 1917, by more than the necessary two-thirds majority, the vote being 282 for and 126 against. The following day the Senate concurred in the House amendments and the famous joint resolution was promptly transmitted to the states for ratification.

"Ratification by fifteen states was secured during 1918. Beginning January 2, 1919, thirty additional states ratified by February 25, making forty-five in all ratifying the Eighteenth Amendment. Connecticut, Rhode Island and New Jersey failed to ratify.

"On January 16, 1919, ratification day, the thirty-sixth state ratified, making the required number, and thus, according to the amendment itself, national prohibition became operative at midnight, January 16, 1920.

"On July 22, 1920, the prohibition enforcement bill passed the House of Representatives after two months' consideration, by a vote of 287 to 100, and passed the Senate September 5, without a record vote. The bill was sent to conference and differences were settled, and on October 15, it was signed by the President of the Senate and the Speaker of the House, and transmitted to the President the following day. On October 27, the President vetoed the bill. By one of the swiftest and most decisive votes in the history of Congress the bill was passed over the President's veto and, therefore, became a law. The bill covered the whole subject of enforcement for both war-time and constitutional prohibition and defined intoxicating liquors as any beverage containing more than one half of one percentum of alcohol by volume. This closed another act in the long struggle for the victory of a great principle.

"On November 18, 1921, the Willis-Campbell bill was passed. The main provisions of the bill are the prohibition of the use of beer or malt liquors for medical purposes, the extension of prohibition to Hawaii and the Virgin Islands, prohibition of the prescription of more than one-fourth of one gallon of vinous liquors within ten days and the prohibition of more than 100 prescriptions to a physician in three months, unless some extraordinary reason is given, and stops importation of spirituous and vinous liquors until the present supply is not sufficient to supply the current needs for non-beverage uses, and prevents search and seizure of a private dwelling without a search warrant.

"March 13, 1924, United States-Great Britain Treaty: The United States-Great Britain treaty to cope with the rum smuggling problem was ratified by the United States Senate, March 13, 1924, by a vote of 61 to 7. The treaty had the signatures of Secretary Hughes and the British Ambassador, Mr. Geddes, on January 24. This treaty has somewhat inaccurately been referred to as the twelve-mile limit agreement. The fact is, no specific limit is placed. Under the terms of the treaty, any ship suspected of smuggling liquor under the British flag would be liable to search and seizure if intercepted within an hour's sailing distance from shore, the speed of the ship being the measure. It has been estimated that this averages about 12 miles, though in the case of faster ships, the zone of possible seizure might be much broader; the estimate led to naming it the twelve-mile treaty.

"In reciprocity, the agreement grants British ships the right to carry sealed stores of ship liquors within American waters for use on the return voyage. The question has been raised whether this is practical under a recent Supreme Court decision, but it was possible to secure this agreement with Great Britain only by writing it into the treaty and taking a chance on its interpretation by the court."

CHAPTER VI

PATRIOTISM AND WAR PROHIBITION

FIFTY years ago, the "call" of the Woman's Christian Temperance Union was, in reality, a "call to the colors." "For Native Land," was included in the winning rally-cry of these women patriots as they sought the annihilation of the greatest enemy that imperiled the home and the nation. They reverenced their country's flag "with its red for love; its white for law, and its blue for the hope that our fathers saw, of a larger liberty," and they saw this symbol of a great nation floating over legalized breweries and distilleries. With invincible determination the white ribboners joined hands for the destruction of these un-American institutions, and were at the front in purifying Old Glory from the stains of the liquor traffic. The leaders who dared, and scores of the rank and file were "minute" women, bravely voicing the danger that confronted the republic.

In 1883, many of the saddened women of the "solid south" responded to the loving impact of the white ribbon women of the north. In the civil war, these southern women had suffered the loss of homes, husbands and sons. The story of their enlistment in the peaceful, non-sectional war that was to save their homes, husbands and sons, already has been told. The "solid south" became "solid" for prohibition. The women who were God's messengers in helping to bring together the embittered sections of the United States, were staunch generals in the army of peace. Their guns were ballots, their bullets were ideas. Their message was both religious and patriotic.

In 1887, for the first time, the National Woman's Christian Temperance Union convened south of the Mason and Dixon line—in Nashville, Tennessee. As Frances Willard greeted this assembly of delegates from the north, south, east and west, with every southern state represented, she told of the "tugging at her heart" when she first saw the ocean, the Alps, St. Peters at Rome, and the city of Jerusalem, and fervently said: "At this hour I am in the presence of one of God's mightiest spectacles of the moral sublime, and it is too great for me—it is high, I cannot attain unto it. For today the National Woman's Christian Temperance Union has been made welcome in the conservative metropolis of southern education, the home of Mrs. President Polk and the vicinity of Andrew Jackson's 'Hermitage.' There is a spirit in Nashville's air today that makes of every breath a sacred inspiration. The people here may not know it, but history will know, that since this city was founded on the banks of the Cumberland, no assembly of a significance so far-reaching has ever before been convened within its borders. Here, side by side, sit the blue and the gray. Prohibition first of all is the fixed point whence we calculate all others—no saloon in politics or law, no sectionalism in law or politics, no sex in citizenship, but liberty, equality, fraternity in politics and law now and forever more. When in all history were such matchless issues espoused?

"The women who uniformed their sons in southern gray and said, like the Spartan mother of old, 'Come ye as conquerors, or come ye no more,' are here tonight with those women who belted northern swords upon their boys in blue with words as pitiful, as brave. The women who embroidered stars and stripes upon the blessed flag that symbolized their love and faith today have only gentle words for those who decked their 'bonny flag of stars and bars' with tenderness as true and faith as fervent. What hath God wrought? Surely a winsome thing is the human heart. The bloodless warfare of today, where women share the field with men, makes us forget the past.

'O veterans of the Blue and Gray, who fought on southern field

The purposes of God are true, His judgment stands revealed;

133

The pangs of war have rent the veil, and lo His high
  decree,
One heart, one hope, one destiny, one flag from sea to
  sea.'

"When the troops were mustered out in 1864, we little
dreamed that just ten years later we should be together in
line of battle, but behold—here are the women who went to
the polls pleading with voters to do the right in Michigan
and Oregon, side by side with those who went in Tennessee
and Texas. The south is 'solid' still, but it is for home
protection; the 'free ballot and fair count' have come, but
it is through local option contests; the northern and the
southern heart are fired alike, but it is by the ringing bugle
blast of 'Prohibition.' "

In the year 1917, a state of war between the United
States and the imperial German government was declared.
The National Woman's Christian Temperance Union seized
the tragic opportunity for service. Five hundred thousand
white ribboners made articulate the patriotism of their organization. Many of the leaders attended the extraordinary
session of the Sixty-fifth Congress, which opened April 2,
1917, and was formally addressed by President Wilson. A
resolution declaring the United States at war with Germany was passed in the Senate (82-6); and in the House
(373-50).

On April 4, after the war resolution had been adopted,
Senator Sheppard introduced as a vital war measure, a
resolution calling for an amendment of the Federal Constitution. He declared that the adoption of this amendment
would be a measure of preparedness as "prohibition is
necessary to the efficiency of our man power and conservation of our resources." The mothers of the country, so
many of them in the W. C. T. U., were saddened but
heroic. An unspoken cry, an inarticulate prayer, went up
from every home. There was an out-reaching response in
the heart of the national president, Anna Gordon, as she

The Georgia W. C. T. U. War Service Flag. The Stars represent sons, husbands and brothers of white ribboners.

Medal presented by the French government, in gratitude for distinguished W. C. T. U. war relief service, to Miss Lella M. Sewall.

National W. C. T. U. Ambulance used in war service in France.

sent broadcast immediately after Congressional action, this significant call:

"Our Woman's Christian Temperance Union has been a foremost factor in educational work for peace and international arbitration, but we are loyal daughters of our country and we are face to face with war. We shall meet the situation with sublime courage, with Christian optimism and with the self-sacrifice of the patriot. Let us be worthy of Frances Willard's characterization of our organization: 'There were never such women as our white-ribboners, so large hearted, so generous, such patriots, such Christians.' Let us give to our soldiers and sailors our best service. We are fortunate at this critical hour to have in both Senate and House of the United States Congress, many strong prohibition friends. Prohibition, as a war measure, will be vigorously pushed by the National W. C. T. U., as well as by other temperance agencies centered in Washington. Already, our friends in Congress are considering how they can best safeguard our boys. The prohibition program of this extraordinary session of the Sixty-fifth Congress ought to fully meet the ardent, prayerful hope of mothers whose boys may soon be subjected to the awful fortunes of war. The enactment of this Congress called to deal with war measures, should be in accord with the mighty progress of public sentiment in favor of a sober nation—a sentiment which today is insistently calling for national prohibition." The instant, enthusiastic response to Miss Gordon's call was the wide-spread adoption of the slogan: "Every white ribboner, a prohibition patriot."

The National W. C. T. U. co-operated with government plans for women's war service, and were members of the advisory committee of the Woman's Committee of the Council of National Defense, of which Dr. Anna Howard Shaw was appointed chairman, and of the advisory committee of the Women's Liberty Loan Committee. They were also members of the National Temperance Council, the United Committee on War Temperance Activities in the Army and Navy, the National Legislative Conference, and the Commission of Nineteen, on National Constitutional Prohibition. A magic increase in the spirit of co-operation was shown in the organization of the United Committee on War Temperance Activities in the Army and Navy. In this coming together of the mighty forces of temperance and philanthropy, representing also leaders in the church, eighteen noble bodies were patriotically united. The president of the National W. C. T. U. was elected vice-chairman of this responsible committee. Each society was given its special work, and a budget of one hundred thousand dollars supplied the funds, each society administering its own war budget.

The stupendous task of planning the war activities of the National W. C. T. U. was valiantly undertaken by the National W. C. T. U. War Work Committee. This committee consisted of the national general officers, and six National W. C. T. U. superintendents, whose departments were closely related to the activities occasioned by the war. They were: Margaret Dye Ellis, of Washington, D. C., superintendent of the department of Legislation; Ella Hoover Thacher, superintendent of the department of Soldiers and Sailors; Lella M. Sewall, superintendent of the Flower Mission and Relief Work; Mary E. Brown, superintendent of the department of Moral Education; Lucia F. Additon, superintendent of the department of Temperance and Labor; Ella Black, superintendent of the department of Foreign Speaking People.

The burden of decision necessarily rested upon the three resident general officers, the national president, Anna A. Gordon, the corresponding secretary, Frances P. Parks, and the treasurer, Margaret C. Munns. The organization owes much to Mrs. Parks' initiative and daily, systematic supervision of the committee's plans and problems. The machinery of the National W. C. T. U. department of Work Among Soldiers and Sailors was especially adapted to service along Red Cross lines and for years had been mobilized for duty of this nature. As the liquor and vice interests had established themselves near military centers, all good citizens in the vicinity of recruiting stations and mobilization and training camps were urged by the W. C. T. U. to see that the soldiers were not subjected to temptation.

For thirty years the devoted superintendent of the department of work for Soldiers and Sailors, Ella Hoover Thacher, had been visiting naval training stations and forts and holding gospel temperance meetings with the men. As she again visited these military stations she found her knowledge of conditions and friendly acquaintance with military and navy officers most helpful in the promotion of war activities. The work for soldiers, sailors and marines and for general relief work was standardized by Red Cross rules. Mrs. Thacher, through her state associates, had her special plan of work well in hand. This included purchasing electric fans, furnishing fruit and delicacies for army base hospitals, social welfare work and activities in the army training camp and mobilization centers, serving coffee and doughnuts or cake and lemonade to soldiers and sailors as they entrained, and giving to each a copy of the "Soldiers Temperance Songster" and a total abstinence pledge-card. The co-operation of women and men in all the churches, especially in the vicinity of the camps, was sought.

In 1918, on the resignation of Mrs. Thacher as national superintendent, Mrs. Richmond Pearson Hobson, upon the earnest solicitation of the National W. C. T. U. officers, loyally assumed the duties of national superintendent. In this position she met with marked success and was aided by her distinguished husband, Captain Hobson, the hero of the "Merrimac."

The prohibition of the liquor traffic in the District of Columbia went into effect September 8, 1917. This caused great rejoicing among the mothers of the country, for hundreds of their soldier and sailor sons thus escaped the alluring temptation of the saloon. The W. C. T. U. of

Washington, D. C., with the aid of the District W. C. T. U., Mrs. Emma Sanford Shelton, president, and the generous gifts and supervision of Mrs. Thacher, opened a recreation and rest room which was gratefully enjoyed by sailors from the nearby forts and soldiers from military posts. The following incident, illustrating the efforts of a former United States President to protect the young recruits of the Civil War from drink, often was told in that rest room. When Abraham Lincoln, Commander-in-chief of the army and navy, happened to see in the streets of the capital city, a young soldier starting to enter a corner saloon, he laid on his shoulder a firm, detaining hand. The lad, looking up, saw a kind, fatherly face, and recognized at once, the President of the United States whose framed picture held an honored place in his country home. "I never want to see the United States uniform going into a place like that," said Mr. Lincoln, as he gently led the young soldier into safer surroundings. At a meeting of veterans many years later, an old man in a faded uniform told this story, and said, "I was that soldier boy, and it was Abraham Lincoln who saved me from the curse of drink. The thought of that noble, sorrowful, fatherly face has ever been with me."

The patriotic service of the W. T. U. included successful educational and social work in camps, in reconstruction hospitals, the sending of motor ambulances, motor field kitchens, providing hostess houses, hospital mothers, stereomotorgraphs, cheer-up books for the blind, comfort kits, knitted articles, hospital delicacies and flowers lavishly contributed; it supplied speakers in camp, literature for the soldiers, sailors and marines, and slides showing the scientific value of total abstinence. It is impossible to depict in detail the stirring patriotic scenes enacted; for every state W. C. T. U. was alive to its opportunity. In their local and special meetings, while carrying out their scheduled W. C. T. U. programs, groups of white ribboners all over the country made comfort bags and hospital and Red Cross supplies. The constant contact of white ribboners of twenty thousand local unions with the members of women's clubs, missionary and patriotic societies and leaders of community centers was mutually helpful.

In sixteen states, in response to the government's needs, miracle cities sprang up. In a peculiar way, white ribboners were interested in the training camps to which the citizen soldiers of their own state reported for duty. Never in the history of the world has any government provided so carefully for the all-round welfare of the enlisted man. The war department recognized the necessity of protecting them from alcohol, gambling and vice, and "white zones" relentlessly enclosed every camp and cantonment. The comprehensive scheme by the Committee of Protective Work for Girls, included the appointment of policewomen who worked under direction of the city police. The National W. C. T. U. promoted the plan for the care of girls issued through the Department of Health and Recreation of the Woman's Committee of the Council of National Defense. The policewomen helped in the solution of the tremendous problems growing out of the mobilization of a million and a half of men in more than eighty training camps. The spirit of youth, combined with patriotic fervor and a disposition to hero worship, made an appalling problem in communities frequented by men from nearby camps. The policewoman patriot, with her large sympathy, clear understanding of girlhood danger, her sisterly care backed by authority, was enabled to protect the girls ignorant of danger and, whether desired or not, to give help.

Plans issued by the Woman's Section, Social Hygiene Division of the Committee on Training Camp Activities, received the support of the W. C. T. U. Whether the approach was made through the patriotic appeal, the religious motive, or scientific fact, the common goal, a "white life for two" had long been familiar to the W. C. T. U. Properly chaperoned entertainments, with music and refreshments, were given by the young people. White ribbon girls by setting a high social standard, exerted a restraining influence over those young women who foolishly failed to observe toward men in uniform the proprieties that prevail in times of peace. "Keep the home fires burning" was one of the most popular songs rendered in the camps by the Young People's Branch of the W. C. T. U.

The example of the National W. C. T. U. corresponding secretary in sending out helpful war bulletins, was followed by some of the state presidents. "Patriotism of a practical type has characterized the W. C. T. U. from north to south, from east to west," said Mrs. Parks in one of her able documents. "It is illustrated from the Old Bay State to the Land of the Golden Gate, from the Canadian border to the Gulf of Mexico. The patriotic service of the W. C. T. U. is so attractive and appealing and so carefully co-ordinated that men, as well as women, are flocking to our aid with money and personal help. The International Film Company has taken pictures of some of our large Comfort Bag Shops. White ribboners are sending out hundreds of thousands of these indispensable articles. Conspicuous work at Fort Sheridan and the Great Lakes Naval Training station is being accomplished." Many mothers were interested in holding up for their sons and other soldiers a high standard of purity. It was the patriotic white ribbon mother of college sons who wrote the clean life pledge, which was signed by four thousand men of the First Reserve Officers Training Camp at Fort Sheridan. It reads as follows:

"1. We undertake to maintain our part of the war free from hatred, wanton brutality or graft, true to the American purpose and ideals.

2. Aware of the temptation incident to camp life and the moral and social wreckage involved, we covenant together to live the clean life and to seek to establish the American uniform as a symbol and guarantee of real manhood."

"A mother's a mother, the world over." The appeal for war relief took fast hold on the hearts of "organized mother love," Miss Willard's name for the W. C. T. U. In every cry for help from the famished and orphaned children of Europe, each true woman heard the cry of her own child. Nearly three thousand fatherless children were adopted at a cost of over one hundred thousand dollars. White ribbon women also made eighty-one thousand, five hundred garments, costing approximately six thousand dollars. These were "turned in" through the committee, Children of the Frontier, and also through the Red Cross. In their relief work W. C. T. U. women also included those at home. In all these activities there was co-operation with the following agencies: Home Service of the Red Cross, Y. M. C. A., Y. W. C. A., War Camp Community Service, Women's Committee of the Council of National Defense, Fatherless Children of France, and the Belgium and French Relief Society. In practically every state flowers in abundance were distributed in the base hospitals and among the families in service. Miss Lella M. Sewall, of Boston, National W. C. T. U. superintendent of Flower Mission and Relief Work, who promoted the adoption of French orphans, received from the French government, in gratitude for distinguished service, the artistic, inscribed medal pictured on another page.

At the beginning of the World War, an army of workers, a large number of them women, worked at high pressure to turn out the war orders for the Allies. The entrance of the United States into the conflict increased the demand for women workers, many of whom received sisterly advice and aid through the W. C. T. U. department of Women in Industry. Over one million women were employed in essential, war, industrial work. The Committee on Women in Industry of the Council of National Defense recommended certain standards for government contracts which would prevent unjust profiteering. The W. C. T. U. materially aided in pushing the suggestions of the committee. The recommendations for the protection of women and children included tenement house work, child labor, safeguarding of mothers, wages, hours of work, seats, extra heavy and hazardous occupations, heavy lifting and exposure to heat and cold. It was immensely gratifying to the Committee of Women in Industry to receive assurance from the Secretary of War that all army clothing produced under government contract would be made under clean and sanitary conditions. It was also encouraging to have the chairman of the Department of Women in Industry, Miss Agnes Nestor, so honored. In co-operation with the National Council of Women, the National W. C. T. U. prepared to engage in definite work under the Labor Department of the Federal government which arranged for military and general relief and for the establishment and maintenance of employment bureaus for women who were obliged to take the places of men called to the colors.

"The woman touch," said Frances Willard, "is to brighten every nook and corner of the earth." Since people of almost every "nook and corner" have come to America, the land of opportunity, the "melting-pot" of the nations, it was the "woman touch" through the W. C. T. U. department of Americanization, with Mrs. Ella B. Black, superintendent, that expedited throughout the war, the contact with foreign speaking people, especially with the wives and mothers. In all the states having a large percentage of foreigners, the state presidents, and the state superintendents of Americanization actively participated in the program for the beneficent "woman touch."

With a large city of the middle west as the central point of service, the state in which it was located, with eighty-seven thousand, five hundred and forty-seven foreign-born women, among them Italians, Bohemians, Roumanians, Hungarians, Syrians, Poles, Croatians, Greeks, Swedes and Chinese, adopted as its watchword, "America First." Already, the city had opened Americanization headquarters with a salaried worker. Great emphasis was laid on the education of both the new Americans themselves and volunteer workers on their behalf who were trained to proceed carefully and intelligently. The initiative taken by the W. C. T. U. of the metropolis led other organizations to engage in similar efforts on a co-operative basis, the W. C. T. U. superintendent acting as chairman of the visiting committee. In New York City, thickly populated with foreigners, a paid worker labored among the Greeks and emigrants from the region of the Balkans, doing humanitarian, Christian service. The foreign-born women of New York City numbered over a million. The worker persuaded both men and women to invest their beer money in liberty bonds and war-savings stamps. Foreigners were prevailed upon to take out naturalization papers. The chief cause of poverty was found to be not a low wage, but expenditure of money for liquor. A survey of twenty-two states was made. In the population of these commonwealths, there were 2,945,615 foreign-born white women, also Spanish, Japanese, Italian, French, Slav, Polish, Hungarian, Lithuanian, Slovak, Crotian, Russian, Greek, Swedish, Jewish, Albanian, Syrian, Bohemian, Scandinavian and Mexican. About thirty-eight per cent spoke English. When the battle-cry of democracy sounded, calling the men of America to arms, it found their wives and daughters also ready and longing to do their bit. "How can I help?" was the cry on every side. Many entertainments were held for the benefit of soldiers and sailors. Libraries and writing facilities were provided in recreation rooms. Christmas packages, scrap-books, candy, flowers, victrolas, records and "smilage" books, found their way to the boys. Hospital cots were equipped and large sums of money donated. Books were contributed to the number of nearly one hundred and four thousand, and nearly 168,000 magazines. "Save, Serve, Sacrifice" and "Bar the barley from the bar and bake it into bread," became the rally-cries as the problems connected with the high cost of living confronted the nation.

Flashing, electric signs gave to the public the slogan, "Food Will Decide the War." Women in the grain producing states considered themselves responsible for a large grain crop. In Kansas, the women farmers, including

143

W. C. T. U. women, early organized. There was a great demand for women as farm hands. The liquor traffic annually destroyed enough grain and fruit to feed starving millions—turning it into poison that was corrupting the life of the nation. The W. C. T. U. women made known the futility of this waste of grain and fruit. Sixty-eight million four hundred thousand bushels of grain were used each year in the production of beer. Bread or beer was the vital issue. The W. C. T. U. sought the protection of soldiers and civilians and not of beer. British brewers were well named food destroyers.

The National W. C. T. U. president in an appeal to the women said, "We patriotically observe seven wheatless, fourteen meatless and twenty-one wasteless meals each week. We have purchased liberty bonds. We knit and sew, we conserve and preserve. We dry and can, we waste not a slice of bread nor a grain of sugar. We eat war bread, we follow the excellent advice, 'Use corn-meal, common sense, and calm.' The six million loaves of bread we send to our Allies are saved in this way. Why do the powers that be continue to waste foodstuffs daily in the manufacture of beer? The amount saved, if breweries could be eliminated, would send to our enlisted men and the Allies six million loaves of bread." Foreign-speaking wives and mothers appealed to the President at Washington for aid. They plead for food for their children. Miss Jeannette Rankin, Congresswoman, advocated their cause. They said, "We don't know much about politics, but we know we can't get food. If the government wants to take our sons to be killed in France, it must pass the food bill so we may feed the children left at home or our young men will go to war only over our dead bodies." An investigator visited fifty schools of the east side of New York City, with an average attendance of one thousand, two hundred children, and forty-three principals told her the children were falling behind in their lessons because they were under-nourished and had as a result become a prey to disease.

144

The following memorial in favor of food conservation, which was also a vital factor in securing war prohibition, was addressed to the Commander-in-Chief of the Army and Navy, and signed and endorsed by 6,000,000 women. The assembling of this memorial was an herculean task—directed by Mrs. Lenna Lowe Yost at the Washington (D. C.) W. C. T. U. Legislative Headquarters. The memorial read:

"To Hon. Woodrow Wilson, President of the United States:

"Believing that the women of the United States are loyally doing their utmost in our national crisis to carry out all government plans for the conservation of food; and

"Realizing that there is still an alarming waste of foodstuffs in the production of malt and vinous liquors; .

"We, in behalf of mothers, wives and daughters, sisters and sweethearts of enlisted men, appeal to you, as Commander-in-Chief of the Army and Navy, to prohibit the further waste of these foodstuffs in the production of malt and vinous liquors during the period of the war."

The document embossed on parchment in handsome book form was presented to President Wilson with the following letter from the National W. C. T. U., the promoters of the conservation petition:

"March 1, 1918

"National W. C. T. U. Headquarters,
    "Washington, D. C.

"Mr. President:

"We deeply appreciate the privilege of presenting to you a memorial representing six million women patriots of the United States.

"We believe this is the first petition in the history of our country in which all leading organizations of women, civic, fraternal, social, patriotic, and religious, as well as hundreds of notable women in the educational and official life of the republic have united. It comes to you, Mr. President, as the voice of the womanhood of America. It comes

145

to you, our Commander-in-Chief of the Army and Navy, at the time of an appalling crisis which peculiarly concerns the mothers of the nation.

"Educated by the government to believe that food will win the war, these women whose magnificent war service and sacrifice everywhere are attested, plead for the maximum conservation of food materials for the duration of the war. They earnestly and respectfully ask that all food materials now used in the production of malt liquors be devoted to food supplies, desperately needed by our army and the armies of the Allies.

"On behalf of these six million petitioners, Mr. President, we thank you for the steps in this direction already taken, and we beg your early and favorable consideration of the prayer of the memorial we have the honor to place in your hands.

"(Signed)   Anna A. Gordon,
"President of the National W. C. T. U."

White-ribboners were keenly alive to the strategy of the situation. While warring against crowned autocracy they also were gaining ground in their fight to annihilate King Alcohol. Their great petition to President Wilson aroused favorable public opinion. The grain, Congress said, would henceforth be fed to the men and not to the breweries and distilleries. If not wasted in time of war, why wasted and turned into poison, in time of peace?

It was the famous psychologist, Professor William T. James, of Harvard College, who said that people seldom unlocked their hidden abilities. At the psychological moment every W. C. T. U. woman used the key that unlocked all the resources of her devoted motherhood. The boys must be fed! War prohibition must come! Mother-love in determined action is irresistible. White-ribboners worked at white heat.

A white-ribboner originated the slogan: "Nail the flag to your hoe, your spade, your rake, and enter heart and soul into the food growing movement." In great patriotic parades many people were seen carrying over their shoulders a hoe with the flag tied to it, fit emblem surely of practical patriotism. W. C. T. U. women turned waste land, vacant lots, yes, and even back yards into patches for cultivation of potatoes and other foodstuffs. In one year, three hundred girls enrolled in canning clubs, and their net saving amounted to $38,000. Thousands of college girls spent their summer vacations on this type of work. Hundreds of cans of dehydrated vegetables, and hundreds of packages containing jellies, marmalade and grape juice, were sent to the front. To these were added games, puzzles, recent magazines, scrap-books, song-books and home papers for home troops. This was the "woman touch" that kept up the morale of the homesick boys, for hidden among the packages were loving letters from mothers, wives, sisters, and sweethearts.

At harvest time, the popular slogan became, "Not one ear of corn for whisky, but millions for food for the hungry men, women and children of America and Europe." William Jennings Bryan asserted: "We cannot afford to allow $145,000,000 worth of grain to be converted into alcohol when it is needed for bread. To urge an increase in garden space and yet be indifferent to the conversion of the products of our prairies into alcohol would be saving at the spigot and wasting at the bunghole." Rev. Charles Stelzle, field secretary of the Federal Council of Churches, said that the toil of 75,000 farmers for six months was required to furnish the grain used to make the country's liquor. He declared that the 300,000 persons in America who serve the liquor traffic were needed for the legitimate work of the country. It was stated authoritatively, that Great Britain would not at this time (1917) have been facing a near famine, if in 1914 she had prohibited in the manufacture of alcoholic liquors, the use of grains.

In the interests of food conservation even Mother Goose was "Hooverized"—much to the delight of the children, who, as they recited the following lines, awakened to patriotic action many carnal-minded epicures:

"Old King Cole was a merry old soul, and a merry old soul was he.
To help conserve food, he dined as a rule on cornbread and milk, don't you see?"

"Mary, Mary, quite contrary, how does your garden grow?
Beans and peas and spinach, too, with canned goods all in a row."

The intensity and anxiety of these war-beclouded days were relieved by the buoyancy and loyalty of the young people and the boys and girls of the Loyal Temperance Legion. As, on public occasions, they gave the salute to their nation's flag each one earnestly said: "I pledge allegiance to my flag and to the republic for which it stands, one nation indivisible, with liberty and justice for all."

Eager to express their youthful patriotism, children repeated in concert: "It's your flag and my flag, and oh, how much it holds, your land and my land, secure within its folds. Your heart and my heart, beat quicker at the sight. Sun-kissed and wind-tossed, red, blue and white. The one flag, the great flag, the flag for me and you—glorified all else beside, the red and white and blue." Often, older people as well as children, gave another interpretation of the salute to the flag in which foreign-speaking children joined: "I give my head, my heart, and this right hand for God and home and native land. One country—one language—one God, to whom be praise forevermore." Little Dorothy, six years old, was told one day at school that she must salute the flag. That noon she was almost an hour late in reaching home for lunch. "Dorothy, where have you been," said her mother, as the child came up the front walk. "Teacher said we must salute the flag" replied the small patriot, "and I have been saluting them all the way home, because there's one on pretty nearly every house!" White-ribbon women were deeply interested in the service flag whose blue and gold stars represented their sons in the army and navy—those living and those who had paid the supreme sacrifice. In hundreds of homes this "child of Old Glory" was seen.

The Georgia W. C. T. U. through its president, Mrs. Lella A. Dillard, with the help of another white-ribboner, made a notable service flag, eighteen feet long by six feet wide. The stars represent sons, husbands and brothers of the W. C. T. U. members. A few of the stars are for nephews, their names being sent in by mother-aunts, and daughters who did war work are also represented. The design of this world's service flag is strikingly unique and beautiful, for the magic initials, W. C. T. U., form the background of white, that is studded with the stars of blue and gold. In the summer of 1919, at Columbus, Ohio, during the exhibit of the National Woman's Christian Temperance Union at the Methodist Centenary Exposition, this flag from Georgia, revealed to the visitor, the patriotism pervading all the activities of the white-ribbon women.

"Space is nothing to spirit; the deed is outdone
    by the doing;
The noblest are reared by example and blos-
    som by nursery wooing.
Back of the foreguard and leader stands silent,
    heroic some other,
And colossal behind the achievement stands
    meekly that angel, the mother."

In the midst of their conservation work, American women were deeply stirred by the sufferings of European womanhood. The National Council of French Women, including one hundred and fifty societies; the French Union of Woman Suffrage with eighty original groups; The Society for the Improvement of Woman's Lot; the Fraternal Union of Women, representing more than a million French women, appealed to the women of all countries to unite with them in denouncing the infamous and sinister attack on the common life of humanity through its womankind. This appeal met with a warm response in the heart of every W. C. T. U. woman. A petition to the Peace Council asking for the punishment of men who had violated the persons of women under their power and asking that the women so outraged should be considered "wounded in war" was circulated. The national W. C. T. U. vice-president, Mrs. Ella A. Boole, earnestly promoted by addresses and correspondence the circulation of this petition, co-operating with the Committee of Protection of Women Under International Law.

For her masterly and unique service, Anna Howard Shaw was the recipient of a governmental decoration. Later, at a W. C. T. U. luncheon where she was the guest of honor, she called attention to the handsome medal from the government that she was wearing and said most unassumingly, that it was a decoration to which every white ribboner and every woman who helped in the national defense had equal claim with herself. She told with enthusiasm of the loyalty of the women's societies in following directions so that duplication, overlapping, and useless war work were prevented. The hope shared with millions of other women, that she was helping the war that would end war, was expressed in these eloquent words:

"The mothers of this country, the mothers of men, build their own lives into the lives of their sons until they reach manhood—and how much is embraced in that word 'manhood!' The mother looking into the eyes of the young man whom she held in her arms as a tiny, helpless baby, knows that she beholds the most marvelous thing in all the world; that in all the universe of God, there is nothing more wonderful than a strong-limbed, clean-hearted, clear-brained young man, just as he stands on the border-line of life, and in an hour this country calls him out, and in another hour he may lie dead. When she looks into his face, that woman knows the meaning of war. That is the 'bit' our country asks of its women. A whole lifetime of service, of love, and then it is all swept away from her, and from him, and yet they wonder that women do not want war. We do not want war—we do not want war—and the reason you and I want to see this war brought to a finish, if it takes the last man and the last loaf of bread, and the last woman in order to do it, is because we hope that after it is done there will be no more war. The men have laid down their lives that this world may be a safe place and that men and women may know the meaning of democracy, which is that we are one great family of God. That, and that only, is the ideal of democracy for which our flag stands."

In closing her address, Dr. Shaw gave this message sent her by General Pershing—a message expressing appreciation of American women and their loyalty: "All ranks of the American Expeditionary Forces unite in heartfelt thanks to the women of America for their love and their prayers. The patriotism of our incomparable women, than whom there are not others more noble, shall be our constant inspiration until the great capital task which has been entrusted to us shall be accomplished. Accept our best wishes for the coming year and our firm confidence in our final success."

In 1889, Hon. John D. Long, Secretary of the Navy, wisely took alcoholic drink away from the enlisted men. In 1917, Hon. Josephus Daniels, then Secretary of the Navy, prohibited the use of alcoholic liquor by officers of the navy, thus making that department of the government, bone dry. In an interview, Secretary Daniels being asked to give his reasons for the issuance of the famous "Wine Mess Order," said:

"Shortly after I had become Secretary, a gentleman came into the department to plead for the restoration of a young relative of his who had been dismissed from the navy for intoxication. I showed him the record which proved that this young officer had not only been drunk, but had at the same time made a public exhibition of himself.

I explained that there was no course to be pursued but to act firmly and finally in approving the court-martial which had recommended the young officer's dismissal. When I made it plain that the young man must inevitably pay the penalty, this gentleman protested earnestly, and with much feeling insisted that his young relative had received injustice at the hands of the navy. 'Now that he is the product of your system,' said my visitor, 'you have turned him out in disgrace.' He then went on to tell me the following story. 'I am a Friend, a Quaker,' he said, 'and the boy's father was a Quaker. When his father died, he was a little shaver and the lad came into my home and always has been to me, as a son. I never even had so much as a glass of wine in my home and when the boy left for Annapolis to enter the Naval Academy, he did not know what the taste of liquor was like. I gave him to the American navy pure-hearted, unsullied, believing absolutely in the old-fashioned Quaker ideals in which he had been reared. In the seven years you have had him in the navy, you gave him wrong ideas about drinking. You taught him that it was all right for a gentleman to have his toddy. You legalized the "wine mess." You had a code that made a youth feel that he was narrow-minded if he turned down his glass at the table, but now that my boy has been ruined by you and your system, the navy kicks him out and puts a stigma on him.' "

Secretary Daniels, in continuing his story, said: "When this sorrowful man went out, I could not throw off a stinging sense of justice in his accusation. I realized that the issuing of a 'wine mess order' meant that it would be resented. If I was at any time tempted not to take the step, the reflection that every year there came into the navy hundreds of young men, some of whom might find their undoing in indulgence, made my duty plain. However, as the days went by, after the action was taken, the order increasingly won over the approval of the officers themselves. One of the ablest admirals of the navy, a man whose name is known in naval circles all over the world, told me that he had never known such a revolution in the navy as had been brought about by the wine mess order. 'On the very day that you issued the order,' he said, 'I had stocked up my closet with the usual wines and liquors as was customary to be used when I entertained guests on board ship. I did not, therefore, like the order, but when I first read it, I immediately called the steward and told him to pack all drinkables up and remove them from the ship. To me, an order is an order. In my long service, whether I liked it or not, my loyalty to lawful commands has never failed. My own opinion is that the wine mess order is the wisest thing you have done as Secretary.' The statement of this admiral is typical of the opinion of the vast majority of the commissioned personnel of the navy."

In 1917, for the first time in its history, Harvard University gave its graduates and undergraduates a commencement week free from the use of champagne and cocktails. This patriotic act made strong sentiment for the protection of the boys in camp. Other colleges took similar action.

After the armistice, November 11, 1918, a million men in uniform returned from overseas to resume the duties of civilian life. They had been protected from drink in the camps and at the front. The duty and problem that confronted the nation was the adequate protection of these brave men from the enemies at home. The National W. C. T. U., as one of its after-war relief measures, adopted whole-heartedly a new "God-child," the Fort Sheridan Reconstruction Hospital. The wounded had started to come home, some with bodies badly broken. Five thousand of these boys were to be cared for, re-educated if need be, at this great hospital. The commanding officer warmly welcomed the W. C. T. U. hospital mother, Mrs. Louise Chez. Several states made liberal contributions to the Fort Sheridan Hospital fund. The Young People's Branch assumed responsibility for "cheer-up" books for blinded soldiers and sailors. The Loyal Temperance Legion raised a fund to print in Braille a beautiful story carrying the children's message of good cheer, to soldiers, sailors and marines who had lost their sight. Relief work under the Flower Mission department, for families of soldiers and sailors, continued as long as necessity demanded. The Iowa W. C. T. U. adopted as one of its special benevolences the United States Army reconstruction hospitals at Fort Des Moines with a capacity of three thousand five hundred beds, with Mrs. Dessa Carleton as the hospital mother. The "boys" were greatly comforted by these sympathetic, gracious women.

Of the 100,000,000 bushels of grain which each year had been turned into alcoholic liquors, a large proportion now provided necessary food. A number of distilleries continued making alcohol to find its way into perfumes, toilet water, bay-rum, medicine and industries where denatured alcohol is used. Revenue records state that during that fiscal year (1917-1918) nearly 11,000,000 gallons were shipped to Allies for powder manufacture.

The extraordinary work of the allied, temperance and philanthropic organizations brought victory after victory. The Sixty-fifth Congress prohibited the use after September 8, 1917, of food-products in the manufacture for beverage purposes, of distilled spirits. July 1, 1919, under the provisions of the war prohibition bill enacted by the Sixty-fifth Congress and sustained by the Sixty-sixth, in special session, the Federal government prohibited for the period of the war and of demobilization, the manufacture and sale of alcoholic liquors. It will be recalled that on November 1, 1917, the capital city of our great country became dry. The long desired goal—National Constitutional Prohibition—was now almost in sight. One of the greatest upheavals of the war was this revolt against alcohol. The value of sobriety in the army, navy, and in aviation, had been effectively demonstrated.

Throughout the war "Co-operation" had been the keynote of action, but the National W. C. T. U. while co-operating, did its own work in its own way; and all its patriotic funds passed through the hands of the resourceful National W. C. T. U. treasurer, Mrs. Margaret C. Munns. Harry S. Warner, executive secretary of the United Committee on War Temperance Activities in the Army and Navy, later said, "The W. C. T. U. is largely responsible for the splendid work accomplished." The following facts and figures prepared at National W. C. T. U. headquarters, summarize the magnificent patriotic work the Woman's Christian Temperance Union accomplished:

Sent to the President at Washington, D. C., petition of 6,000,000 women for war-time prohibition, as a conservation measure.

Participated in forty-five successful campaigns for ratification of the Eighteenth Amendment.

Enrolled ninety per cent of the half million members in the Red Cross society; seventy-five per cent of the half million members were workers in Red Cross shops.

Prepared hundreds of thousands of special comforts for men in service, outside the Red Cross. Contributed to the Red Cross for field kitchens, $41,573; for ambulances, $13,600.

Prepared comfort bags, at the estimated cost of $176,585.

Furnished through the United Committee on War Temperance Activities in army and navy, stereomotorgraphs, at the cost of $9,430.

Contributed for hospital tables, electric fans, grafanolas, $3,779.

Co-operated in every camp community, in war-camp community service.

Established and maintained hostess houses, recreation centers and rest-rooms from Camp Devens, Massachusetts, to Camp Las Casas, Porto Rico—from Camp Lewis, Washington, to Camp Lee. Virginia.

Extended service of women police officers to camp communities.

Introduced the hospital mother as a new welfare worker in reconstruction hospitals. Maintained resident hospital mother at General Hospital No. 28, Fort Sheridan, Illinois.

Contributed hospital furnishings and equipment valued at $5,911.

Contributed, through the Young People's Branch, cheer-up books for use of permanently blinded soldiers, sailors and marines at Evergreen Hospital, Baltimore, Maryland, valued at $1,523.

Contributed diet kitchen for Evergreen Hospital, $3,500.

Subscribed for Victory Bonds and Liberty loans.

Adopted 2,800 French orphans.

Contributed to Armenian, Serbian, Belgian and other relief funds, $25,774.

According to James Russell Lowell, democracy in its best sense is merely the "letting in of light and air." In the hope of helping to secure a Christian democracy such as Mr. Lowell so well described, the National W. C. T. U. carried on its extraordinary war activities. The exalted spirit of the organization which, from earliest days, had declared for "the establishment of courts of national and international arbitration which should banish war from the world," is seen in this resolution passed at the forty-fourth annual W. C. T. U. convention which assembled during wartime, December 2-7, 1917, in the capital city. It reads: "While we deplore war as wholly evil in its inception, we yet believe that when it became necessary for our nation to enter the present world conflict we came in on this high moral ground, namely: To vindicate the principles of peace and justice in the life of the world as against selfish and autocratic power and to set up among the really free and self-governed people of the world such a concert of purposes and action as shall bring peace and safety to all nations and make the world itself at last free."

The W. C. T. U. women were now cheerfully meeting the second test of patriotism—the practice of severe economies in the reconstruction days. "During the coming years," said the national president, in 1918, "as we traverse the road to the victory of National Constitutional Prohibition, let us heed the words of a seer given to Israel of old. 'They march everyone on his way, and *they break not their ranks.*'"

CHAPTER VII

THE EIGHTEENTH AMENDMENT; ALLEGIANCE TO THE CONSTITUTION

THE passage of the Eighteenth Amendment to the Constitution of the United States, January 16, 1919, was one of the greatest moral triumphs of history.

It was a twentieth century Declaration of Independence, and assured to the one hundred and twenty-five million men, women and children of this mighty Republic the guarantees of the United States Constitution, "life, liberty, and the pursuit of happiness." In celebration of this patriotic event, a United States flag was raised over a worsted mill. It was made of wool from American sheep, sorted by an American, carded by an Italian, spun by a Swede, warped by a German, dressed by an Englishman, drawn in by a Scotchman, woven by a Belgian, supervised by a Frenchman, inspected by an American, scoured by an Albanian, dyed by a Turk, examined by an Irishman, pressed by a Pole; and these loyal workers of foreign birth were all *Americans* and sang in unison, "My country, 'tis of thee, sweet land of liberty, of thee I sing." This victory of Federal prohibition, this moral mountain peak, viewed by all the nations of the earth, is destined to make not only in honored law, but in living reality, a sober nation and a sober world.

It is a wonderful story—the intensive campaign of the National Woman's Christian Temperance Union for National Constitutional Prohibition, and for the steady growth of prohibition areas—state, county and municipal—throughout the entire republic.

The list of the prohibition states and territories and the dates of their prohibition enactments is as follows:

Maine (Constitutional) 1851	Mississippi (Statutory) ...1909
Kansas (Constitutional) ...1880	Tennessee (Statutory) 1909
N. Dakota (Constitutional) 1889	W. Virginia (Constitutional) 1914
Oklahoma (Constitutional) 1907	Alabama (Statutory) 1915
Georgia (Statutory) 1908	Arizona (Constitutional) ..1915
N. Carolina (Statutory)...1909	Virginia (Statutory) 1916

Colorado (Constitutional) .1916
Oregon (Constitutional) ...1916
Washington (Statutory) ..1916
Arkansas (Statutory) 1916
Iowa (Statutory) 1916
Idaho (Constitutional) 1916
South Carolina (Statutory) 1916
Nebraska (Constitutional).1917
S. Dakota (Constitutional) 1917
Dist. Columbia (Statutory) 1917
Alaska (Statutory) 1918
Indiana (Statutory) 1918
Michigan (Constitutional) .1918
New Hampshire (Statutory 1918

Montana (Constitutional) .1918
N. Mexico (Constitutional) 1918
Texas (Constitutional) 1919
Florida (Constitutional) ...1919
Utah (Constitutional) 1919
Ohio (Constitutional) 1919
Nevada (Statutory) 1919
Wyoming (Constitutional) 1920
Kentucky (Constitutional) 1920
Porto Rico 1918
Canal Zone ....
Island of Guam 1918
Territory of Hawaii......1918
Virgin Islands 1919

In the remaining fifteen states much territory had been won for prohibition through county or local option elections.

The temperance and church allies have remarked frequently and emphatically that the systematic work of the W. C. T. U., especially the laws the organization secured regarding the teaching of scientific temperance in the public schools, laid the changeless foundation on which this phenomenal Federal victory was built. In co-operation with the allies, the W. C. T. U., which in 1875 began its National Constitutional Prohibition campaign, followed the "gleam," which now brightened their prohibition pathway. What were the steps so bravely taken?

On September 10, 1911, Mrs. Lillian M. N. Stevens, then the revered president of the National W. C. T. U., issued this proclamation: "In the name of the World's and National Woman's Christian Temperance Union, we hereby make this proclamation for a great crusade to carry the vital truth to the people themselves in all lands, and through them to place prohibition in the organic law of all nations and ultimately in the organic law of the world; and to this high end we invoke the guidance and blessing of Almighty God and the co-operation of men and women of all lands who love their fellow men, and to America, the birthplace of the local, state, National, and World's Woman's Christian Temperance Union, we hereby proclaim that within a decade, prohibition shall be placed in the Constitution of the United States; and to this end we call to active co-operation all temperance, prohibition, religious and philanthropic bodies; all patriotic, fraternal and civic associations, and all Americans who love their country."

In December of the same year, Congressman Richmond Pearson Hobson of Alabama introduced into the Sixty-third Congress a resolution providing for a referendum to the states on the question of a prohibition amendment to the United States Constitution. In the Senate, the measure was ably championed by Senator Morris Sheppard of Texas. Mammoth mass meetings held in Washington, D. C., by the W. C. T. U. and other temperance organizations, stirred the entire nation. "On to Washington" was the cry. In 1914, soon after Mrs. Stevens, the statesmanlike National W. C. T. U. president, had been called to her heavenly reward, a hearing before the House Judiciary Committee occurred at Washington, D. C., and Anna Gordon, acting national president, went to this hearing directly from Mrs. Stevens' funeral service in Portland, Maine. She was introduced by Mrs. Margaret Dye Ellis, and said that she brought a message written by Mrs. Stevens' own hand. It was a plea for National Constitutional Prohibition—from one facing eternity; and was sent to those who had it in their power to bring to fruition this important bill. Miss Gordon read the sacred message:

"The movement for National Constitutional Prohibition is meeting with greater favor than I dared to hope on that memorable evening, September 10, 1911, when on behalf of the World's and National Woman's Christian Temperance Union, I made the proclamation—and I dare to hope almost everything for the temperance cause. I know we are to win. The destruction of the liquor traffic will glorify God in heaven, and on earth will hasten the establishment of the kingdom of our Lord and Saviour, Jesus Christ." Breaking a reverent silence, the chairman of the committee said: "The Judiciary Committee of the House of Representatives of the United States have learned with profound regret of the death of Mrs. Stevens, and desire to express to the W. C. T. U. their sincere sympathy."

Who can measure the impact on unawakened consciences of such an "other-worldly" appeal. It had irresistible power, for it came from one who unselfishly loved humanity, even unto death. On December 22, 1914, the memorable day of decision, Congress did not adjourn for either the noon or the evening meal. A thousand people sat throughout the debate. Across the entire length of the house over the speaker's desk was fastened a scroll recording the number of individuals endorsing the resolution and sent to Congress from National W. C. T. U. headquarters. Every state was represented upon this scroll. Nearly 12,000 organizations and assemblies endorsed the resolution, representing an aggregate of some 5,000,000 people. Adding to this large number the petitioners whose names were sent directly to members of Congress, it is safe to say that 10,000,000 American citizens petitioned on this subject— ten times as many as ever petitioned any government.

A majority vote for the bill was secured, but not the necessary two-thirds. The liquor forces, though they called this "a big defeat" for prohibition, were alarmed, as they knew that a majority vote was really a victory and meant disaster for their trade. Congressman Hobson, shortly before the vote was taken at nearly midnight, held the respect of every auditor as he made an eloquent speech. In this challenge he stated that if the vote soon to follow did not submit this question to the states, in 1916 the bill would again be the paramount issue. In 1915, at the National W. C. T. U. convention held in Seattle, Washington, the National W. C. T. U. president declared: "The fact that a two-thirds majority vote was not obtained at this, the first trial of National Constitutional Prohibition in the United States Congress, does not daunt us. The united temperance forces of this nation will patiently continue their righteous clamor until the United States Congress hears and heeds and hands over to the sovereign people of the states of this Republic this mighty question, which will not be settled until it is settled right.

"The Supreme Court of the United States has declared that no one has an inherent right to sell alcoholic liquors, and that no legislature has the right to bargain away the public health and the public morals. A legislature does this when it passes a license law. Local option makes it easier for the liquor men to handle the situation. This is why they prefer it to a Federal prohibition law. Across our continent already gleams the white way of prohibition. Good roads are the order of the day. We have a Lincoln highway from the Atlantic to the Pacific. Let the allied temperance forces complete a trans-continental highway from Washington to Washington; a highway in which the wayfaring man shall not err; a highway safe for the feet of little children; a good road of prohibition named in honor of the father of our country—the Washington prohibition highway."

National Constitutional Prohibition brought its own spectacular and moral appeal to the boys and girls. As National Prohibition Guards they rallied to the defense of the home with Miss Mary B. Ervin, national general secretary, as their enthusiastic leader.

Under the supervision of Mrs. Stella B. Irvine, national superintendent of the Sunday School Department, an immense petition, national in character, and signed by Sunday school scholars of all grades was sent to Congress. It read: "We the undersigned young people, members of the Sunday schools of the various states, are trying to fit ourselves for the duties of citizenship. There is prevailing in our nation a deadly disease—alcoholism—and against its ravages we have no adequate protection. We appeal to you to eradicate the cause of this disease to make it unlawful for anyone to sell or traffic in any manner in alcoholic liquors for beverage purposes. We appeal to you for the opportunity to grow up in an atmosphere free from this pestilence. As the future citizens of this United States we earnestly plead for National Constitutional Prohibition."

During the session of the Sixty-fourth Congress, a prohibition resolution similar to the one sponsored by Congressman Hobson, was introduced in the House by Edwin Y. Webb of North Carolina; and in the Senate by Morris Sheppard of Texas. It was favorably reported, but not brought to a vote.

In her Washington Letter, a popular feature of the weekly *Union Signal*, Margaret Dye Ellis tells the dramatic story of the Day of Decision in the Sixty-fifth Congress—December 17, 1917. She wrote: "The victory is ours. Praise be to God!—The greatest day in the history of the temperance reform has come and gone. The referendum bill for National Constitutional Prohibition has passed the House of Representatives by a vote of two hundred and eighty-two in favor to one hundred and twenty-eight against, and the Senate concurred in this the following day by a vote of forty-seven to eight. Monday, December 17, 1917, had been set apart as the day when the House would take final action on the measure. This body convened at eleven o'clock, the doors being opened at ten o'clock. A large group of white ribboners stood for half an hour awaiting entrance. In this company were the president and the entire official staff of the National Woman's Christian Temperance Union, it being the first time the general officers had all been in the Capitol building together. As we waited, some of us quietly repeated that beautiful psalm, beginning 'I will lift up mine eyes unto the hills, from whence cometh my help.' The great galleries filled as soon as the doors were opened, and all day, until six in the afternoon, that great 'crowd of witnesses' sat almost motionless. The members of the House came in leisurely; and just before the hands of the clock reached eleven, Speaker Champ Clark, with smiling face and wearing the customary carnation pinned to his coat, ascended the steps of the rostrum and, with a sharp rap of his gavel, called the House to order. The blind chaplain, Rev. Dr. Couden, offered a fervent prayer.

"Congressman Webb, standing in front of the Speaker's desk, opened the discussion by exhibiting a poster bearing the sentiment of a number of leaders of labor organizations,

163

commending and endorsing prohibition. It was a reply to
Samuel Gompers' statement that a majority of the leaders
of labor were opposed to the proposed amendment. About
fifty speeches, pro and con, were made during the day.
As five o'clock, the hour set for the vote, drew near, the
interest, if possible, grew more intense. Three amendments
were offered which were overwhelmingly voted down, and
at five minutes past five the roll-call began. Silence prevailed
as the historic roll-call proceeded and the ayes and noes
responded. This was the culmination of a struggle that has
been fought over and over for so many years. Tally-sheets
were in the hands of scores of people, and as the ayes began
to gain, there was a rustling of leaves and an atmosphere
of expectancy.

"Not until the speaker announced the result, two hundred and eighty-two in favor, to one hundred and twenty-
eight against, were the friends of the measure absolutely
sure we had won the great victory. Then the floodgates of
enthusiasm burst forth. Even though the Speaker had twice
warned the galleries, 'to refrain from any demonstration,' it
was impossible to stop them, for both floors and galleries
evidenced their delight. It was noticeable that those who
had opposed the referendum hurried away, evidently greatly
surprised at the result. Ex-Speaker Cannon, who had not
responded to his name when called by the clerk, rose just
before the vote was announced and asked that his name be
called again. This was done, Mr. Cannon responding "aye,"
most heartily. The national president with the national
official staff, waited upon Mr. Webb to congratulate and
thank him, in behalf of thousands of white-ribboners.

"During his address in the House, Mr. Webb read a
letter from the National W. C. T. U. president, which appears in full in the *Congressional Record* of Monday, December 17, 1917. It is a concise résumé of the work of the
W. C. T. U. in its efforts to secure a Federal prohibition
amendment. Addressed to Congressman Webb, it reads:
'It is an honor to present to you, and through you, to the

House of Representatives, the appeal of five hundred thousand members of the Woman's Christian Temperance Union, praying for the passage of the joint resolution providing for a referendum to the states on National Constitutional Prohibition. This appeal comes from a host of home-loving women who, with untiring energy and unstinted devotion, have wrought marvelously for the moral and spiritual advancement of our country. This appeal comes from half a million patriots who answered promptly the call to the colors. The nobility of woman's sacrifice, the fine quality of her patriotic service, her keen discernment in the adjustment of industrial conditions for women and children, her tender ministrations at home and on the battlefield should entitle her to the granting by the Congress of this appeal.

" 'In addition to the petition of women members of the National Woman's Christian Temperance Union, I beg to present a huge petition of the endorsers of the Joint Resolution for a referendum to the states on National Constitutional Prohibition, secured through the efforts of the Woman's Christian Temperance Union, and representing eight million men and women of our Republic. Adding to these the petitions sent directly to members of Congress it is safe to say that our appeal is backed by more than eleven million people. If these petitioners could be massed in solid phalanx in our Capital City you would see more than thirty times the population of the District of Columbia.

" 'Unquestionably it is an appeal for an act of true democracy, an appeal for a patriotic economic measure. Autocracy and alcohol must be overthrown. "Speed up" is the urgent cry echoing back to us from the awful battle fronts of Europe. "Speed up" on prohibition legislation is the respectful appeal of the Woman's Christian Temperance Union to the Congress of the United States. We pray that in this crucial time of a stupendous world crisis the House of Representatives will rise to this exalted opportunity and give to the legislatures of the various states the chance to deal with a question so enormously vital to the economic and moral interests of our republic. When the war is over and a righteous peace has been secured, only the clear brain of a sober nation can be entrusted with the solution of the mighty problems that will then confront the greatest democracy on earth—the United States of America.'

"The House resolution gave the states seven years in which to act; the Senate resolution passed August 1. 1917. by a vote of sixty-five to twenty, gave the states six years to act; hence the need of ratification by the Senate of the House resolution. This was done on Tuesday, December 18, without the formality of a roll-call, but by a rising vote, forty-seven to eight. Having received a two-thirds vote in both Houses, the resolution does not require the approval of the President. Ratification requires the approval of three-fourths of the states of the Union, thus removing the struggle from the Congress to the state legislatures. It will mean hard, persistent work to bring the states up to the required standard. The liquor hierarchy knows it means the death-knell of their trade if the necessary thirty-six states ratify this resolution, so we call to our never failing, always ready constituency, 'Prepare for the battle.' Money without stint will be used by the liquor power to prevent the election to the legislatures of men favorable to the amendment. We have many good men in every state and they are the one to fill our legislative halls. I hail you comrades of long hard years—let us still press on to complete victory."

It is significant that the Crusade Psalm opens and closes with a song of praise. Throughout the fifty years of W. C. T. U. pilgrimage toward the mountain height of Federal prohibition, W. C. T. U. hymnology contains a victory note clearly sounding. An early song leader in the National W. C. T. U. conventions. Mrs. Alice Osborne Harris of Boston, gave the W. C. T. U. a "Victory" paean set to a Swiss mountain melody. "Victory" with cornet accompaniment became an instant favorite—later adapted by Mrs. Frances W. Graham to prophesy the coming of a national prohibition victory. After the passage of the Eighteenth Amendment, Mrs. Graham again adapted the song to prophesy a world prohibition victory. "Victory" has been the musical peak of each annual convention, inspiring thousands of earnest toilers with the conviction that "prohibition will come, surely come." Often the cornet obligato has been played on the "golden" cornet given to the National W. C. T. U. by Mrs. F. A. Bent of Maine, who was wont to call it "Maine's prohibition bugle." In late years, Miss Rose Bower of South Dakota has served as National W. C. T. U. cornetist.

THE TEXT OF
THE EIGHTEENTH AMENDMENT TO THE
FEDERAL CONSTITUTION

"Resolved by the Senate and the House of Representatives of the United States of America in Congress assembled (two-thirds of each House concurring therein): That the following amendment to the Constitution be and hereby is, proposed to the States, to become valid as a part of the Constitution when ratified by the legislatures of the several States as provided by the Constitution:

"Section 1. After one year from the ratification of this article the manufacture, sale, or transportation of intoxicating liquors within, the importation thereof into, or the exportation thereof from the United States and all territory subject to the jurisdiction thereof for beverage purposes is hereby prohibited.

"Section 2. The Congress and the several states shall have concurrent power to enforce this article by appropriate legislation.

"Section 3. This article shall be inoperative unless it shall have been ratified as an amendment to the Constitution by the legislatures of the several States, as provided in the Constitution, within seven years from the date of the submission hereof to the States by the Congress."

The W. C. T. U. entered whole-heartedly into the campaign for the ratification of the Eighteenth Amendment. The distillers of the country put up a two billion dollar fund in an effort to defeat National Constitutional Prohibition. Their leading lawyer, when asked by a journalist what he thought of their chances for success, replied, "I do not care to make any comment. This prohibition is going through. It is like a great prairie fire sweeping across the country and cannot be stopped!"

Throughout this and previous exciting campaigns, the flying of the flag between stately trees in front of Rest Cottage and the National W. C. T. U. headquarters, Evanston, Illinois, was a notice to the community that the prohibition cause had achieved new triumphs. On one of the trees between which the flag was suspended was a brief explanation. Students of the Northwestern University, passing, stopped to read, and occasionally expressed their delight by a cheer.

On January 29, 1920, in Washington, D. C., thirty-six states—three-fourths of the forty-eight commonwealths—having ratified the amendment, the acting Secretary of State. Hon. Frank L. Polk, signed the proclamation declaring the ratification of the Eighteenth Amendment to the Constitution of the United States. It was a great occasion. A group of notable temperance leaders, both men and women, were present. The pen first used by Secretary Polk was presented, for the organization, to the president of the National W. C. T. U. The handle of the pen is of shining silver and it has written many white-ribbon letters to white-ribbon women who have given one thousand dollars each to the Jubilee Fund.

The honor roll of states that have ratified the Federal Prohibition Amendment and date of ratification is here recorded:

1. Mississippi, January 8, 1918.
2. Virginia, January 10, 1918.
3. Kentucky, January 14, 1918.

4. South Carolina, January 23, 1918.
5. North Dakota, January 25, 1918.
6. Maryland, February 13, 1918.
7. Montana, February 19, 1918.
8. Texas, March 4, 1918.
9. Delaware, March 18, 1918.
10. South Dakota, March 20, 1918.
11. Massachusetts, April 2, 1918.
12. Arizona, May 24, 1918.
13. Georgia, June 26, 1918.
14. Louisiana, August 8, 1918.
15. Florida, November 27, 1918.
16. Michigan, January 2, 1919.
17. Ohio, January 7, 1919.
18. Oklahoma, January 7, 1919.
19. Maine, January 8, 1919.
20. Idaho, January 8, 1919.
21. West Virginia, January 9, 1919.
22. Washington, January 13, 1919.
23. Tennessee, January 13, 1919.
24. California, January 13, 1919.
25. Indiana, January 14, 1919.
26. Arkansas, January 14, 1919.
27. Illinois, January 14, 1919.
28. North Carolina, January 14, 1919.
29. Kansas, January 14, 1919.
30. Alabama, January 14, 1919.
31. Iowa, January 15, 1919.
32. Colorado, January 15, 1919.
33. Oregon, January 15, 1919.
34. New Hampshire, January 15, 1919.
35. Utah, January 15, 1919.
36. Nebraska, January 16, 1919.
37. Missouri, January 16, 1919.
38. Wyoming, January 16, 1919.
39. Wisconsin, January 17, 1919.
40. Minnesota, January 17, 1919.

41. New Mexico, January 20, 1919.
42. Nevada, January 21, 1919.
43. Vermont, January 29, 1919.
44. New York, January 29, 1919.
45. Pennsylvania, February 25, 1919.
46. New Jersey, March 9, 1922.

There are two states yet to ratify, Connecticut and Rhode Island. The Connecticut legislature has adopted a state enforcement code. When National Constitutional Prohibition became effective, one hundred Connecticut towns were under no-license, and sixty-eight towns under license. In 1922, the legislature of Rhode Island passed a prohibition enforcement act by an overwhelming majority in both houses.

With vivid, logical oratory, Deborah Knox Livingston, in speaking of the victory for prohibition, said: "No greater piece of constructive legislation was ever added to the Constitution of the United States than that embodied in the Eighteenth Amendment. Perhaps no amendment to the Constitution was ever so thoroughly considered, from so many angles, as was the Eighteenth Amendment. For more than half a century the political, social, educational, and economic aspects of prohibition have been discussed by the press, the pulpit and platform, as well as by the people themselves. There was no 'putting over' upon the people of the United States the law of national prohibition; on the contrary, the people put through the Constitution this great and beneficent law, and because it is an act of the people themselves, we believe it will be a part of the Constitution as long as the government stands. Law enforcement is the great political challenge of our day. The challenge must be met by an enlightened citizenship! By a revival on the part of its citizens of obedience to the law and order of our country; by the election to office of men and women who are not afraid to do their duty, irrespective of consequences, whether or not those consequences result in their political or social ostracism. The election of such officers is accomplished only through the combined efforts of all clean, decent, and courageous citizens."

A strong enforcement code, the Volstead Act, defining intoxicating liquor as a beverage containing more than one-half of one per cent of alcohol and providing enforcement machinery, was enacted by the Sixty-sixth Congress in special session. Many otherwise well-informed people, and those in favor of the return of beer and wine think that the percentage of alcohol in drink considered intoxicating, was decided by the drys. It was the liquor people themselves who asked that one-half of one per cent of alcohol should be classed as fermented. This one-half of one per cent was fixed upon when near beer began to be made— before that, all beers had been classed as fermented liquor.

The real reason for Congress adopting one-half of one per cent as a standard was because the states that had tried it, clearly demonstrated that a higher percentage made prohibition enforcement impossible. "While recognizing that there are limits beyond which Congress cannot go in treating beverages as within the power of enforcement," said former Chief Justice White of the Supreme Court, "we think that those limits are not exceeded by the provisions of the Volstead Act wherein liquors containing one-half of one per cent of alcohol by volume, and fit for use for beverage purposes, are treated as within that power."

At this time, the beneficial effects of national prohibition that had been in operation some months, were apparent. In spite of only a partial enforcement the transformation was magical. When later on it became apparent to the defeated, but still organized liquor forces, that they could hope for no legal support from the Supreme Court or any other department of the Federal government, they organized with unprecedented subtlety and systematic strategy, a conscienceless campaign of nefarious nullification. These representatives of the Association Against the Prohibition Amendment and of the Personal Liberty League, sent out as a rally slogan—"The Liberty Bell Must Ring Again." The

171

liberty bell of July 4, 1776, did ring again on January 16, 1919, and January 16, 1920—but, though having ears to hear, the nullifiers heard it not. The truly American liberty-loving, home-loving and nation-loving people heard it, and on every suceeding birthday of the Eighteenth Amendment they have sent rejoicing notes of that pealing bell around the world.

It was significant that during the campaign, the United States Public Health Service issued the following warning against alcohol: "Alcohol, as ordinarily taken, is not a stimulant, but a depressing drug. Your brain and nervous system govern your body. Alcohol not only reduces the efficiency of a nation, but life insurance experience has shown that the death-rate among steady drinkers supposed to be temperate—even within the bounds of so-called moderation —is nearly double that among average people."

The Anti-Prohibition organizations announced a definite campaign for the following definite purposes: To get the Volstead Act out of the law and keep it out; to work for the repeal of the prohibition amendment. These organizations called for a million members—members who would work for the repeal of the Volstead Law and favor state's rights as to prohibition. Knowing these facts, the National Woman's Christian Temperance Union met organized evil with organized good and inaugurated a lively five-year campaign for a million members who would work for the observance, enforcement and retention of the Volstead Code and the Eighteenth Amendment.

"What this country most needs is a good glass of beer for a nickel," said the president of the National Personal Liberty League. The plan of this organization, which is aligned with the breweries, is to arouse voters to obtain an amendment to the Volstead Act which will permit the manufacture and sale of beer of not less than 2.75 per cent alcoholic content. It is well known to the allied temperance forces that three-fourths of the drunkenness existing before the Eighteenth Amendment went into effect, was due to beer-drinking. As early as 1922, the Association Against the Prohibition Amendment announced a new slogan—"Out of the Dry Trenches by 1924." From their headquarters in Washington, the Association sent out this announcement: "Beer and light wines within two years and possibly by next summer." This is the promise held out to the thirsty by the Association, which is organizing through the country to carry the Congressional election for the consummation of this program.

The W. C. T. U. believes that the men who, today, are saying, "We don't like the Eighteenth Amendment and we'll not obey it" are not fully civilized, for they have not come to a realization that the only freedom that has an enduring basis is one founded on absolute loyalty to and observance of constituted law and authority. They forget that personal liberty ends where public injury begins. "The Eighteenth Amendment," said the late president, Warren G. Harding, "is the will of America and must be sustained by the government and public opinion, else contempt for the law will undermine our very foundations. There is only one position for a public official or a law-abiding citizen: *Support the Constitution and obey the laws as they are enacted.* The Constitution of the United States should command the respect and obedience of every American citizen, otherwise our government cannot long endure."

"The authority of the law is questioned in these days all too much. The binding obligation of obedience against personal desire is denied in many quarters. If these doctrines prevail, all organized government, all liberty, all security are at an end," said Calvin Coolidge, when, as governor of Massachusetts, and confronted with lawless police officials in the capital city, he was superbly successful.

The opinion of many voters opposed to the return of beer and wine is voiced by Colonel Hayward, U. S. District Attorney of New York, who says: "The beer memorial to Congress which Governor Alfred Smith sponsored was a beer pledge over which the wets hoped to cross to the

Island of Hootch." This discerning attorney also states that "When two popular songs are sung and there occurs a discord as one side sings, 'The Sidewalks of New York,' and the other, 'The Star Spangled Banner,' there should be no doubt which side you should choose." "The signature of the governor to the bill," he asserts "was a violation of his oath to support the Constitution of the United States. The state law was the result of one hundred years of legislation."

When the authority of the Eighteenth Amendment was nationally threatened, President Coolidge invited the governors of thirty-seven states to meet with him at the White House. A determined program for the rigid enforcement of the prohibition laws, that divides the burden of responsibility between the Federal and state governments, was adopted. "Enforcement of law and obedience to law," said the President, "by the very nature of our institutions, are not matters of choice in this republic, but the expression of a moral requirement of living in accordance with the truth. They are clothed with a spiritual significance in which is revealed the life or the death of the American ideal of self-government. The great body of the people are thoroughly law-abiding. This great law-abiding element of the nation is entitled to support and protection. I propose to give that support and protection to the limit provided by the Constitution and the law of the land against every lawless element. The executives are required to enforce the law." On another occasion the President, in appealing for better law enforcement, said: "It is the duty of a citizen not only to observe the law, but to let it be known that he is opposed to its violation."

"Everybody is ready to sustain the laws he likes," says Charles Evans Hughes, the Secretary of State. "That is not, in the proper sense, respect for law and order. The test of respect for law is where the law is upheld even though it hurts. And we cannot afford in this country to

174

W. C. T. U. Mother-Child Center, Detroit, Michigan (above).
Children of W. C. T. U. Americanization Center, St. Louis, Missouri.

have a Constitutional provision, which is the fundamental law of the land, ignored, betrayed."

On the fourth birthday of the Federal prohibitory law, January 16, 1924, three-fourths of the people of the United States rejoiced in the benefits it had brought to their homes. The clamor for beer and wine comes largely from the foreign element, the Association Against the Prohibition Amendment and similar liquor organizations. The amount of alcohol consumed by the average beer drinker, is injurious. Forty-three American Life Insurance Companies show by their records that "policy holders who at the time of applying for insurance, were in the habit of drinking two glasses of beer daily had an average death rate eighteen per cent higher than the normal death rate."

Scientific experiments have all tended to show that the man who drinks his pint of wine, or his two or more glasses of beer daily, is just as surely submitting his mind to the injurious effects of the drug as is the man who chooses the whisky road. It is the drug effect of alcohol for which beer and wine are drunk. If not, then there is no beer or wine question. There are palatable non-alcoholic drinks made from grains and fruits that do not produce the harmful results of alcohol. If the drinker does not desire the drug effect, he will not use such drinks; if he prefers beer and wine, he prefers them for the drug effect of alcohol. Wine, as generally understood, is the fermented juice of the grape. Wine contains the habit-forming drug. A one-half pint of ten per cent wine contains as much alcohol as a single one and six-tenths ounce drink of whisky and sends as much alcohol into the blood of the drinker. "The general moral," said Francis William Newman, "is that the light wine gives the taste for strong wine. The national taste has to be altered if a great national calamity is to be wiped out. Total disuse alone can enable us to regain the unsophisticated taste of childhood." The above scientific facts are vouched for by Miss Cora F. Stoddard. Before national prohibition, the police courts of the big cities were filled with men intoxicated by beer and wine. A Boston policeman, after forty-one years' service, has said, "My experience is that the beer drinker becomes more gluttonous, more degraded, and often more brutal than any other kind of drunkard."

The Federal Prohibition Commissioner, Roy A. Haynes, strongly supported by President Coolidge, in his fearless attitude toward law breakers has made this patriotic and uncompromising statement: "Shall the saloon come back into our homes through the front door? No, ten thousand times, no. Then, in the name of decency, let it not come back through the cellar door or the back door. Shall it come back through the upper world, with the approval of our best citizens upon its return? Then in the name of honor, let it not come back through the underworld of our life, with only the blessing of criminals and law breakers upon it. To say that it is impossible for America to enforce any law is to do violence to American tradition and to underestimate the American spirit. American will-power is the alchemy that has ever turned apparent impossibilities into startling achievements, and now is the time when it must be determined positively and definitely whether or not we are able to make and enforce our own laws. This, in my humble judgment, is the greatest problem confronting America today."

Commissioner Haynes gives the following valuable statement of the definite benefits that have resulted from the national prohibition of liquor traffic in the United States of America:

"Prohibition has reduced the arrests for drunkenness more than one-half.

"Prohibition has reduced the arrests for drunkenness among women by more than one-half; in some localities as much as 80%.

"Prohibition has cut heavily into the number of arrests for offenses against chastity.

"Prohibition has reduced by one-half, the deaths from alcohol and alcoholic insanity.

"Prohibition has lowered the national death rate to an extent that can now be measured in figures.

"Prohibition has materially cut down the population of state penal farms, prisons and almshouses, releasing thousands of citizens for useful work.

"Prohibition has had a marked influence in the reduction of the number of cases of juvenile delinquency as shown by court records, bespeaking not only the force of example at home, but an increased sense of responsibility and exercise of restraint on the part of the parent.

"During the three years prohibition has been in operation, there has been a steady falling off in industrial accidents and an increase in the worker's efficiency.

"During the same period, there has been a rapid improvement in school and college attendance.

"There has been a continuously increasing activity in home-building. The volume of new homes built in 1922 was five times greater than that of 1918, the last wet year.

"There has been a definite movement toward more wholesome forms of social life and recreation. During each month of the year 1922, there were social and recreational buildings constructed that represented an expenditure of $9,164,000, or an outlay for these purposes of $2,200,000 a month greater than that of 1918.

"There was, as shown by figures given by the Comptroller of the Currency on savings banks, an increase in savings banks deposits.

"There has been an astonishing increase in the strength and membership of our churches since prohibition enforcement became a fact. In 1921, church membership increased 1,200,000; in 1922, there was an increase of more than 950,-000 over the previous year. For every day of 1922, 3,000 persons joined the church, twelve ministers were licensed or ordained and seven congregations were organized. During the year an average of $7,172,000 was expended each month for the erection of churches and other religious or memorial buildings.

"The amazing tendencies in our national life which we have witnessed since prohibition enforcement became a fact cannot be overlooked or unfelt even by those most determinedly opposed to the law. The reduction in the death rate, the increase in longevity, the elimination of the brothel, the rapid disappearance of crimes against chastity, the falling off in cases of destitution due to intemperance, the reduction in the burden of juvenile courts, the lowered rate of alcoholic insanity, the abandonment of institutions for the cure of drunkards—all these point with inexorable definiteness and certainty to the fact that prohibition, even imperfectly enforced as yet, is weaving something new and worth while into the fabric of American life."

The Federal Prohibition Commissioner depends upon the support of the women. He says, "The womanhood of America can co-operate with the Federal government in a great campaign—not in destroying stills and arresting violators—but in a great campaign of preaching and living law observance, a program of promptly assuming the responsibilities of citizenship, as serving on juries, meeting nullification propaganda, and inspiring the young and old with a proper appraisal of the fundamentals of Americanism—a campaign of active participation in political and citizenship problems, for bad men are elected by the good women who stay away from the polls on election day." Women are resourceful and will ever find it possible to convert "disreputable beer-kegs into substantial bee-hives." Already in one locality this has been done and while the beer-kegs still retain their sting, it isn't of the variety formerly administered.

Leading journals are filled with articles giving the benefits that have accrued to the nation since the legalized liquor traffic was abolished. There is space for only a few typical statements showing the blessings that have come to the American workman, to the American home, and to the

American people who seek safety in travel and on the street.

In an address delivered recently at a citizenship conference in New York City, Warren S. Stone, national head of the organization of Locomotive Engineers, said: "Prohibition has come to stay. Every time you take a railroad journey, you ride behind one of the men I represent. They are skilled men, keen, cool, bright, wide-awake men of the very highest type, men who can think and act quickly; men with nerves of steel. We who have spent most of our lives in the cab of a locomotive, know the infinitesimal fraction of a second that oftentimes means safety. That alcohol does slow down the brain action is conceded by all.

"Every law-abiding citizen who loves his country and is interested in its future welfare, is vitally interested in the enforcement of the Eighteenth Amendment. In my opinion, the future of our country depends entirely on the enactment of fair laws and the enforcement of the same. If the fact is brought home to the American people that it is the intention of our state and national officers to rigidly enforce the prohibition law, I am certain it will create a more respectful attitude toward the general laws of this country. Every law-breaker, regardless of his social position, or whether he be rich or poor, should be required to pay the penalty of the law he has violated. And when every violator is made to pay the penalty of the broken law, it will not be very long until the American people will have a more wholesome respect for our laws than they have at the present time.

"There are some people laboring under the delusion that they are going to have the prohibition law modified or abolished. Someone should awake them from their Rip Van Winkle sleep. I wish that they could go with me for thirty days as I travel over this broad land of ours and see the homes being erected everywhere, note the accounts being opened at the savings banks; see the families all out together in the parks, recreation and community centers; see the children taken out of the sweat-shops, see them well fed, wearing shoes and warm clothing, and in school; see prosperity and sunshine now existing where formerly there was only squalor and misery. All this is a result of prohibition—why, they had just as well talk about stopping the waves from beating on the shore, or the sunlight descending from heaven, as to imagine they can stop the onward march of the prohibition movement. Again, I say prohibition has come to stay."

No doubter of the value of prohibition can escape the logic of this statement made by another speaker at the conference:

"Did you ever hear it said there is just as much liquor used now as ever there was—a remark that would be funny if it were not tragic. Not so long ago I had business in New York. There was a base-ball game played that day, and I took the time to go because I knew I was going to speak to this conference, and I wanted to tell those gathered what I saw. I went out to the ball-grounds and there were about seventy-thousand people present, and I not only watched the game, but I watched the crowd. I did not see a single man or woman intoxicated, and there wasn't an instance of disorder. And such conditions obtain all over this country today. I have no need to tell you about New York and other places. What about the situation in your own home city or town? Is it not a fact that a drunken man on the streets today is a rarity—a curiosity? Of course, I say there are entirely too many if there are any at all. But that is not my point. My point is that any man who is fair, and looking for facts in every community in the United States, will say that conditions have improved tremendously, and even if we make no greater progress than we have made up to this hour, the Eighteenth Amendment would have been magnificently worth while."

Recently, the National Federation of Settlements, after an exhaustive inquiry in forty-five cosmopolitan centers passed the following resolution: "Believing that practically full enforcement of the Eighteenth Amendment is vital to the safety and well-being of the nation and is practically feasible in every community, resolved, That the National Federation of Settlements heartily approves the efforts of those who are striving to enforce this amendment and calls upon all the duly constituted authorities strictly to enforce all the laws for securing its operation as the law of the land." Commissioner of Correction, Frederick A. Wallis, of New York City, declares that "The present population of the various institutions of the department of correction has been much less since the Volstead Act became effective, than it was in the same number of years prior to the Volstead Act." This decrease in prison population is probably due to the fact that the multitude that had free access to liquor in the past, cannot now obtain it so easily, and fights and brawls have been greatly reduced and disorderly-conduct cases are fewer.

The value of prohibition is evidenced on the Bowery in New York City. A view of the Bowery, according to *The Survey*, shows that since prohibition went into effect the bread line, even in the crisis of unemployment, has been discontinued: "Before prohibition, many good people were worried about the disappearance of the saloon—the 'poor man's club'—and certain labor leaders with moist idiosyncrasies predicted all kinds of dire consequences. The problem took care of itself. Those qualities which made the bar-tender popular behind the mahogany bar, are now better appreciated and rewarded behind the lunch or ice-cream counter. The assertion, or belief, that men really like to wallow in the mire of the bar-room belongs to the days of Sodom and Gomorrah. Witness the drunkards of yesterday adorned in white collar, multicolored silk shirt, with stiff hat, brown shoes and a 'nobby' suit and necktie, a trifle gaudy, somewhat loud—screaming, if you please—but it heralds the awakening of a man just as the thrush and the violet betoken the coming of spring."

"We have heard much and often, through the newspapers, that the American Labor movement unanimously wants and votes for light wines and beer," says Mrs. Raymond Robins, social economist. "There is no such unanimity. In Chicago, the president of the Federation of Labor, John Fitzpatrick, is a total abstainer, and has been one for all the long years that I have known him, and Steve Sumner, organizer of the Milk Wagon Drivers' union, is a prohibitionist and appeals so persuasively that he has succeeded in getting every member of that union to sign the pledge. There are no laboring women who do not know the hideousness of the political control of the liquor interests. It mattered not what bills were introduced in the state legislatures for bettering the industrial conditions of women and children; it mattered not whether we worked to secure the protection of children, the enfranchisement of women, or the eight-hour day, we were opposed by the liquor interests. Whether we asked to have the children of the richest land in the world taken out of the mines and factories and put into the schools, whether we asked for the shorter work-day or the right of women to the ballot—it mattered not how simple the request—we were met by the united opposition of the liquor interests—including light wines and beer. These same interests are seeking to regain their lost political control by using unthinking folk, and especially the younger men and women, to do their bidding and work for the return of these conditions of humiliation and disgrace—and this in the name of liberty. With Mr. Robins I went to Chicago eighteen years ago. We made our home on the top floor of a tenement house in the old Seventeenth Ward, a river ward with 75,000 folk in less than a mile square, representing twenty-three or more different nationalities with a different ethical, political, religious and economic heritage, yet holding in common one purpose—the building of a home; and one faith—the hope of a better life.

"In the early days, we had practically three saloons to every four street corners. To know our neighbors we had to know saloons and saloon-keepers, and to meet with the working women in their trade union gatherings, we met often in the saloon parlor because good people would not permit us to meet elsewhere. In those days, in New York and Chicago, or many another large city, a union of young girls had no other place for its meetings. Today, with a growing conception of the value of life, schools and churches have opened their doors and young girls are welcomed whether they come to study literature in their clubs or economic conditions in their union.

"We need to restate our reasons for the enactment of the Eighteenth Amendment, because there have come into maturity young men and young women to whom this story is not known. We must restate the reasons for our faith. I want them to know that we are living not only under the 'Thou shall not' of the Old Testament, but that we are living also under the 'Thou shalt' of the New Testament; that we are living not only under the law, but that we also live under grace. We want our message to contain not merely 'Thou shalt not drink,' 'Thou shalt not be a bootlegger,' 'Thou shalt not break the law,' but the greater word—'Thou shalt be fit,' 'Thou shalt be free,' 'Thou shalt have life more abundantly.' We want the understanding of the young men and women of the nation and their free assent to the task in hand."

The Metropolitan Life Insurance Company gives this cheering statement: "Deaths from alcoholism among 15,-000,000 industrial policy holders, decreased 17.5% during the first quarter of 1924 as compared to the same period in 1923. The death rate from alcoholism so far in 1924 is 2.8% per 100,000 among its policy holders." One of the latest scientific statements concerning alcohol recently given by Professor W. D. Lewis of the department of chemistry of Northwestern University should have wide publicity. "All alcohol of whatever kind," Professor Lewis says, "from the alcohol of fermentation to wood alcohol, is deadly poison. Its action differs from that of other poisons only in the rapidity of reaction. Every kind of alcohol has a malicious effect upon the blood, nerves and tissues, and these effects have been proved to be permanent. Wood alcohol, when taken into the body, forms formaldehyde and formic acid." In view of these facts, Professor Lewis' assertion that only a chemist in a laboratory can tell the difference between wood alcohol and a common alcohol of fermentation, assumes a new signficance.

The Woman's Christian Temperance Union believes that the American people are determined that the Eighteenth Amendment shall be enforced. A story is told of a man in a railway car in England who took in with him a large mastiff. A guard came in and told him that he must put the dog into the baggage car. "Is that so!" said the man, smiling politely. "You put him out." The guard moved toward the dog, but the dog showed his teeth and the guard went out and locked the door. At another station a similar scene occurred. At a third station no guard came in. The man said to himself complacently, "I have carried my point." Then he began to wonder why they stayed so long at that station. Seeing a guard passing, he called to him from the window and inquired why they were remaining so long. The man answered, "You were twice notified to put out your dog. You did not do it and so we have side-tracked you and the train has been gone an hour." Is it not the opportune time to side-track legislators and political parties that pay no heed to the demand of the protectors of the home— and let the law-obeying people travel on to a higher civilization?

Representing the National Woman's Christian Temperance Union of nearly half a million voting citizens, the national president recently spoke before the platform committees of the Republican and Democratic parties. The committees were asked to embody in their platforms a declaration for law enforcement, with special reference to the maintenance of the Eighteenth Amendment.

Today, there are needed officials like these of whom J. G. Holland in "Wanted" wrote, "Men whom the lust of office cannot kill; Men whom the spoils of office cannot buy;

Men who possess opinions and a will; Men who love honor; Men who will not lie; Men who can stand before a demagogue, and brave his treacherous flatteries without winking."

The great scientist, Dr. C. W. Saleeby, quoted in an earlier chapter, makes a declaration of profound significance when he points out that the prohibition movement is a question of preserving the life of nations from generation to generation: "On the day American prohibition came into force," writes Dr. Saleeby, "I said it was the greatest health measure in history. The home's greatest enemy has been turned out. The homes of the people have been protected. Motherhood, the first sacred circle around the future life of the race, is protected and the home is made safe." In many of the large cities today there are figures to prove this assertion. Dr. Saleeby verified his statement with well-accredited statistics.

Professor Amos R. Wells, the brainy and brave editor of *The Christian Endeavor World,* Boston, Massachusetts, in the following lines on "Prohibition Enforcement," well expresses the determined purpose of the allied forces of the home—the purpose to destroy this racial poison:

"We have put out the fire that was burning our house,
    And they bring us a match to light it again.
We have got the wild animals trapped in their lair;
    They would smash the obstructions and open the den.

"We have cured the disease that was sapping our life;
    They would feed us with germs of that very disease.
We have planted an orchard with promise of wealth;
    They would poison the ground, they would girdle the
    trees.

"We are out of our wilderness weary and worn;
    They would turn us right back to those desolate ways.
We have lighted a beacon that flashes afar;
    They would put out the light, they would darken our
    days.

185

"We have battled too hard to be caught by a trick,
We have traveled too far to be turned at the goal.
We will hold all our gains to the very last inch,
We will win all mankind to the very last soul!"

Mrs. Mabel Walker Willebrandt, Assistant United States Attorney General, whom Jack O'Donnell in *Collier's* calls "prohibition's white hope," is a member of the W. C. T. U. She is hated and feared by liquor law breakers. "Give me the authority," she says, "and let me have my pick of three hundred men and I will make this country as dry as it is humanly possible to get it. There is one way it can be done—get at the sources of supply. I know them and I know how they could be cut off. I have no patience with this policy of going after the hip-pocket and speak-easy cases. That is like trying to dry up the Atlantic ocean with a blotter!" The story as Mr. O'Donnell tells it, reads like a romance. This American up-to-date young woman, a judge, is the heroine. In her conflict with lawlessness, she pierces the enemy's armor with the sword of law. Mr. O'Donnell sums up, in the following paragraph, the prowess displayed by this "first legal lady of the land": "She is the woman who broke up the Big Four bootleg ring of Savannah, Georgia; put George Remus, one-time real king of booze venders, in Atlanta Penitentiary; wrote most of the opinions which hamper booze running and rum smuggling, and is the one person in official Washington who could and, if vested with proper authority, would make America almost bone dry. Mrs. Willebrandt doesn't bow to any political god and she places honesty above party expediency.

Under the direction of the gifted national W. C. T. U. director of the Christian Citizenship department, Mrs. Ida B. Wise Smith, the W. C. T. U., national and state, is pushing its own progressive citizenship and law enforcement program. In co-operation with other organizations, that met for conference in Washington, D. C., Fred B. Smith, chairman, the following program was adopted.

"Scientific temperance instruction in the public schools; pledge signing in churches and Sunday Schools; a ten years' program of training in sobriety and clean living; systematic distribution of prohibition data; churches and right-minded members of clubs should discourage efforts to circumvent the law and cultivate clean recreation and fellowship; increased use of appeals to the eye. Conferences with movie producers for elimination of scoffing at prohibition and creation of scenes depicting value of abstinence and prohibition; training of young people in citizenship; promotion of respect for law; must not honor law breakers whether in high life or low. The strength and perpetuity of the nations lie in the moral character of the people. Forces of nullification and lawlessness are everywhere at work. The forces of education must reconceive their task, gird themselves for new adventure and organize for at least a ten years' campaign."

The W. C. T. U., represented by the national president and Legislative superintendent, is a vital factor of the Woman's National Committee for Law Enforcement. The recent convening in Washington, D. C., of this influential committee meant that the leading women of the nation are determined to secure allegiance to the Constitution and observance of law. The general chairman of this inclusive patriotic committee is Mrs. Henry W. Peabody of Boston, Massachusetts; first vice-chairman, Mrs. William F. McDowell of Washington, D. C.; editor, Mrs. Elizabeth Tilton of Cambridge, Massachusetts. "Forward into the moral battle," "Up and doing" are the earnest watchwords of this campaign.

Mrs. Carrie Chapman Catt expressed her appreciation of the W. C. T. U. of which she is a member, when she said, "There is something that we women who never did aught to bring prohibition should do now. Some of you, like myself, were busy along other lines perhaps, or perhaps you were indifferent; but at the same time, while we were at work elsewhere, there were women who were working night and day with a sacrifice, with a power of which we of this time have little idea. Some of you may perhaps be old enough to remember, as do I, the time when churches did not work in fellowship with each other; and the greatest cause that brought their union about was the Woman's Christian Temperance Union. There never has been a woman leader in this country greater nor perhaps so great as Frances Willard. In those early days, when those women—when the world did not sympathize with them, when the vision that made them follow the light was not visible to others—in those days they labored, and now they have achieved. I am not forgetting what the men did. But I do not believe the people of this country would ever have achieved prohibition had it not been for those women."

Among the many noted women friendly to the Woman's Christian Temperance Union, is the distinguished author of "America the Beautiful," Katherine Lee Bates. Speaking at the Washington Conference, Professor Bates, referring to "America the Beautiful," said: "What strength, what uplift it may have, it draws from the American response. It is yours as much as mine, save for the wording."

Repeating the second stanza,

"O beautiful for pilgrim feet,
　　Whose stern, impassioned stress
A thoroughfare for freedom beat
　　Across the wilderness!
America! America!
　　God mend thine ev'ry flaw,
Confirm thy soul in self-control,
　　Thy liberty in law!"

Professor Bates said: "America is still a wilderness to be made beautiful with law and order, self-mastery and self-sacrifice. Freedom sought and found through such brave effort, such mighty labor, has yet to be interpreted, to be distinguished from license, to be recognized as a force of construction, not of destruction. Is not this great convention gathered here to remind liberty that her true name is obedience?

"It is perhaps easier for women than for men to keep the Beatific Vision clear of the confusion of the senses. It is not material prosperity that matters most, but to build in beauty, in peace, in honor, in love, those shining walls of the new Jerusalem. Why do we not build it here and now; why wait? For brotherhood there are no national bounds. I have sometimes been asked to write a fifth stanza to this song, making it international in scope, but songs write themselves. Yet in my thought I fling the last line around the globe. Our prayer for brotherhood not content with embracing the broad lands from Atlantic to Pacific, would enfold Asia and Africa and Europe in its return flight from the Pacific to the Atlantic.

'America, America,
God shed his grace on thee,
And crown thy good with brotherhood
From sea to shining sea.'"

Mrs. Kathleen Norris, the noted author, who also addressed the Washington Conference, gave this vivid word-picture of the Woman's March of Allegiance, which was the leading factor in securing for the state of California the Wright Enforcement Act. Mrs. Norris said in part: "We had in California what they call a 50,000 rock-bottom wet vote. We called together a mass meeting of the women who were interested. Mrs. Paul Raymond hoped for three hundred women and sent out invitations to more than 10,000! She organized the largest luncheon ever given in San Francisco. There were 1,700 women at that luncheon, and as one of the wet papers remarked disgustedly the next day, 'The town boiled with women.' Each one of the women who came found a card at her place which said, 'I am in sympathy with the enforcement of the law. I can work.' We rounded those women up into an enormous committee, and each one went back to her district and did what she could. That was the first step. After that we stormed the newspapers. Don't think that letters do not count. I am a newspaper woman and I say this to you in all seriousness: Letters from responsible women are a tremendous influence in any newspaper office. One hundred letters from one hundred voters and taxpayers will carry whatever points those women are trying to carry. We ended our campaign two days before election with that thoroughly horrible experience—a street march! It is a terrible thing to contemplate, it is a glorious thing to do. You don't walk, you float! We hoped to get seven hundred women in our march, and it rose to seven thousand. We started at ten o'clock at the Ferry Building and walked a short mile. They cleared the streets for us. We had two bands and some carriages. Most of us walked. It seemed to have a psychological effect upon the people and the press, that was incalculable. That night the wets staged a parade in which a large truck full of beer barrels was represented with 'Columbia' the figure of our liberty and our nation riding on those barrels. We carried the state, broke up the fifty thousand rock-bottom wet majority, and added thirty-five thousand dry votes to California's usual vote. California adopted a state enforcement code. California went dry." The Woman's Committee, including thousands of white-ribboners, by its far-reaching publicity, make it known that Mrs. Willebrandt, Assistant Attorney General of the United States, says: "The Eighteenth Amendment is a part of the Constitution made so by the same legal steps, although by a far greater number of states and legislative majorities, than the fourth, fifth, fourteenth and fifteenth amendments which every bootlegger claims for his protection while breaking the Eighteenth Amendment."

Three influential lawyers of Connecticut and New York City, the loyal sons of a white ribbon mother, are the authority for the following historical facts: The general court of Connecticut, held April 5, 1638, adopted eleven articles known as the Fundamental Orders. This was the oldest of American constitutions. It was the guide in the formation of the constitutions adopted by sister states as

Mrs. Culla J. Vayhinger

Mrs. Deborah Knox Livingston

Mrs. Frances W. Graham

Mrs. Mary Harris Armor

Catharine Waugh McCulloch

well as a foundation later for the Federal Constitution and the system of representation in the American republic.

The following is a beautiful concept of national and international law which is found in "The Laws of Ecclesiasticall Politie," written in 1554 to 1600, and dedicated to Thomas Hooker, the founder of Connecticut:

"O law of law, there can be no less acknowledged than that her seat is the bosom of God, her voice the harmony of the world; all things do her homage. The very least has felt her care; and the greatest is not exempt from her power; both angels and men and creatures of what condition soever, though each in different sort and manner, yet all with uniform consent admiring her as the mother of their peace and joy."

Generations later, with the same high appreciation of order and harmony, Abraham Lincoln said: "Let reverence for the law be breathed by every American mother to the lisping babe that prattles on her lap; let it be taught in schools, in seminaries and in colleges, let it be written in primers, spelling books and in almanacs; let it be preached from the pulpits, proclaimed in legislative halls and enforced in Courts of Justice and, in short, let it become the political religion of the nation, and let the old and young, the rich and the poor, the grave and the gay, of all the sexes and tongues and colors and conditions sacrifice unceasingly upon its altars."

CHAPTER VIII

THE NINETEENTH AMENDMENT

THE passage by the United States Congress of the Nineteenth Amendment (the Susan B. Anthony Bill) in May, 1919, and its ratification in September, 1920, giving the women the right to vote on equal terms with men, caused great rejoicing among the new electorate.

W. C. T. U. women were especially jubilant over the Nineteenth Amendment, for it passed Congress at the psychological moment to aid the enforcement of the Eighteenth Amendment. The leaders of the liquor trade who for more than two decades so bitterly have fought all woman suffrage measures were in consternation.

This victory for women, ended a seventy years' campaign of agitation in which the Woman's Christian Temperance Union had a mighty part. The text of the Amendment (Susan B. Anthony) reads: "The right of citizens of the United States to vote shall not be denied by the United States or by any state on account of sex." This bill was presented by the Hon. Jeannette Rankin of Montana—the fortieth time the measure had been introduced. For the first time, a woman was sponsor in Congress for any bill— and this was a measure giving equality of citizenship to her sex. At that period, there were ten million women of voting age in the United States. Susan B. Anthony and Lucy Stone were pioneer workers together for this bill. The writer, recalling the elderly, benignant face and strong, womanly personality of Lucy Stone (Blackwell) can scarcely believe the truth of an incident occurring in Lucy Stone's early career, often related by her in the later and happier years. A Boston clergyman was asked to give a pulpit notice of a lecture soon to be given by this unafraid pioneer, and announced that on such a date in a certain Boston hall, "a hen would crow!"

In the height of prohibition and suffrage campaigns, Frances Willard and Anna Gordon were frequent visitors at the office of *The Woman's Journal* on Park Street, Boston, Massachusetts, where, in converse with Lucy Stone, Henry Blackwell and their white ribbon daughter (Alice Stone Blackwell), then a student at Boston University, there were witty scintillations and constructive argumentations— a plenty. Speaking at a suffrage hearing on Beacon Hill often was on Miss Willard's program, and also conferences with such elect spirits as Dr. and Mrs. Joseph Cook, Rev. Edward Everett Hale and Bishop Phillips Brooks. It is well to recall this galaxy of forward-looking friends who in the 'effete East' bravely and gaily battled for woman's emancipation.

Early in its history, under the leadership of Frances Willard, the National W. C. T. U. made public sentiment for woman suffrage—as a temperance measure. At the national convention held in 1875, forty-nine years ago, this courageous resolution was passed: "Since women are among the greatest sufferers from the liquor traffic, and realizing that it is ultimately to be suppressed by means of the ballot, we, the Christian women of this land in convention assembled, do pray Almighty God, and good and true men, that the question of the prohibition of the liquor traffic should be submitted to all adult citizens irrespective of race, color or sex."

Commenting, in her autobiography on these early days, Miss Willard says: "In 1875, I remember writing a declaration to this effect: 'Resolved, that since woman is the greatest sufferer from the rum curse, she ought to have power to close the dramshop door over against her home.' I told the women that I had no home in that word's highest and most sacred sense, and I never would in this world, although I hope to in a better; and that if I could brave an adverse public opinion for the sake of other women's homes, surely they could do so for the sake of their homes. These words I could hardly speak for the ache in heart and throat, and I saw tears in many a gentle woman's eyes as I made my simple plea."

In 1876, at the National W. C. T. U. Convention held in Newark, New Jersey, Frances Willard encountered decided opposition to her appeal for woman's ballot—as a temperance measure. A lady from New York, gray-haired and dignified, who was presiding the night Miss Willard made her first public plea for woman's ballot, said to the audience: "The National W. C. T. U. is not responsible for the utterances of this evening. We have no mind to trail our skirts in the mire of politics." As Frances Willard left the church, one of the chief women bitterly said to her: "You might have been a leader in our national councils, but you have deliberately chosen to be only a scout." Miss Willard, however, was not dismayed, for she knew that the majority of the audience, though timid, really sympathized with her.

The white-ribboners who courageously promoted sentiment for woman's ballot, were building better than they knew. They were declaring not only for the cause of temperance, but for the "diviner womanhood that should bring in the era of sweeter manners, purer laws! for the mighty forces which should level up, not down, and which should draw manhood up to woman's standard of purity in the personal conduct of life."

In 1877, at the Chicago W. C. T. U. Convention, this resolution received the majority vote: "As the responsibility of the training of the children and youth rests largely upon woman, she ought to be allowed to open or close the rum-shop door over against her home." In April, 1878, supported by the organization, Frances Willard sent a memorial to Congress asking the Senators and Representatives to recommend such legislation as would, in the District of Columbia, and the territories, make legal the sale of intoxicating liquors as a beverage, only when the majority of the men by their votes and the women by their signatures, should ask that such sale might be legalized.

In presenting this memorial, Miss Willard said: "First among the powerful and controlled instincts of our nature, stands that of self-preservation, and next to that, if, indeed, it should not take superior rank, comes that of mother-love. It is as deep and resistless as the tides of the sea. The stronghold of the rum power lies in the fact that it has upon its side two of the most powerful of human appetites—in the dealer, the appetite for gain; and in the drinker, the appetite for stimulants. As God has provided in nature an antidote for every poison, and a compensation for every loss, so in human society He has ordained against alcohol—that worst foe of the social state, an enemy, beneath whose blows it is to bite the dust. Brothers, there is not one of you to whom some woman's life is not a dear and sacred thing."

At the national W. C. T. U. convention held the same year in Baltimore, Maryland, Frances Willard, referring to this memorial, called it the Home Protection Petition. Speaking in heart-to-heart fashion, she related to the assembly this personal experience: "The thought of the Home Protection Petition came to me on my knees one Sunday morning in the room of a veteran Crusader in Columbus, Ohio. I knew it meant criticism, but I acted according to my conscience and my light. A Baltimore lady said to me yesterday, 'Persimmons are nice when they are right, but they pucker the mouth when they are green.' This Home Protection Petition is a green persimmon in Maryland, but, my friends, it is a ripe one yonder on the prairies, and you surely wouldn't forbid us to gather and partake of it."

Several years later, Frances Willard found a strong friend in the famous astronomer, Maria Mitchell, who gave her a "Home Protection" audience at the National Woman's Congress. At the same national convention, Hannah Whitall Smith of Philadelphia, always progressive, stated her viewpoint as follows: "The commission has come to some of us, in a heavenly vision, that God is preparing the Christian women of this country to wield a weapon in our warfare against the liquor traffic which will be by far the most effectual weapon God has yet given us."

In 1881, a committee on "Franchise," consisting of Frances Willard, Mary Livermore and J. Ellen Foster, was appointed. In 1882 the department of Franchise was formally adopted, with Mary Clement Leavitt as national superintendent. Mrs. Zerelda Wallace succeeded Mrs. Leavitt in 1883, and following her, the national superintendents have been: Rev. Anna H. Shaw, Mrs. Theresa A. Jenkins, Dr. Louise C. Purington, Miss Marie C. Brehm, Mrs. Ella S. Stewart, Dr. Maude McIlvain Sanders and Mrs. Deborah Knox Livingston.

With the complete enfranchisement of women, the department of Suffrage was merged into that of Christian Citizenship, and led by the inspiring National W. C. T. U. director, Mrs. Deborah Knox Livingston, suffrage sentiment in the W. C. T. U. swept onward. "We have come to the day of a new dream," said Mrs. Livingston, "the dream of a better America, in which democracy is a religion, rather than a quasi-fiction of government; in which love of country is a supreme passion; in which the duties of citizenship are co-equal with the privileges of citizens. The W. C. T. U., because of its methods of organization and the personnel of its membership, seems to be the best equipped of all national organizations of women to make American citizens of our foreign-born women. In our ranks are enlisted professional women, industrial women, and women of the farm. In other words, our membership is drawn from all classes of society. One of the most fascinating stories of the development of 'the woman movement' is that of woman's struggle for educational privileges and advantages on equal terms with men. One hundred years ago the term 'higher education' had no meaning for women. Even in Colonial days the grammar and elementary schools were intended only for the education of boys. Seventy-five years ago there was not a single college for women in our country, and not one of the men's colleges had opened its doors to the other sex. In Northampton, Massachusetts, today the seat of the largest college for girls in our Republic, it was voted at a town meeting in the early eighteenth century that no town money be appropriated for the education of girls. Now more girls than boys graduate from public schools, and the tremendous growth in the last seventy-five years in the education of women is one of the marvels of the woman movement."

Many readers of this history have been privileged to hear Frances Willard tell a racy incident of her early days on the farm. She reveled in it with keen delight! "When I was a child," she said, "my father returned one night to Forest Home in Wisconsin. Sitting by my mother's chair, I listened to their conversation. With a good deal of spirit, father told of the encouraging news about Neal Dow and the fight for prohibition in Maine. He ended by saying, 'I wonder if poor, rum-cursed Wisconsin will ever get a law like that?' I was much impressed as I saw mother silently rocking in her dear old chair before she gently said, 'Yes, Josiah, there'll be such a law all over the land some day when women vote.' Father looked at mother with astonishment, and in a keen, rather sarcastic voice, said, 'And pray, how will you arrange it so that women shall vote?' Mother's chair moved a little faster as she looked into the flickering flames of the grate and slowly answered, 'Well, Josiah, I say to you as the Apostle Paul said to his jailer, "You have put us into prison, we being Romans, and you must come and take us out!" ' "

At the age of twenty-one, Oliver Willard, the only son of the Willard family, went with his father to cast his first ballot. Frances, then a girl of sixteen, watching from the window with her younger sister, their departure to the polls, turned to Mary, and with an ache in her heart, said: "Don't you wish we could go with them when we are old enough? Don't we love our country just as well as they do?" and Mary, just a little scared, said, "Yes, of course we ought. Don't I know that? But you mustn't tell a soul—not mother, even, or we should be called strong-minded."

Working in its own way, but in co-operation with other women's organizations, the W. C. T. U. brought conviction on this controversial subject to many conservative home, church and missionary women who had turned their backs, as well as their consciences, on the seemingly "bold advocates" of "woman's rights."

The wonderful spirit that dominated white ribboners is illustrated by this serio-comic incident: The Indiana W. C. T. U. appealed to the state legislature for a law that would protect the young from the ravages of the liquor traffic. This petition was signed by 20,000 influential women, including the wives and mothers of many substantial men of the state. In a tirade against the bill that was introduced, the youngest member of the house vehemently said: "I understand that this bill is backed by a petition of 20,000 women; but, gentlemen, the signatures of 20,000 women in this state mean no more to us than the signatures of 20,000 mice." This egotistical dictum so stirred Indiana's great-heart, Mrs. Zerelda Wallace, the stepmother of Gen. Lew Wallace, author of "Ben Hur," that she decided to devote her life to bettering the political standing of women.

In the old Colonial days it was New England that set the nation's pace. It is well to recall the fact that the pilgrim foremothers, as well as the pilgrim forefathers, were founders of a race. Westward their descendants went. Beyond the Rockies, and in the Middle West the women who helped the men conquer the wilderness were chivalrously given a voice in the affairs of state. Certain western states began to show the benefits coming from woman suffrage, and the women of the east slowly learned that "a force which when indirect, is helpful, will be more helpful when it becomes direct; for the most benignant and pervasive force in human life will not change in character when to its indirect power it adds the concentrated force of woman's ballot."

In the northwest, one of the earliest leading suffragists and white ribboners was Mrs. Elizabeth Boynton Harbert, editor of the "Woman's Kingdom" in the *Chicago Inter-Ocean.* Later, Miss Mary Allen West and Mrs. Susanna

198

M. D. Fry were live wires. Miss Jane Addams, the noted sociologist and the distinguished head of Hull House, in speaking a decade ago, declared: "At the beginning of civilization, women were the originators of some of the greatest trades. The great trades which women discovered are agriculture, building, architecture, spinning, weaving, sewing, tanning, pottery and cooking. It was not by accident that the primitive women stumbled upon the paths leading to civilization. Necessity spurred their minds to activity. Their physical weakness and offspring kept them from the chase but their minds were illumined instead by the discoveries which they made."

When Harriet Martineau visited America in 1840, she put it upon record that she found but seven employments open to women, namely, teaching, needlework, keeping boarders, washing for the operatives in cotton mills, typesetting, work in bookbinderies, and household service. Miss Addams, in 1912, optimistically viewed the suffrage situation when she said: "Whether or not the voters in a given community express themselves in favor of equal suffrage cannot impede its progress. The future historian will merely be able to read whether or not the voters in that city or state were at a given moment sensitive to the democratic movement of that time or indifferent to it. The forward progress of the world is a steam roller which only the blind are willing to oppose." In rural districts as well as in the large cities women did their "bit." In a certain community in the conservative state of Maine the voteless women were in the habit of picking blueberries in hot July weather, to earn money with which to pay their husband's poll taxes. These women remind one of the cheerful giver of holy writ. Cheerful in that connection really means hilarious. How still more hilarious today are these dutiful wives as they use some of their blueberry money to pay their own poll taxes!

In 1880, at the invitation of the Brooklyn W. C. T. U., Rev. Henry Ward Beecher, made his first speech in favor of woman suffrage. He said in part, "It's a thundering fact! I am ashamed to say that while enthusiasm is never wanting on the part of the saloon-keepers for the work of the devil, we never can get up enthusiasm for the work of the churches. Instead of giving out the heat of a common flame, they are like scattered brands, but the enemy is organized. It is a shame and an outrage that it should be so, but it is. I have something new to say about women. I am going to announce a heresy. For the cause of religion, morality and temperance, I plead the right of women to vote."

Later, at a W. C. T. U. meeting arranged for Frances Willard in Plymouth Church, Mr. Beecher presided. He escorted Miss Willard to the platform, and after introducing her, asked if he might sit beside his wife in the audience, saying, "I almost never get the chance to do so in this church, you see." When Miss Willard had finished, he walked up the steps smiling, pointing toward the lecturer as he came, and then turning to the audience said in his dramatic way, *"And yet—she cannot vote! Aren't you ashamed, men, that this should be?"*

In recounting this remarkable episode, Miss Willard said: "I had spoken strongly in favor of prohibition as the best method of dealing with the liquor traffic, and Mr. Beecher said distinctly, 'Not a word has been uttered but that we all know to be just and true and right.' His first temperance speech when he was an Amherst collegian, was in favor of a law against the liquor traffic. After these two sermons, in a sentence he proceeded to make a collection speech that outdid all I ever heard elsewhere for wit and wisdom. Of course, everybody stayed through, and the baskets came back actually full—I have never seen them thus except on that occasion."

As early as 1883, Rev. Joseph Cook of Boston, declared himself in favor of woman suffrage, and made this revolutionary statement: "The five great powers of modern society," he said, "are not England, Russia, Austria, Germany and France, but the parlor, the pulpit, the press, politics, and the police." And as the leader of these marshalled powers, he emphasized the parlor, which might, if it would, control all the rest.

In one of her early lecture tours, Mary Livermore, after giving a logical suffrage address to a large audience, talked with an intelligent brewer who said: "When you give women the right to vote, a prohibitory amendment is sure to follow, and women haven't a grain of sense on the temperance question. They are crazy fanatics on that subject, and they will not stop till the whole liquor business is destroyed root and branch." After the amendment bill for suffrage was submitted to the states, the liquor organizations spent thousands of dollars to defeat it at the polls. In secret circulars sent to their henchmen, the distillers and brewers emphatically declared that women, if given the ballot, would vote out the saloons and utterly destroy the liquor business.

Just as in the campaigns for prohibition, so in the public discussions for woman suffrage, argument was met with argument. "How much simpler it would be," declared Anna Shaw, "if the women, instead of spending all their time trying to boost up the men could go to the ballot-box and vote like men—exactly as the women in the parliament of Finland have been able, not only to influence the Finnish parliament, but to cast their votes in the interests of the prohibition measures which the women of Finland everywhere desired to have passed. Talk to women about keeping the children off the street! What can a man be thinking of who stands out in the street and looking over across the street, sees his own door open and one of his own children putting his head out, and then stands shooing him back, saying, 'Go back, go back to your mother's home; don't dare to come out on your father's street, for if you do you are lost, and if you are lost it isn't your father's fault, it is your mother's fault for letting you out.' Now, that is the cry which we women all over this country have heard. If the men could make the streets safe and clean without women and still will not do it, then the women under God are bound

201

to go out and help the men to make them clean, for if there is any right which a woman has under God, it is the right to protect her children from any form of degradation and vice, legalized or unlegalized.

"God laid upon women the obligation of motherhood and child rearing. It is the business of mothers to rise up and protest against the forces which will prevent the mother from protecting her child. If there is any crime greater than another perpetrated by a great Christian country, it is the curse of protecting the business which destroys all the life's work of a mother. It is the right, and ought to be the purpose of every woman of this country to demand every ounce of power which will enable her to do for her children the very best and noblest service. The distiller is armed with the ballot, the brewer is armed with the ballot, the saloonkeeper is armed with the ballot, the bartender is armed with the ballot, the drunkard—the male drunkard—is armed with the ballot. The home maker, the child rearer, is powerless against such a foe without the ballot which determines political conditions in this country, and it is the crime of our day."

Among the young women who, in the early years, believed in woman suffrage was Mary E. McDowell. Miss McDowell had the courage to organize W. C. T. U. work for young women in Evanston and Chicago, and she also gave social prestige to the evening gatherings over which she presided—often in her parents' hospitable home. Later, Miss McDowell became the head of the Chicago University Settlement, and ever since has been a well-known power in the civic life of the metropolis. In all the reforms she has instituted, she has upheld the principles of a white-ribboner. Soon after starting the settlement work in the stock yards district, she instituted measures for reducing the death rate of the babies of the neighborhood.

It is interesting to see the influence woman's ballot had in giving Miss McDowell the victory in a notable campaign. For nearly twenty years she fought against the city's dumping its garbage into the deep holes made in her neighborhood, by excavating clay for the manufacture of brick. The owners of the "clay holes" received large incomes by renting these "holes" to the city. Garbage by the hundreds of tons was dumped into them and little ones died like flies from the diseases bred from the decomposing offal. The impetus of the struggle against the city's system of handling garbage carried Miss McDowell to Europe, which she visited in 1911 to study European systems of the disposal of city refuse. For two years after her return, she conducted a city-wide campaign for the scientific study of garbage disposal by municipal commission. When the state of Illinois gave women the ballot, she won her fight and the commission was appointed and made its survey. Miss McDowell is now the City Commissioner of Public Welfare—the only woman member of the mayor's cabinet. This is a department of municipal social service. In speaking on the subject of garbage, this story wittily reflecting on the aristocratic "Boston-ese," is one Miss McDowell enjoys telling: A recent arrival in a city of the middle west, a lady from Boston, entered a leading emporium and asked for a "refuse chalice." The salesman, nothing daunted, immediately handed her a garbage pail. "How did you know what the customer wanted?" later he was asked. "Oh," he replied laughingly, "I saw that she must have come from Boston, for I once lived there long enough to learn the refined language of the Back Bay district."

In the later years of the nineteenth century many victories for women were seen. Catharine Waugh McCulloch, of Evanston, Illinois, the legal advisor of the National W. C. T. U. is a Master in Chancery. Four times, each time for a period of two years, the judges of the Superior Court have given Mrs. McCulloch this important appointment. It will be recalled that she was the first woman in the United States to win an election as Justice of the Peace. Mrs. McCulloch strongly urges W. C. T. U. women to "crusade in the court room." "The white-ribbon," she says, "strikes terror to evil doers!" Mary Bartelme is the first woman to be elected a judge of the Circuit Court of Cook County, Illinois—a district of three million people and the largest that ever elected a woman to such an office. In Ohio, a prominent woman lawyer, Florence Allen, has been elected a judge of the Superior Court. These women judges co-operate with the W. C. T. U. "When we women are fully enfranchised," said Mrs. McCulloch, "we will elect judges and clerks who are true to their duty. If we had one honest and intelligent judge in every precinct of every community in the United States, fraud would be impossible. When the women have the vote all over this country, those people who have exploited child workers, those who are cornering the food markets when many are starving, those who break laws made to safeguard the community, in that day the great army of women voters will be like unto an army of Jehovah." One of the good W. C. T. U. women who served on juries in Washington territory, and always got complimented by the judge for doing her duty, has sent her fees to the National W. C. T. U. treasury—a good example to follow!

Mrs. Thomas Edison, the daughter of an original Ohio Crusader and of Lewis Miller of Chautauqua fame, recalls the days when her mother, with other dauntless women, visited the saloons and pleaded with the men to close their doors. They were subjected to insult and had buckets of water thrown over them. "When I look back to those days," Mrs. Edison writes, "and note the growth of our great cause, I cannot be discouraged. I am proud to remember that my father was one of the pioneer advocates of woman suffrage."

Julia C. Lathrop, first director of the Federal Children's Bureau, said: "Not so-called anti-suffragists, but the liquor interests are the worst opponents of woman suffrage. Over forty years of education and agitation by the W. C. T. U. helped to give this nation a Federal Child Bureau."

The contagion of "The Ballot for Women" reached even the children. In a state amendment campaign, a manly Loyal Temperance Legion boy distributed ballots and leaflets. He saw the mother-hearted leader weep when brewers and distillers won, and the flag of our country protected their places of business. Charlie was not a mere looker-on— he was in it, and was himself a part of this battle for the protection of the home instead of the saloon. Going with his little sister to their leader, he said earnestly, "Please don't feel so sorry. When I grow up I'll vote the saloons away, and Mary will vote, too."

Many leaders, interviewed by politicians seeking office, are being asked what women voters most want. In substance, the answer received is one suggested by Mrs. Ella A. Boole: "If you want the women to vote for your party, give them a platform they can endorse and candidates for whom they do not have to apologize." After four years of suffrage, many women previously conservative, are so happily at home in the use of the ballot, that observers are reminded of that irresistibly funny little picture that two decades ago went the rounds of the illustrated papers. It was a chicken with a little of the shell he had just left still clinging to his back, and looking down at the broken prison from which he had just pecked his way out, he was made to say with a great gravity, "Nobody can ever convince me that I've been in there."

In Illinois, in the first encounter of white ribboners with the liquor trade—after women were given the ballot—the victorious results was announced in these rythmic lines: "Mary had a little vote, That roamed the state about; And everywhere that vote went in, John Barleycorn went out." Now, women voters in both states and nation are giving to the lawless liquor element more unwelcome information about "Mary." There is nothing obscure about this versified challenge:

Mary has a little vote
That keeps our nation dry;
It jumps right over party lines
Ask nullifiers why.

It serves America so well—
It "follows *her*" you know—
That nullifiers sadly learn
Where Mary's vote will go.

The gratitude of W. C. T. U. women toward brotherly men in professional and business life, who have given them the ballot, is boundless. It must not be forgotten, however, that Petruchio, that famous creation of Shakespeare, is still at large. He said of his wife: "She is my goods, my chattels. She is my house, my household furniture, my field, my barn—my anything." Today, the man like-minded with Petruchio, is the unscrupulous politician—the "masculinity complex."

Susan B. Anthony, in her later years when asked if she were not tired of shaking hands, answered that she was not more so than when there were no hands to shake! This pathetic and characteristic statement of a warrior-soul is a revealing one. It visualizes the hardships, the controversies, the weariness of body, if not of soul, of the long struggle for woman's emancipation.

When, in the past, problems pressed and perplexed white-ribboners, they found that the only way out was to advance. Going forward into the dark, light has come. Their example is commended to those who now without experience, are saying, "What shall we do who carry the fray for civilization on today?" Women in public life, delegates to recent national political conventions, many of them white-ribboners, have amazed old school politicians by their high purposes. The spirit of the marching mothers of the Crusade has been in them. Take the testimony of a noted woman author who gives a vivid account of the women who assembled for conference at one of the political conventions. This is the pen picture in brief:

"The women delegates of the north and the south fighting a common enemy chanted, 'In the beauty of the lilies Christ was born across the sea, with a glory in his bosom which transfigures you and me. As he died to make men holy let us die to make men free, His cause is marching on.' Then with zealous inspiration a woman went down on her knees and lifted her voice in prayer. 'God give us strength,' she plead. A younger woman took up her word. Woman after woman followed, as men, veterans of many a political campaign, crowded into the doorway, stricken by wonder at this most amazing spectacle. 'If the women take politics this way,' a former state governor whispered, 'we might as well go back to our farm. We cannot stay in the game with them on these terms.' 'It's a children's crusade,' said a great lawyer. 'They are setting out for a Jerusalem of faith without even a leader. They may not get there, but their going will light the torch for those who will.' Such must have been the spirit of those women who went through Ohio years gone by, kneeling in the streets before the saloon. Out of their praying came two Constitutional amendments, the Eighteenth and Nineteenth." Is there not great reason for rejoicing that over the women of this republic a great wave of political crusading fervor is sweeping?

Mrs. Margaret B. Platt, who has given, in Washington by the Atlantic, and in Washington by the Pacific, superb white ribbon service, asks these significant questions: "What manner of mothers shall tomorrow give us? Are changed conditions to bring us changed ideals of womanhood? Will the man of the future as he searches back in the mind's treasures to the throne-room of his childhood, find in the chief place there, one in true womanly guise, gentle and tender, pure and loving, yet clothed with dignity and strength and courage, fully able to guide the high-strung, youthful spirits 'along life's treacherous highway?' Will the words

207

of God and the evening prayer at mother's knee linger as sweet perfume in memory's chalice? Will he say with another: 'I see you oft, in my dreams at night, and you whisper soft, "My child, do right." ' "

Was it not in God's plan that woman, the born conservator of the home, should prove the Nemesis of the arch enemy of the home, alcohol?

CHAPTER IX

Our Golden Jubilee

IN this Jubilee Year, this year of our Lord, 1924, the W. C. T. U. gratefully chronicles a golden history, a golden present and prophesies a golden future. A half century ago, in 1874, the National Woman's Christian Temperance Union was organized. Today it is a mighty host with a membership of half a million and a large following of co-operating, home-loving women. In the last fifty or one hundred years, how wonderfully the point of view in regard to the liquor traffic has changed! An incident that occurred during the administration of John Quincy Adams, President of the United States, illustrates this. In 1825, while Mr. Adams was campaigning one day near Worcester, Massachusetts, greatly to his surprise there came to meet him and his mounted escort, a winsome young matron, who in order to reach him had ridden sixty miles on horseback. Courteously addressing the President, this young mother earnestly pleaded that for the sake of her husband and three young children he would work for the outlawing of the liquor traffic. With characteristic chivalry, Mr. Adams told the anxious mother how much he appreciated her solicitude, but said most emphatically, "Madame, what you ask is an impossibility. I might as well expect to legislate against the winds and the tides as to try to prohibit the legalized liquor traffic." This was the sincere opinion of a President who was one of the most able among American statesmen of the old school—a lawyer and a diplomat. Today, a man of such a mental make-up could not be elected United States President. The "impossible" has been accomplished. In 1874, a multitude of devoted, daring women from all over the land came to the aid of the children and children's children of that devoted, daring mother. Even the "winds and the tides" of the legalized liquor traffic had to obey the behest of these crusading women. The W. C. T. U. of this golden Jubilee Year is patriotically declaring, "Allegiance to the Constitution"—the Constitution of a gov-

ernment that has outlawed the legalized liquor traffic.
White-ribbon women also rejoice in the United States Supreme Court, whose decisions have ever been in favor of
sobriety and justice; and in a United States Congress that
by a large majority is strong for the observance and the
enforcement of law. One hundred and twelve million free
people are benefited by Federal prohibition. Nine-tenths of
the homes are enjoying unprecedented prosperity. The
President of the United States, the majority of governors,
and a large per cent of the electorate are supporting the law
enforcement program of the Federal Prohibition Commissioner. Surely never before has the vision of the W. C.
T. U. been so fully realized. In the customs of society and
in the laws of the land the Crusaders' dream of fifty years
ago is becoming a reality.

In 1919, in preparation for the year of Jubilee, 1924,
the National W. C. T. U. entered upon a five-year intensive
drive for money and members. It was a noble resolve,
heroically carried out. The story, in outline, follows: It
was in 1915, at the national convention held in Seattle,
Washington, that the national president, Anna Gordon, introduced the plan for a Jubilee celebration. "In 1924," she
said, "will come the Jubilee Year of the National Woman's
Christian Temperance Union. I recommend the appointment of a committee to lay foundation plans for a fitting
observance of the fiftieth year of our organization—plans
that shall include the raising of a thank-offering Jubilee
Fund." By request, Miss Gordon appointed the following
committee: Mrs. Deborah Knox Livingston, Mrs. Lenna
Lowe Yost, Mrs. Paul Raymond, Mrs. William F. Mc-
Dowell, and Mrs. C. P. Lindsay. In 1918, Mrs. Livingston,
chairman of the committee, in consultation with the national
general officers, having recommended a campaign for a million dollars and a million members, it was decided to begin
at once the financial drive. Mrs. Elizabeth Perkins, of
Michigan, was invited to come to National W. C. T. U.
headquarters as the executive secretary for the intensive
campaign.

GENERAL OFFICERS NATIONAL W. C. T. U., 1924
Anna A. Gordon, Pres. (in center); Ella A. Boole, Vice-Pres. (at top);
Frances P. Parks, Cor. Sec. (left to right); Margaret C. Munns, Treas.;
Elizabeth P. Anderson, Rec. Sec.; Sara H. Hoge, Ass't. Rec. Sec.

Mrs. Perkins co-operated with the national treasurer, Mrs. Margaret C. Munns, the state, county, and local key-women; the ten national field representatives, as well as with the ten members of the National Jubilee Committee. A quota of Jubilee money to be raised, based on membership, was given to each state, the time limit for all being from March 20, 1919, to March 20, 1920. The budget of $1,000,-000 was to cover the following activities: Child Welfare, Health and Social Morality, Americanization, Women in Industry, Education and Information, World Prohibition, Headquarters (Evanston and Washington), Equipment and Repairs, Field Service and Administration. In the forceful campaign for the Jubilee Fund, Mrs. Elizabeth Perkins was in daily consultation with the resident general officers. Ably assisted by the editor of *The Union Signal*, she issued from week to week, through the official organ, informing, strong, convincing appeals.

When the drive for a million dollars approached completeness, the appeal for 1,000,000 members secured the right of way. It was in the spring of 1920 that the national corresponding secretary, Mrs. Parks, who ingeniously sponsored the campaign for a million members in 1924, first sent out the membership campaign plans. This Jubilee call was extended to every mother, every teacher and every church member. "Alone, we can do little; united, we become batteries of power."

"Be a million-aire," was Mrs. Parks' appeal. "Count one," she said. "You need the Woman's Christian Temperance Union! and the Woman's Christian Temperance Union needs you! You need the W. C. T. U. to help secure the high type of education in your community, state and nation; further wise, and prevent unwise, legislation; awaken intelligent enthusiasm for the privileges and responsibilities of citizenship; uplift and protect child life; meet the colossal appeal for higher standards of social morality and health; educate public sentiment in reverence for law; uphold the Eighteenth Amendment. The W. C. T. U. needs you to help emphasize the value of total abstinence; build public sentiment for the retention and enforcement of national and state prohibition laws; enlist the aid of all women in industrial circles in upholding prohibition; teach foreign-born mothers the value of total abstinence and to understand the spirit of the Eighteenth Amendment; line up all women in a systematic study of the duties of citizenship; publish abroad the beneficial results of prohibition; work for world peace, purity and prohibition." How naturally one drive helped the other! Experienced workers in the financial drive already in the field found that it was dollars received that made it possible to plan conferences and campaigns in which more dollars came in—this time each Jubilee dollar meaning a Jubilee member.

At the present time, through the energetic co-operation of the state W. C. T. U. presidents, nearly all the state unions have completed their assigned quotas for the Jubilee Fund. Each state retains in its treasury ten per cent to cover the cost of the campaign. From the offices of the corresponding secretary and treasurer there have been sent out each year, special Jubilee Fund and membership appeal leaflets that have caused many to join the W. C. T. U. women in their March of Allegiance to the Constitution of the United States.

It was during this period of activity that an ardent advocate of prohibition, a gentleman from Switzerland, in his search for facts regarding the success of prohibition in the United States, visited National W. C. T. U. headquarters. He had heard, as he journeyed through the United States, wild tales of the utter failure of prohibition, and even from some of its friends, a doleful prophecy that it probably would have to be modified, because it could not be enforced. Of course, such an absurd statement had been denied by advocates of prohibition who really understood the situation and he had been informed that the United States never would abandon its dry law. But the contradictory statement troubled him, and he wanted some indisputable evidence that he might carry back to his home to assure his people that America had not really backslid in the fight for its anti-liquor law. In the course of his tour of inspection of the headquarters building, he came to the room of the National W. C. T. U. corresponding secretary, Mrs. Frances P. Parks, where hangs the wonderful W. C. T. U. membership map which strikingly visualizes the local unions in each state—black pins showing the unions of long-standing, and red pins, the new ones that have been organized since the inauguration of the membership campaign of 1920. In some areas the pins are in exceedingly close proximity.

When this map was explained to him, the visitor cried with enthusiasm, "There is my answer; there is the proof I long have sought that America will not give up prohibition; that it will keep right on fighting for better enforcement and never let go of what it has won. This map shows something definite and tangible—it is proof that the women of your nation are determined to keep prohibition. Now, I can return to my home and tell my friends that *I know America will not go back.*" Above the map is the statement, "Ten thousand local unions are engaged in the Jubilee membership campaign to mobilize a million women. This map shows where they are."

In a mid-west town of probably thirty-five thousand homes, an active union decided on a membership drive. At four in the morning on the appointed day, a committee appeared at the local dairies and attached to the milk bottles for morning delivery, a notification that the local union of G—— would that day open a membership drive, and requested a courteous reception of the lady who would follow the milk bottle. Mrs. Frances Parks, who tells this story, remarks happily, "Needless to say, there was a big membership increase in that union."

A festive, colorful feature of the 1923 membership drive was its culminating celebration on July 21, of the birthday anniversary of the national president—a red-letter day. Miss Gordon received a delightful surprise. Twenty-five thousand new "Allegiance" members suddenly appeared in her office, converting it into a bower of loveliness—thanks to Mrs. Parks' clever, decorative scheme. These

213

invisible guests were impersonated by lovely flowers, floral cards and many ingenious state devices. The "gather the posies while you may" idea originated in flowery California. Each one of the five thousand new members from California (North) is still represented in Miss Gordon's office by a beautiful floral card bearing her name. California (South) sent gay little "Jubilee ladies"—tiny dolls in gold colored gowns, one for each local union that had measured up to its allotted increase in membership. Iowa sent a $2,375.00 corn necklace—each grain representing a new member who had paid her dollar dues; Kansas, a huge sunflower with a thousand autographed petals; Georgia, an exquisite white rose with local union names on its petals. There were greetings from Maine with pine tree cone decorations; garden posies from Wisconsin; rhododendrons from West Washington; sweet peas from Minnesota; laurel from Connecticut; wild roses from Iowa and North Dakota; golden-rod from Nebraska; violets from Rhode Island; columbines from Colorado; bitter-root from Montana; blue-bonnets from Texas, with lilies, marigolds, carnations, gladioli, roses and every imaginable flower from all along the line, and best of all, there was a soul in every flower. Evanston's new members were represented by a large cluster of the L. T. L. children's flower, the field daisy.

In her official letter of grateful appreciation, the national president said: "To the law-defying element in our republic, this riot of emblematic W. C. T. U. activity in the shape of an imperishable garland of human flowers and gracious gardeners, represents the challenge of the Woman's Christian Temperance Union to continued consecration to its holy task for the new crusade—law observance, law enforcement, trained citizenship and devotion to our coming citizens, the youth of this youthful pilgrim land."

In April, 1921, the National W. C. T. U., through its general officers, sent a proclamation to the women of America. It was an earnest plea for co-operation. "We are facing a great crisis," the national officers said: "Camouflaged as defenders of 'personal liberty' the friends and adherents of the outlawed liquor traffic are organizing and massing their forces to secure the annulment of the Eighteenth Amendment to the Federal Constitution by weakening the enforcement code or securing such interpretations of the law as shall permit the manufacture and sale of intoxicating liquors, contrary to the spirit and letter of the Amendment. The Woman's Christian Temperance Union, with its 500,000 members who are engaged in twenty-five different kinds of social, economic, and moral service —in city and in town, among women of all creeds, classes, and color—is now engaged in the Jubilee membership campaign to mobilize a million women. It invites every woman of our country who believes in the broad-gauged program of the W. C. T. U. to unite with us, through the local union nearest her home, and help in the accomplishment of the great tasks just ahead. We sincerely hope that through our united efforts—for God, and home, and every land—the womanhood of America may stand up and be counted—together—as well as one by one."

The Jubilee membership plans are still systematically marshaling the forces to unity of action. Year by year, in spite of losses by death, a fine net gain has been reported and the campaign will be carried over into the new era. In these manifold far-reaching ways the loyalty of the white-ribbon women was manifested. The day of preparation was over!

"The Year of Jubilee has come," triumphantly and hopefully exclaimed the National W. C. T. U. president in her message given at the national convention held in Columbus, Ohio. "Let us make it a continent-wide celebration —a triumphal march 'from sea to shining sea,' a March of Allegiance to the Constitution of the United States. Let us visualize to this nation the moral power of united womanhood, when for a great cause its patriotism is released." Mrs. Lella A. Dillard, president of the W. C. T. U. of Georgia, gives this graphic picture of the convention as it celebrated the fiftieth anniversary of the Crusade. "On the opening day—a processional—the Marching Mothers of the

215

Crusade of 1873, ballotless women kneeling and praying, despised and rejected by all but the spiritually discerning. Then, the triumphant March of Allegiance through the crowded streets of Columbus. The governor of the state and other officials in the procession, bands playing, magnificent floats, marching of thousands of enfranchised women conscious that their possession of the ballot meant that never again would there be a return to the old days when the home was despoiled, children defrauded, and women's hearts broken."

Through *The Union Signal* white ribboners have learned of the gratifying success of the fifty national-state Jubilee meetings aided at National W. C. T. U. headquarters by the up-to-date, enthusiastic, executive secretary of field service, Mrs. Jennie M. Kemp. Miss Anna A. Gordon, Mrs. Ella A. Boole, Mrs. Margaret C. Munns, Mrs. Elizabeth P. Anderson, Mrs. Ida B. Wise Smith, Mrs. Mary Harris Armor, and Mrs. Laura P. Miller, were the National W. C. T. U. speakers whose routes were planned by Mrs. Kemp.

Almost unanimously the states report the great value of these meetings. Interest and enthusiasm were aroused and notable people participated. The publicity was unusually good and many new members were obtained. State presidents say, "Never in our history have we ever done anything which has advanced our organization like the Jubilee meetings." This was especially true in the states where the celebrations under the National W. C. T. U. auspices were followed by fifty state meetings. Among the many prominent people participating and bringing greetings there have been governors, mayors, Supreme Court justices, editors, and state and college officials.

In most instances, the "get together" was at luncheons or banquets, the light of candles typifying the shining of the truths that were presented in the after-dinner speeches. The national president, Miss Gordon, was in the southern states; Mrs. Boole in the extreme west; Mrs. Munns in the middle west; Mrs. Anderson in the northwest; Mrs. Smith in the southwest, New England, and the middle west; Mrs. Armor in the south and middle west; Mrs. Miller in the middle west. The number of miles traveled by this national group was 52,821. The co-operation of state presidents in arranging these important gatherings was most praiseworthy.

What was the keynote of the speeches made at these Jubilee gatherings? Was it not the achievements of the past, and the present, and the boundless opportunities of the future? The oratory of the W. C. T. U. is far-reaching and enduring, for it is based on facts. It makes vivid the many-sided, progressive, co-operating program of the W. C. T. U. How great have been the results! For the benefit of those who are "listening in," the National W. C. T. U. radio announcer will broadcast the illuminating messages of the directors and superintendents of the following departments:

Americanization; Anti-Narcotics; Child Welfare; Christian Citizenship; Evangelistic; Exhibits and Fairs; Flower Mission and Relief Work; Health; Institutes; Legislation; Medal Contests; Medical Temperance; Parliamentary Usage; Peace and Arbitration; Prison Reform; Publicity; Sabbath Observance; Scientific Temperance Instruction; Scientific Temperance Investigation; Social Morality; Soldiers and Sailors; Sunday School; Temperance and Missions; The Bible in the Public Schools; Women in Industry; Work Among Negroes.

The national publicity director, Mrs. R. Scott Dunkin, a graduate of Columbia University, and formerly on the editorial staffs of New York newspapers, tells, first of all, the reasons why the W. C. T. U. should put good things in cold type—and have them there for keeps. Kindly "stand by!" Listen to Mrs. Dunkin and many others: "Publicity," says Mrs. Dunkin, "is the logical, modern method of interpreting an organization to the public. No matter what its glories, past history, notable achievements and progressive contributions to human development, unless an organization actively tells about its work, only a very limited public will realize more than its existence. Today, many talk of 'child welfare' as if it were a comparatively new study and yet for the past fifty years the National W. C. T. U. has been interested in the study of the child as apart from children in the mass. It has had a special department devoted to the study of child welfare and yet few, except those interested, have known of this splendid, progressive, nation-building work. It is because the W. C. T. U. did not make use of its opportunity to 'shout the glad tidings.' A great many people speak of 'Americanization' as if it were something entirely new, yet for fifty years, the W. C. T. U. has been working among the foreigners in America, helping them to know the customs of their adopted country and making them feel at home here through acting the part of real neighbors, understanding, sympathetic friends.

"Because the W. C. T. U. has spent its time working, instead of talking about itself, a comparatively small number know of this activity. Instead of having one limited interest, in reality the W. C. T. U. has twenty-six departments of work embracing every angle of a wide-visioned, progressive, humanitarian program for the betterment of community life. Through the various avenues of publicity, the public is now being informed as it should be. The time will come when, instead of being the most misunderstood organization, the W. C. T. U. will be recognized by women everywhere as the representative woman's organization."

A strange voice is now heard. Impressed by the speech just made, someone personifying the printing press is saying: "I am the voice of today, the herald of tomorrow; I am light, knowledge, power; I epitomize the conquests of mind over matter; I weave into the warp of the past the woof of the future; I am the record of all things mankind has achieved."

The announcer gives these additional facts: In the early years, the exchanges received by the editor of the W. C. T. U. national organ were innocent of all allusions to temperance work. The persistent publicity work, however, soon began to show results. The only difficulty experienced

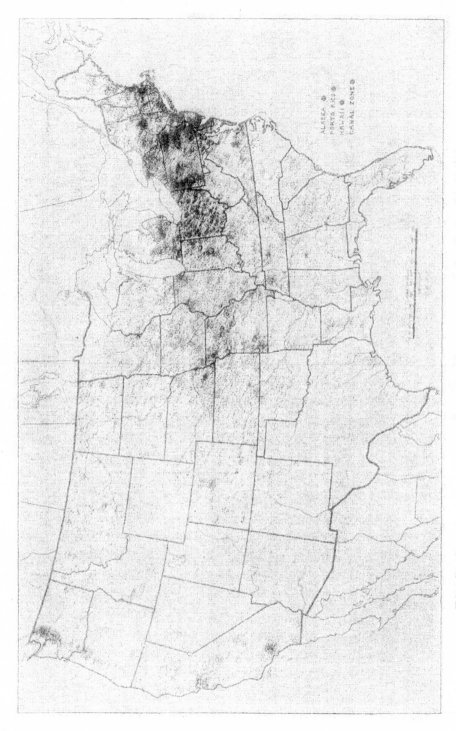

Distribution of the Woman's Christian Temperance Union in the United States.

Each Dot Represents a Local Union.

by the editor of *The Union Signal* was to choose the best out of the multiplicity of published temperance articles. This widespread change in the secular and religious press was largely due to the expert work of the national organ and of the "Press" department, as it was then called, which secured weekly and monthly temperance columns in religious weeklies and in the cosmopolitan and local newspapers. *The Champion,* an influential liquor organ of Chicago, thus bewailed this consummation: "There is not a day when the American press in almost every state of the Union does not indulge in violent tirades against the saloonkeeper. He is held forth to the world as a ghoul and a blood-sucking vampire—as a thief, robber and a murderer—as a most dangerous, abhorrent, God-forsaken character of our civilization. In the large cities especially, the saloonkeeper is tossed and kicked abut like a football by every religious mountebank, temperance crank and sham reformer, from the pulpit or the rostrum, or by means of some dishonest, lying newspaper." No wonder *The Champion* hated *The Union Signal* and also every white-ribboner who had the acumen of a successful pen woman.

The next speaker, Mrs. Frances P. Parks, national superintendent of the department of Organization, and chairman of the board of organizers and lecturers, which also includes evangelists, calls attention to the broadcasting stations all over the land where the experts of this department are sending out, with scientific and educational facts, womanly and compelling appeals which annually bring to the organization hundreds of new members. Mrs. Parks gives the following list of national organizers and lecturers: Mrs. Mary Harris Armor, Mrs. Florence E. Atkins, Mrs. Ellen A. Dayton Blair, Miss Rose A. Davison, Mrs. Lyversa M. De Silva, Mrs. Fannie A. Drummond, Mrs. Lulu Thomas Gleason, Rev. Lida M. Herrick, Miss Louise E. Hollister, Mrs. Emma H. Howland, Mrs. Azuba Jones, Mrs. Lora S. La Mance, Mrs. Jeannette H. Mann, Mrs. Matilda E. Patterson, Mrs. Viola D. Romans, Miss Roena E. Shaner, Rev. Mary Sibbitt, Mrs. Jackson Silbaugh, Miss

Christine I. Tinling, Mrs. Ida D. Van Valkenburgh. National evangelists: Mme. Layyah Barakat, Mrs. Lem Gilreath, Mrs. Ella Kroft, Rev. Etta S. Shaw.

"The purpose of the Young People's Branch," says the national general secretary, Mrs. Maude B. Perkins, "is to unite the young people of the community, county, and state in a campaign for the enforcement of the prohibitory law; to keep alive the civic consciousness concerning the value of total abstinence; to educate the young men and women as to the effect of narcotics upon the human system; to study the meaning of a single standard of purity and live it—that we may emphasize the essentials of Christian citizenship and thus perpetuate the heritage that has come to us from the mother organization.

"Many of our early boy members are now prominent teachers, preachers, university professors, and leaders of life in various communities. Many have said that their college training aided them to make a living; but the principles and training of the young people's organization had helped them to make their lives. A state senator of New Jersey says that it was through identification with our young people's organization that he had an arrest of thought along temperance lines and so is now able to work forcefully in that direction. A prohibition enforcement agent in another state had his training in a young people's society. Scores of young men state that our work has had a vital influence in shaping their lives.

"Our girls also pay tribute to our organization. In early life, one of our young women wanted to go as a missionary, but her health would not permit. When she came into our society, she confided to me her ambition, and I told her that all international work was not necessarily done in the countries across the sea. Since that time, she has worked officially and effectively here for our young people whom we have sent to other nations. A young woman of New York state, trained in our principles, gave fine service in South America. Students from other lands have felt the impress of our work and are now pushing these principles in the Orient and elsewhere.

"The young people have done valuable research work, making surveys as to the beneficial effects of prohibition in their respective communities; they have carried on correspondence with the young people of other non-prohibition countries, imparting information regarding the value of the dry law in this country; they have conducted, in their own branches, citizenship study classes to which members of other young people's societies have been invited; and in their own circles have been influential in building up sentiment for total abstinence and prohibition."

The announcer makes this historic statement: "In the beginning, the Woman's Christian Temperance Union met the challenge of the American liquor traffic, with the challenge of America's youth. Frances J. Barnes, of New York, cultured and devoted, the first national 'Y' secretary, gave herself freely to the task of winning young women and young men for an unpopular reform. Later, she gave her organizing and social program to the youth of the world."

The voice of the national secretary of the Loyal Temperance Legion Branch, Miss Mary B. Ervin, is now heard: "Inspire America's youth with civic ideals." she says.

"In Athens, long ago, boys were taught this pledge: 'We will never bring disgrace to this, our city, by any act of dishonesty or cowardice, nor ever desert our comrades; we will fight for the ideals and sacred things of the city, both alone and with many; we will revere and obey the city laws and do our best to incite a like respect and reverence in others; we will strive unceasingly to quicken the public's sense of civic duty—that thus, in all these ways, we may transmit this city greater, better and more beautiful than it was transmitted to us.' Such a pledge taught to the American youth today and passed on to future generations would make our own loved land truly 'America the Beautiful.'

"That we may celebrate our Jubilee Year in a manner worthy of this great event, worthy of the years of service

221

and sacrifice of our blessed foremothers, worthy of that splendid army of Loyal Temperance Legioners that helped make 'King Alcohol tremble' and totter from his throne when fhey 'grew up,' in honor of these worthy heroes of the past and in appreciation of the bigness of our task yet ahead, we need a MILLION boys and girls enlisted in the ranks of the Loyal Temperance Legion. These million members will want their fathers and their mothers to vote against beer and wine, and to talk against it, and to obey the laws of the land, and, above all, they will have had instilled into their plastic minds, the principles of clean living and right thinking.

"May the white-ribbon forces of America realize anew that the 'law-makers of twenty years hence are forming their habits and opinions now,' and may we catch a vision of the far-reaching influence of our labor of love in capturing this generation for law observance and for Christian citizenship. Enlist the children today and help make America 'greater, better and more beautiful than it was transmitted to us.' The imperative need of today is a larger number of consecrated leaders to keep before the youth of America the watchwords, 'Love, Loyalty, Light,' and to inspire in them the Christian patriotism embodied in our Loyal Temperance Legion movement."

"Hats off to the past, coats off to the future," said Mrs. Culla J. Vayhinger, the late national director of Americanization. "What is our past? A half century of toil and sacrifice to educate public sentiment in the United States to the belief in total abstinence for the individual, and prohibition for the state; to place the ballot in the hands of women; to establish a single standard of purity for men and women; to better working conditions for wage-earners, especially women and children. What is our future?

"Victory always brings new obligations. Enforcement officers tell us that from sixty-five to ninety per cent of the violations of the prohibition law must be laid at the door of the foreigner of our country; but again, a noted judge of Chicago says that ninety per cent of the foreigners coming before him for violations are ignorant of the law and its penalty, to say nothing of being ignorant of the reason which led to its enactment. Surely, our organization, which had so large a part in writing the law, has the responsibility of teaching these foreigners. The foreign-born women in this country are potential voters—largely through our efforts. It is our task to help them to become safe and intelligent voters. We must not fail.

"The foreign centers in our large cities are the greatest liability of our government. These foreigners are not anarchists and traitors to the flag under which they have come to live, but they do not know 'Old Glory' and that for which it stands. One generation of foreign-born, or children of foreign-born parents taught conscientiously by Christian Americans would make of this liability an asset. When foreigners first leave the ship at Ellis Island, let us extend to them a friendly hand. Let us enlist in this line of work, women who will be Christian American neighbors to the neglected foreign women, especially mothers."

"Stand by," says the announcer while you have Mrs. Vayhinger's picture of a day in a W. C. T. U. Americanization Center: "The clock in front of the jewelry store, owned by Mr. Cerevegna, marked eight o'clock as a young American woman, probably thirty years old, stepped lightly down Paulina Street, stopped in front of a store building facing on two streets, unlocked the door and went in. The windows were clean and in them was a fine exhibit of picture posters on health, prohibition, total abstinence, law enforcement, peace, good citizenship and child welfare, with the American flag much in evidence. There were pictures of Washington, Lincoln, Lafayette, Kosciusko, and Frances Willard; and in the center of the group a copy of Hoffman's head of Christ occupied a conspicuous position. On a window facing each street, in gold and black letters, were the words, 'W. C. T. U. Neighbors,' and on the door, in the same colors, the words, 'Welcome, Walk In.'

"As the young woman entered the bright, cheery room the telephone rang and a voice at the other end of the line asked if a group of young Italian men and women from homes where the families were crowded into two rooms, might come to the Center the next evening with their own 'eats' and have a party. As she turned from the phone, the door opened and a dirty, unkempt woman entered. In broken English, she told a sorry tale of sickness in the city hospital, dismissal, inability to work, and no place to stay. The teacher heard her story and then called up the Salvation Army to see if they could take care of the case in their woman's quarters. Receiving a favorable reply, she wrote a note to the person in charge, asking her to let her know when the bearer arrived, placed it in the hands of her visitor, took her to the street-car, paid her fare, and asked the conductor to put her off at the right place. Later, she was told over the phone that the woman had put in an appearance, all safe and sound.

"It was nine o'clock when three women, wearing the marks of Russia as their native land, called at the Center. For one hour the teacher with infinite patience and care used her brain and all the ingenuity she could muster to instruct them regarding the various parts of the body. Then she took into her own hand the horny hand of each woman, and carefully guided the stubby fingers in the attempt to make letters that would spell her name. When the lessons were finished and the stories of sick babies, husbands out of jobs, and the troubles of the children in school had been listened to with sympathetic attention, the teacher gave her promise to see what could be done, and the three foreign sisters, filled with more courage and interest because one American woman cared, went out to take up the trials and struggles incident to life in a strange land.

"Each hour brought new visitors and fresh duties. At two o'clock, three white-ribboners came and for an hour they studied with the teacher the correspondence course in Americanization, and then went out with her to call at some of the homes of the neighborhood, in preparation for volunteer work among the mothers. At three-thirty a crowd of boys and girls came scuffling into the Center, and after discouraged looking stockings had been pulled up off of shoe-tops, buttons put into their proper holes, and noses wiped, at the suggestion of the young women from the Young People's Branch who had charge of the Loyal Temperance Legion, an interesting group of children representing Rou-mania, Greece, Italy, Czecho-Slovakia, Poland, Croatia, and Russia were taught the reason why they should love America and the principles of the W. C. T. U. This was a busy day, indeed, though it did not happen to be the date when the Mothers' Club or the Girls' Club met, or when the teacher was to visit the court, or the school, or when there was an evening class or a mothers' party. Our successful Amer-icanization field worker, Miss Charlotte Fraser, visits the Centers."

Miss Helen G. H. Estelle, the national superintendent of Anti-Narcotics, is now heard: "Our department has these objectives: Knowledge of present laws regulating traffic in narcotics; observance and enforcement of existing laws; an anti-narcotic program before every mothers' club, parent-teachers' association and other groups interested in humani-tarian work; greater attention paid to the narcotic work in the public schools through the hygiene and biology classes; viewing of the film, 'Human Wreckage'; a copy of the anti-tobacco law of the state in every place where tobacco prod-ucts are sold. Opium, morphine, codeine, heroin, and co-caine are classed as habit-forming drugs. The W. C. T. U. seeks to protect all from the bane of these narcotics, and especially through education to prevent young people from forming drug-using habits. When children of all nations are educated as to the evil effects of opium and cocaine upon the human system, the drug problem will have been solved."

The next speaker to be introduced over the radio is Mrs. Elizabeth A. Perkins, the national director of Child Welfare. "The Child Welfare Department program of the National Woman's Christian Temperance Union," Mrs. Perkins explains, "is a five-pointed one: To every child belongs the right, to be well born (this also includes future health); to an education; to protection from child labor; to be morally safeguarded; to spiritual training. The work is carried on under four divisions. Division one—research work and a campaign of information and education. Division two—selection by local unions of specific work for immediate assistance. Division three—emphasis on the Eighteenth Amendment and the Volstead Code in their beneficent relation to child life. Division four—to give to mothers our friendship, our literature, our special helps and to urge all mothers to stand with organized mother-love in all that helps child life and to say, 'The legalized liquor traffic in any form, under any guise, shall never return.'

"Through the national official organ, *The Union Signal*, through the state papers of the organization, through special literature, and through two special papers sent out each month from the office of the national director, the organization is a vital factor in stimulating community interest in child welfare, and gives direct help to mothers on the care of children. Pamphlets and mimeographed sheets are available as loan material from the office of the national director. Extensive collections of posters and charts are loaned to W. C. T. U. organizations and for educational meetings, chautauquas, health weeks, baby weeks, and fairs."

The white ribbon electorate are alert listeners as they learn that Mrs. Ida B. Wise Smith, national director of the department of Christian Citizenship, will broadcast: "To be a good citizen," Mrs. Smith declares, "and to render the best possible service to one's country, is the responsibility of everyone who receives the benefits and protection of government. All good citizens should themselves implicitly obey the law; discourage violation by personal indulgence in liquor among friends; courteously protest against jests at prohibition in movies, periodicals, or in social converse; and carry plans for co-operation in law enforcement into every organization to which they belong. A particular activity— one that is colorful and spectacular—is the 'March of Allegiance' that in many of the larger towns features election campaigns.

226

"Rally the greater army for the greater task. Co-operate with public school teachers to secure emphasis on scientific temperance teaching and citizenship study, with law observance specially stressed; secure the same co-operation in colleges; give great attention to the Christian Endeavor, Epworth League, Baptist Young People's Union, Loyal Temperance Legion, and all other young people's societies; assist their Good Citizenship committees to properly plan and function; study all public questions—the policy of every political party toward them, and the attitude of every aspirant for office; pay poll tax, if required in the state; register if necessary, and induce others to do so; attend all caucuses—vote at primaries and final elections; uphold the officers now in charge of law enforcement, offer assistance if needed, commend any good work they do, protest when it is proper to do so, secure removal from office when unfit; as part of this program be sure that at every election officials are secured who will live up to their oath of office."

"The aim of the department of Exhibits and Fairs," says Mrs. Carolyn P. Lindsay, the national superintendent, "is to emphasize by picture play, pageant, float, pantomime, parade, tableau, charade, music, poster, exhibit, contest, or drill, the beautiful and the constructive, the benefits of prohibition, the blessings of total abstinence and law enforcement; to study the exhibit problem intensively and by so doing evolve a thing of beauty, both educative and convincing.

"To embrace every occasion where law enforcement may be presented in some form, either by co-operation or by initiative, indoors or outdoors. To plan well for a place at all fairs and to put on a creditable all-day program.

"Valuable W. C. T. U. exhibits have been attractive features of fairs, expositions and all large W. C. T. U. conventions. The National W. C. T. U. received a bronze medal at the Louisiana Purchase Exposition; a gold medal was given the organization at the Lewis and Clark Centennial Exposition held in Portland, Oregon, in 1905, a similar medal was awarded at the Panama-Pacific Exposition held

227

in San Francisco in 1915. For war relief work, a Belgium Orphan Fund medal of bronze was given in 1914, and, as noted elsewhere, a medal was given Miss Lella M. Sewall, the national superintendent of Flower Mission and Relief Work, for the adoption during the war of fatherless children in France."

The announcer gives this notice: "At National W. C. T. U. Headquarters, Evanston, Illinois, can be obtained a five-reel film, 'Safeguarding the Nation.' It is a scientific, educational exposition of the effects of small quantities of alcohol upon the individual, physically and mentally. The slowing down of the physical powers is shown by illustrations of endurance tests in walking, in feats of strength and in ability to accomplish set tasks. It is clearly visualized through the eye-gate that the nerves do not respond as quickly when alcoholized, even to the extent of wine and beer quantities. An engineer makes more mistakes in distinguishing colors, hence may run past his signal with consequent loss of life; the man who gives the signal for the hoisting or lowering of great beams responds a second too late and a life may pay the forfeit; the man at the great steel plant is pouring the red, molten iron into the forms—instantaneous response to the signal is the price of safety. These interesting illustrations hold the attention while they point the lesson.

"The effect of alcohol on posterity is set forth in the guinea-pig experiments, which are interesting and convincing. The physiological aspect of the question is emphasized and the phenomena of the beating heart, the expanding lungs, the circulation of the blood, etc., are so well done as to cause favorable comment from scientists. As a climax to the result of the study of the effect of alcohol, the whitening United States map is shown as prohibition progress was made and at last the beautiful Capitol of the saloonless nation is exhibited."

Miss Lella M. Sewall, the national superintendent, and her associate, Miss Eva Kilbreth Foster, tell how the beautiful Flower Mission and Relief Work has blessed many countries. The department seeks "to alleviate the sufferings of a chastened humanity; to afford relief increasing and comprehensive in its scope; to meet acute situations with emergency relief, international as well as national, if necessary. Co-operating with other departments, this one not infrequently opens the door to pronounced prohibition sentiment." The remarkable war relief work of the department is told in a previous chapter. The historic setting of the Flower Mission department is well known to all who continue to celebrate Jennie Casseday's birthday. Miss Casseday, it will be recalled, a suffering invalid, became at Frances Willard's request, the first superintendent of this gracious, ministering department. Miss Ethel Austin Shrigley, who preceded Miss Sewall as superintendent, initiated many of the plans so successfully used today.

A woman physician now speaks—Dr. P. S. Bourdeau-Sisco, the national superintendent of the department of Health. "This department," Dr. Sisco says, "was established in the year 1881, at the eighth annual convention. Thus early in the history of the movement was the relation of health to temperance recognized. The department has had thirteen superintendents, three of them having been physicians. During the past forty-three years it has been known at various times as the department of Hygiene, the department of Heredity, and the department of Health, which indicates something of the scope of the work that has been done. Today it is organized in forty-six states and divisions of territory.

" 'To glorify God in our bodies, to keep His word and teach men so, is the tap-root of the temperance reform,' said Frances E. Willard. 'The Health department is the great foundation department,' is the statement of Anna A. Gordon. These sentiments have ever been the department ideals. It teaches that the craving for alcohol is due in part to a condition of lowered physical vitality and an indefinable feeling of inadequacy. It is known that the general movement for better health, the increased interest in all matters of public hygiene, during the past years has been one of the factors in the banishment of the saloon.

"And, now, it is just here that at the present time the work of the Health department also vitally touches the question of law enforcement. It seeks to aid in the enforcement of the law by removing one of the causes of infringement of the law, namely, disease and ill health.

"Moreover, the study of physiology clearly indicates that the human body is governed by law, and that for every broken law there is a corresponding penalty. We know also that the body politic is ruled by law, and that for every broken law there ensues greater or less civic disaster. And so when the department of Health teaches respect for the laws of the body, therein does it also teach respect for law wherever found, not only in the realm of nature, but also in the domain of the state. Thus does the department correlate its efforts with the great objectives of the national organization.

"Its methods include the extensive use of well-chosen literature, health lectures, health demonstrations, the use of the public press for the dissemination of the truths of health, and health meetings held in all the local unions of the organization throughout the land. It stresses the various features of public hygiene, personal hygiene, and mental hygiene, as general and local conditions demand. Its principles are indicated in the following physical decalog:

"I. Thou shalt eat for health. Thou shalt not stuff nor starve.

"II. Thou shalt drink plenty of pure water. Most men eat too much, but drink too little.

"III. Thou shalt work, but thou shalt not overwork.

"IV. Thou shalt obtain sufficient sleep, but thou shalt not be found a sluggard.

"V. Thou shalt recreate, but thou shalt not dissipate.

"VI. Thou shalt dress healthfully: thy body shall be well protected, but no part constricted.

"VII. Thou shalt practice deep breathing, for thy lungs are thy body's ventilators.

"VIII. Thou shalt bathe frequently, for thus thou keepest active the million pores of thy skin.

"IX. Thou shalt covet the sunshine. It is God's great life-giving force.

"X. Thou shalt not worry, for the paths of worry lead but to the grave."

"The price of progress is education," says Mrs. Anna Marden De Yo, national superintendent of the department of Institutes. "The Institute offers a constructive program which will aid in the education and development of W. C. T. U. women while at the same time attracting others. The Institute gives needed emphasis to the benefits of prohibition, thereby creating sentiment to help in holding and endorsing the Eighteenth Amendment. The Institute diffuses a wider knowledge of the far-reaching plans of our great organization!"

"Listeners in" hope to hear the latest plans from Washington, D. C., when the next speaker, Mrs. Lenna Lowe Yost, national superintendent of Legislation, is announced. They are not disappointed. Mrs. Yost says:

"This department aims to present the voice of organized womanhood, the church, and the home, to legislative bodies, local, state, and national, to perfect and unify prohibition laws, and to aid in securing other legislation that relates to human welfare. The Legislative representative keeps watch for the constituency of the Woman's Christian Temperance Union. When an attack is made by the enemy to modify or repeal our prohibition law through legislation, an agency is needed to speak for the organized womanhood of the nation. Many times since the Constitutional Prohibition Amendment was ratified the need for new legislation has developed, and additional legislation from time to time will be found necessary to meet the devices of the violator and to meet constructions placed upon the law by courts or executive departments. Prohibition legislation will always have our first and active support. The prohibition law was secured after fifty years of organized and sacrificial effort on the part of the Woman's Christian Temperance Union.

To establish the principle of prohibition in the fundamental laws of the land has been the goal, all through the years. It has always been the major issue and it will continue to be until the principle is established in the customs of society.

"The Legislative representative promotes other Federal legislation, especially that which has to do with the efficiency of the home, education for citizenship, the health of our people and the highest moral development of the individual. The endorsement of the following measures is recommended: Adequate appropriations for the enforcement of prohibition; the Children's Bureau, to include appropriations for the study of conditions relating to procedures affecting children; venereal disease division of the United States Public Health Service; Women's Bureau. For the protection of the Indian from the drug, peyote. For a Department of Education which shall adequately provide for physical education. The principle for this is found in the Sterling-Reed Bill now pending before Congress. For an increase in the number of army and navy chaplains. The Capper-Hull Bill (S. 2532; H. R. 7036). For an improved industrial program for Federal prisoners, particularly for the new home for Federal women prisoners. For a Federal Industrial Reformatory for boys (Pending Bill, Foster, H. R.). Entry into Permanent Court of International Justice according to the Harding-Hughes proposals.

"To perfect state prohibition laws. For ratification of Child Labor Amendment. For acceptance and enforcement of the Maternity and Infancy Act. For welfare of women engaged in gainful occupations. For better child labor laws where they are below the standard. For uniform laws, especially relating to marriage and divorce.

"The National W. C. T. U. declares its interest in human welfare legislation for the District of Columbia—the nation's capital city, such as a Department of Public Welfare, and will, through the national superintendent of Legislation, direct such activities in the interest of this measure as the organization may find it possible to give. From the Legislative Headquarters, Bliss Building, Washington, D. C., information in regard to Federal and state welfare and prohibition laws, also information on pending bills in the U. S. Congress, is furnished."

Mrs. Lettie Hill May, the national superintendent of The Bible in the Public Schools, gives this information: "The object of the department is to create sentiment for a more active and definite study of the Bible in all schools where it is now used, and to introduce it into others. In order to do this we must arouse public sentiment along this line by using some of the following plans: Secure the co-operation of state, county and local superintendents of public instruction, as well as members of local school boards; hold public meetings in the interest of the department, and get newspaper publicity. Secure the appointment of a superintendent in each state and local union who will circulate diligently the literature for the department. Enroll members of school boards and school teachers as members of the Woman's Christian Temperance Union. Co-operate with other organizations who are doing the same line of work.

"There is a growing enthusiasm in the United States and other nations for bringing the Bible into the public schools; and in this movement a great many organizations are co-operating. In many cities where the school board has appointed a committee to prepare suggestive readings for daily use through the school term, a Catholic, a Jew and a Protestant have been appointed on said committee. It is interesting to note that not only in our nation, but in others, the 'Back to the Bible' slogan is demanding the attention of all thinking people. Theodore Roosevelt said: 'In this country we rightly pride ourselves upon our widespread popular education. It is a great thing to be clever, to be able, to be smart, but it is better to have the qualities that find their expression in the Decalogue and the Golden Rule. Honesty first; then courage; then brains.' "

The voices of young people are now heard as Mrs. Maude Carman Cathcart, the national superintendent of

Medal Contests, gives a demonstration of its educational work.

"Our object," she says, "is to enlist the children and young people in a series of declamatory contests, the selections being on subjects relative to our work published in the recitation books. To use these young people wherever possible, at law-enforcement-citizenship rallies and for ready-made meetings, in the churches and other societies. To utilize this opportunity to keep ever before the public the principles of our organization, and also to enroll new members for the W. C. T. U. To keep a correct address of each medal winner, as each one is entitled to membership in the contest alumni. The department has enlisted thousands of young people and children, promoting the principles of total abstinence and obedience to law, and has greatly helped to build up a clean, honorable, and loyal American citizenship." Mrs. Cathcart then pays tribute to her late mother, Mrs. Adelia Carman, the first national superintendent, who nationally and internationally, for many years, made the department a success.

Mrs. Martha M. Allen, the national superintendent of the department of Medical Temperance, has the special attention of many white ribbon physicians and nurses as she says: "This department began, in 1897, the public campaign against fraudulent patent medicines, especially those containing large quantities of alcohol, and was instrumental in interesting *Collier's Weekly* and *The Ladies Home Journal* in the fight. The department put copies of the 'Great American Fraud' pamphlet into thousands of public libraries, and sent out thousands of copies to persons of influence. The agitation begotten, was a great aid in securing the passage of the National Pure Food Law which requires the statement, on the label, of the presence of opiates and the percentage of alcohol.

"The department began a crusade against the use of whisky in the treatment of tuberculosis of the lungs, aided by a few experts in that disease who did not believe in whisky treatment. The poster prepared by Mrs. Allen, was used by different boards of health in campaigns against tuberculosis and was enlarged and used in the great International Tuberculosis Congress held in Washington. The outcome was that soon all literature on consumption warned against alcohol. We have done much to win better-class physicians to abandon the use of alcoholic liquors as medicine, by the distribution of leaflets at medical meetings. Appeals to physicians, largely circulated, were the means of obtaining strong resolutions from the American Medical Association in 1917, resolutions which had large influence in the securing of national prohibition. The book, 'Alcohol a Dangerous and Unnecessary Medicine, written by Mrs. Allen, was placed in all the medical libraries of the United States and Canada by a philanthropic friend. This book and the leaflets of the department were highly commended by the *Journal of the American Medical Association,* and some other influential journals.

"The agitation kept up by this department with its appeals to physicians and its circulation among them of the best and latest findings against alcohol by practitioners and research workers has resulted in a great change in hospital practice and in the teaching in medical colleges. Very little alcoholic liquor is now used in most of the hospitals of this country, and in some of the largest, no alcoholic liquor has been used since the advent of national prohibition. The best medical schools no longer teach that alcohol is a useful or indispensable medicine; many warn against its use.

"When this department began its work, whisky was looked upon as the sheet anchor of the profession in the treatment of pneumonia and typhoid fever. Now it is a completely discredited drug in all infectious diseases. Whisky and brandy were omitted from the U. S. Pharmacopœia after this department had sent a memorial to all the members of the pharmacopœial convention of 1910 asking for this action and assigning as the reason why such action should be taken that best physicians were not using this agent any longer."

The announcer makes this statement: "Though at present there is no national department of Parlor Meetings and Red Letter Days, of which for so many years Mrs. Mary Davis Tomlinson was the national superintendent (now World's W. C. T. U. superintendent), in many states it still strengthens the local unions by adding many active and honorary members to the ranks. These meetings bring together socially not only white ribboners, but also those who would not attend gatherings in churches and halls. The observance of the national red letter days familiarizes many people with the leaders of the past, who have aided in bringing the victories, and many of the present who are helping formulate progressive plans for the future. These red letter days are: January 16—birthday of National Constitutional Prohibition—Lillian Stevens Legislative Fund Day; February 17—Frances E. Willard Memorial Fund Day; March 20—*Union Signal* Subscription Day; April 14 —Young People's Branch Day (birthday of Frances J. Barnes); May 11—Mother's Day; June 9—Flower Mission Day (birthday of Jennie Casseday); July 4—National Independence Day (birthday of Mary H. Hunt); July 21— Loyal Temperance Legion Day (birthday of Anna A. Gordon); July 31—White Ribbon Missionary Day (birthday of Mary Allen West); August 3—Fresh Air Mission Day (birthday of Lady Henry Somerset); August 28—(birthday of Lucy Webb Hayes); September 28—Children's Harvest Home and *Young Crusader* Day (birthday of Frances E. Willard); World's Temperance Sunday—(*The Union Signal* will announce date); December 23—Crusade and Pioneers' Day."

The announcer says: "The department of Parliamentary Usage owes much to its first superintendent, Mrs. A. S. Benjamin of Michigan, who was elected in 1887 and served with distinction until 1917. Mrs. Benjamin was the acknowledged authority upon all points of parliamentary law and usage and her published 'studies' were widely used. The present national superintendent of Parliamentary Usage, Mrs. I. W. Gleason, elected in 1917, gives these as the high points of her program: 'The aim of this department is to assist an assembly to accomplish the work for which it was organized—in the best possible manner. We are trained in our unions, through parliamentary law, to conform to law and order because parliamentary law teaches discipline, obedience, and respect for law and order; and as our lives reflect action, we impress and are impressed by proceeding always in order. This makes it easier to obey laws that are made for the benefit of city, state, and nation.' "

The national superintendent of the department of Peace and Arbitration, Mrs. Effie Danforth McAfee, says: "This department seeks to do away with the causes which underlie war; with prejudice, race hatred, religious animosity, cutthroat rivalry in commerce and with exploitation. The department seeks to bring about the spirit of co-operation, of fellowship and unity of all in spiritual brotherhood. Drastic laws imposed from without are not so potent as is the guidance of the indwelling spirit and for each individual to manifest the Golden Rule."

Mrs. Minnie Barker Horning, national superintendent of Prison Reform, seeks "to educate for the building of Christian character and for the reformation of life prisoners in the jails and penitentiaries. Efforts are made for proper housing, cleanliness and health safeguards; for the indeterminate sentence and parole; for the appointment of women on the prison boards of every state; for women physicians, guards, and attendants for women prisoners.

"The department assists the families of prisoners by teaching English and American ways when necessary. Foreign prisoners are taught English; employment and aid are given to discharged prisoners. The department helped make favorable public sentiment for the Industrial Home for Federal women prisoners; and for the segregation of the juvenile delinquent."

Mrs. Emma L. Starrett, national superintendent of Sabbath Observance, says: "The department is waging a constructive nation-wide campaign of education to preserve the sanctity of the Sabbath; and to resist legislative enactment for a commercialized Sabbath. As all law is based upon the Ten Commandments and as 'Remember the Sabbath Day to keep it holy,' is a direct command of God, we believe that the enforcement of His law involves the enforcement of all law. The question should be studied from the viewpoint of safeguarding home interests and protection of all in their right for one day of rest and worship as has been ruled by the Supreme Court."

Miss Cora Frances Stoddard, national director of Scientific Temperance Instruction in the Public Schools and Scientific Temperance Investigation, gives by special request extracts from the address she presented at the fifteenth International Congress Against Alcoholism held in Washington, D. C., September 24, 1920. Not only is it of historical value, but it points the way for future work. Miss Stoddard says: "The Woman's Christian Temperance Union early turned to the slow and arduous but constructive task of rearing a whole new generation—several generations if need be—in the principles of total abstinence. For several years after this society was organizing its forces it succeeded in securing the adoption of the Sir Benjamin Ward Richardson 'Temperance Lesson Book' in public schools. Yet public school temperance instruction in its fullness awaited its leader. It was this leader, Mrs. Mary H. Hunt, who twice stood before this Congress, in Brussels, in 1897 and Bremen in 1903, whose vision and capacity for organization finally made temperance instruction of the children of the United States a part of the regular school instruction.

"What were its scope and principles? It was planned to reach all the children. To do this it was made compulsory; hence the twenty years of legislative work that put a law requiring temperance education on the statute books of every state and of Congress for schools under Federal control. It was made a part of instruction in hygiene. The temperance education movement in the United States, beginning forty years ago, not only brought temperance instruction into the schools, but it is also to be credited with introducing instruction in general hygiene. Knowledge of hygiene was good in itself for the rising generation, but by including in it the scientific temperance instruction, the temperance teaching was given a logical, reasonable place in the child's thoughts. Thus the ideal future instruction was the teaching of scientific facts in a form that the child could understand.

"Suitable textbooks were secured and required. These were published by the regular school textbook publishing houses. By the first years of the twentieth century the temperance forces had so far won that scientific temperance instruction was not only a recognized and legal part of the educational system of the entire country, but it had for its assistance a variety of textbooks adapted to all ages of pupils—books whose teaching had kept pace with the scientific progress of the years.

"Another principle of the Scientific Temperance Instruction department has been that thorough teaching should be given in the early years of the child's school course. While provision was made for continuing it into the later years, there has been general agreement as to the necessity of this thorough teaching before the end of the child's sixth school year—that is, before he is eleven or twelve years old. In the case of thousands of foreign-born children later to become citizens, the lower grades are their only chance of being taught total abstinence facts. Handicapped by the necessity of learning a new language, they often leave school to go to work before they reach the upper elementary grades. The fundamental reason for early instruction is always the importance of training to sobriety in the habit-forming period. The Woman's Christian Temperance Union not only had the vision of what was to be achieved, but by the ramifications of its organization it was able to bring public sentiment to bear when and where needed. Fathers and mothers saw in this scientific temperance instruction a chance to save their children from the danger of alcoholism.

"Many factors have entered into the progress of the American temperance movement, but it is generally conceded that the temperance education of the children for more than a generation has been a powerful force in abolishing the legalized liquor traffic. Not until about 1890, had sufficient temperance educational legislation been enacted to make the instruction fairly general, though all through the preceding decade it was being extended. For still another decade, up to 1901, legislative work continued and the struggle was going on to get sound total abstinence teaching introduced into the schools. The children who began school in 1885 were voters about 1900. The children who began in 1890 were coming to their majority about 1905. It is necessary to recall that practically half a lifetime is required before a child taught the truth begins to exert any public influence with it. But all through these years there were coming to maturity ever-increasing tens of thousands of school children who had been taught why alcohol is an enemy to human welfare.

"The enactment of state prohibition laws which culminated in national prohibition began to gain momentum in 1907. Of its sources the Hon. Samuel J. Barrows of the International Prison Commission (1896) said, in 1898, that one reason for the growth of temperance sentiment was the fact that systematic temperance teaching of youth had been going on for years and the result of this education has been telling in the boys and girls who have grown to manhood and womanhood. A new generation has grown up and has found that alcoholic drinks are not necessary for health or happiness.

"The United States Commissioner of Education, Hon. W. T. Harris, had said, in his report for 1900-1901, concerning temperance instruction in the public schools in the United States: 'It may be said that this movement is the most effective one ever devised by the friends of temperance to abate a great evil—one of the greatest evils abroad in the land.' Twenty years later, on the eve of constitutional prohibition becoming effective, the United States Commissioner of Education, Hon. P. P. Claxton, wrote: 'With all persons who are interested in the education of children, in the upbuilding of humanity and the attainment of the highest ideals of democracy, I rejoice at the coming of prohibition for the United States. In the creation of a sentiment which has resulted first in local option, then in state prohibition and now in national prohibition, the schools of the country have played a very important part, in fact, probably a major part. It is a good illustration of the truth of the saying that "Whatsoever we want in the nation in the next generation we should put into the schools of this generation." '

"So much for the past. What of the future? Is the scientific temperance instruction to be continued? The general opinion of the state educational officials is that it should be continued. The reasons given are that it is necessary to acquaint all children now in the schools and especially newcomers of foreign parentage with the reasons for the position the United States has taken against alcoholic drinks. That is important to insure an intelligent public sentiment to prevent or overcome illicit manufacture and sale of alcoholic beverages; that there should be continued warning as to the alcoholic dangers in wine and beer and in home-made fermented beverages.

"Present-day discussions of the alcohol question indicate certain lines of instruction that are still necessary if we are to knit up the loose ends of public knowledge about alcohol. Instruction is still needed along four points: first, that alcohol with its habit-forming power is in even the lighter forms of alcoholic beverages; second, the depressing effects of even small quantities of alcohol upon physical and mental activities and upon self-control; third, the lower resistance to disease which may be due to continued drinking of quantities of alcohol insufficient to cause drunkenness; the fact that alcoholic intoxication is not measured by drunkenness alone, but by every characteristic effect of alcohol showing proven inefficiency or depression at any stage in the drinker's condition below that of visible drunkenness.

"The real 'kings' and 'princes' of the future will be the men and women who rise to their full capacity of powers and exercise them for the common good. Alcohol defeats both these ends. Hence, as one means of insuring that our kings and princes may not 'forget the law and pervert justice' we are putting away alcohol. The American democracy of the future wants no drunkards, but more than that it wants a citizenship free from the minor demoralizations of alcohol. To this end, we must pledge ourselves to maintain the temperance training of all our children, confident that our public schools will go loyally forward in this part of their great responsibiity."

By request, Miss Stoddard gave, in closing, her latest condensed statement regarding scientific temperance instruction in the public schools:

"The Woman's Christian Temperance Union was primarily influential in introducing into the public schools of the United States instruction as to the nature and effects of alcoholic drinks, and other narcotics. The work always has been based on the principles that prevention is better than cure; that childhood and youth are entitled to know the facts of modern science showing the dangers in the non-medical use of these substances; that is to the advantage of the nation that the children be trained to the practice of intelligent sobriety. The laws secured, at the instance of the Woman's Christian Temperance Union, in practically all states requiring such instruction as a part of instruction in physiology and hygiene not only carried this special teaching into the schools, but opened the door legally for all health teaching and training.

"While the instruction is in the hands of the teachers, the Woman's Christian Temperance Union supplements it by reference material and periodicals placed in school libraries, and conducts prize essays and poster contests. Thousands of dollars annually are expended by the local, state and national organizations in awards for these competitions in which nearly 150,000 pupils of elementary and high school grades, teachers, and normal school students participate. Special lecturers are furnished to and welcomed by the schools in some states, in addition to national lecturers who bring information as to material and methods to teachers, colleges, normal schools, summer schools, and institutes. Exhibits of pupils' work and of helpful illustrative material are shown at the educational meetings."

Dr. Valeria H. Parker, a governmental expert in the line of Social Morality and national director of this department, makes the following statement:

"Progress has been made in the five-fold program of social morality which is fostered by our organization. The education of the child for life in home, church, and school; the establishment of community protective measures; the development and supervision of wholesome recreation; the enforcement of laws governing moral conduct; and the establishment of opportunities for treatment of those infected with diseases which especially hamper racial development, are among the responsibilities of the Christian citizens of today.

"A visit to those countries where vice is protected and official attempts are made to regulate prostitution, fills one with gratitude that the United States is among the countries which have abandoned official compromise with this evil. We must not, however, ignore the need of organized and continued activity in constructive work if we are to maintain a nation-wide protection of those forces upon which married love and parenthood are based. Miss Grace Leigh Scott is our successful Social Morality field worker."

The announcer says: "From the beginning the W. C. T. U. bravely has championed the cause of social purity and the White Cross movement, and it has helped to raise in many states the 'age of consent' from ten to eighteen years."

Miss Rebecca Naomi Rhoads, head of the department of Soldiers and Sailors, in speaking of "Our Purpose," says: "This department is devoted to the best interests of soldiers, sailors, marines, seamen, coast guards, and sea-faring men of all classes and lands, and operates on a constructive program co-operating with the government in its welfare work. We aim to bring to these men everywhere, especially in the loneliest and most desolate spots and in the hospitals, good-cheer and the homelike touch; to give them good things to eat, good things to read, and good thoughts to think; to provide for them religious and moral influences and arouse their interest in learning of the danger in intoxicating liquor and habit-forming drugs; to enlist their interest in the enforcement of our prohibitory laws, supplying literature to combat the widespread liquor propaganda. To encourage the opening of homelike places where they can have pleasant social influences, and the right kind of relaxation and amusement.

"A large number of men are still suffering in the hospital from war-time casualties, but I believe that through their recovery the country will soon be freed from the support of these heroes. Every soldier and sailor needs true friends to counteract the temptations which are constantly thrown in his way. In Constantinople, I learned of the unpublished heroism of American sailors when the city of Smyrna was burned. The coast guards have taken on thousands of men for prohibition enforcement work and the W. C. T. U. should remember them with gifts and magazines. Very few soldiers and sailors know the truth about prohibition. They are the victims of an extensive wet propaganda. However, I always have found them responding readily to the truth.

"During recent extended visitations to army camps, including eastern, southern, and middle states, I have been much encouraged because our nation's defenders have taken such thoughtful interest in our great cause and have responded to the religious appeal. At some camps hundreds of boys attended the meetings. I have an encouraging list of signers to the patriotic roll with its total abstinence pledge. The commanding officers and chaplains are all cordial and express appreciation of the work of the W. C. T. U. Soldiers and Sailors department."

"The Sunday School department," says the announcer, "was organized in 1877. Miss Lucia E. F. Kimball of Maine, the first superintendent, served with distinction until 1893. Mrs. Julia Bidwell of New York for one year ably filled the position. The present superintendent of the department, Mrs. Stella B. Irvine, was elected in 1894. In 1881, Frances Willard presented a memorial to the International Sunday School Lesson Committee, asking for a quarterly temperance lesson. In 1885, in part, this request was granted. The memorial of 1890, presented by Miss Willard at the Pittsburgh International Sunday School Convention, asked that the lesson be placed, not on the Sunday given also to the Quarterly Review, but should be assigned a distinct place in the 'Series'—uncomplicated with other subjects. This memorial was granted. The favorable action was confirmed in 1893 by the St. Louis International Sunday School Convention, and again in 1896 by the Boston International Sunday School Convention. Mrs. Irvine has made this great department of Sunday School work known around the world. Her bureau of literature, now carried at the National W. C. T. U. Publishing House, for many years has given to unnumbered Sunday schools the facts needed for use in the Quarterly Temperance Lessons." Mrs. Irvine now speaks: "This department aims to accomplish the teaching of total abstinence with pledge signing in every department in the Sunday school, co-operating with the World's Sunday School department in the World's pledge signing campaign; it aims to promote the training of the youth in Christian citizenship and to enlist the adults of the Sunday school in social and moral reform and in the enforcement law; also, to secure the co-operation of Sunday school lesson writers and publishers of Sunday school lesson helps. The department works to the end that the Sunday school training shall be embodied in the curricula provided for week-day and vacation Bible schools and community training schools."

"Temperance and Missions," says Mrs. Caroline McDowell, national superintendent, "is a popular, progressive department. It is unlimited in its scope and reaches out to every W. C. T. U. activity, extending the helping hand to every human being. The department aims to secure a live temperance secretary in each local missionary society and a missionary secretary in each local W. C. T. U.

"It is the church in action; it co-operates with church and missionary boards in America and other lands. As a vital factor in making known the victorious program of the World's W. C. T. U., the department of Temperance and Missions is not only national, but international. In the United States, it is a powerful ally of all home missionary work and is in helpful touch with the W. C. T. U. department of Americanization. Life and memorial members ($100.00 each) for the World's W. C. T. U. are secured."

"Mrs. McDowell," adds the announcer, "is a generous giver to this work and for several years duplicated the money received for life and memorial memberships in the World's W. C. T. U. Through this department, the World's W. C. T. U. organizers receive much helpful literature. Never have relations between church missionary societies and the W C. T. U. been so close and cordial as today. Through Mrs. McDowell, the W. C. T. U. has kept in close co-operation with evangelistic and missionary circles."

"In its present development, one of the newest national departments is that of Women in Industry," says the an-nonucer. "In 1880, the national Department of Temperance and Labor was created and has had many titles. In 1895, the name was changed to Relation of Temperance and Labor, and Mrs. Mary G. Stuckenberg was made national superintendent. In 1905, Mrs. Mae Whitman became the head of the department. She was followed by Mrs. Lucia H. F. Additon. The present national W. C. T. U. director, Mrs. Laura Parks Miller, was appointed in 1921. Under the title, 'The Spirit of Organized Mother Love,' Mrs. Miller recounts the benefits through this department given and received":

	GAVE	RECEIVED
1875	First Creed of Industrial Justice Adopted in America.	1191 conversions and pledges in next two years — wide influence for temperance.
1881	Friendship with railroad men, J e n n i e Smith's shop meetings, religious and temperance messages.	Better family life, children reared in belief in temperance, S. T. I. made popular, votes for dry territory.
In following years	Street car men, firemen, policemen, postmen, factory and mill workers all included.	With growth of scientific temperance investigation, s u p p o r t of prohibition by employers on economic lines.
In the 80's and 90's	Discussion of "relation of intemperance to capital as well as to labor."	Scientific support of our pledge for growth of "law and custom for
Through the years	Support of measures for physical and moral health of workers such as shorter work day, the living wage, one day rest in seven.	justice as opposed to greed of g a i n," in growing understanding of alcoholism as a result of industrial fatigue.
1917-18 (War Years)	Health laws accelerated, especially for girls and women entering industry.	
Now	Friendship with newer groups of women.	Support by great numbers of "labor" women as well as "h o m e" women.

The national superintendent of Work Among Negroes, Mrs. Marvin Williams, says: "The department aims to build up stronger public sentiment among the negroes of the United States in favor of total abstinence, social purity, and prohibition, to the end that our whole nation may be strengthened by a better type of citizenship, while raising the standards of personal living and an increased number of godly homes. It aims also, to cause an arrest of Christian thinking among the white leaders of the W. C. T. U.

247

in the various states, to the end that a deeper sense of responsibility may be felt for the education in W. C. T. U. principles of the negro race."

"The aim of the Evangelistic department," says its national superintendent, Mrs. Mary Harris Armor, "is, that through faith and prayer—through the study of God's word and dissemination of the same—the Woman's Christian Temperance Union may have increasing moral and spiritual power, and in the midst of the strenuous activities, every woman may hold fast her anchorage to the vital, spiritual things that 'In all things He might have the pre-eminence.'"

The fervent, spiritual power that enabled Mrs. Armor to lead to victory the women of her state when Georgia went dry, has ever been hers, as she has given with fire and logic, in this country and others, her compelling messages. By request, she sends out at this time of religious, social and political unrest, the following call for prayer:

"Some one has said: 'Whoever sets the church to praying will perform the greater service to God and man,' and doubtless this is true, for 'nothing stirs the central wheel of the soul like the breath of God.'

"In the large freedom that has come to woman today, there impends a crisis such as the world never before confronted. In the past, girlhood was compassed about with barriers which, while they meant restraint, also meant protection. Today, there is not a barrier raised in the social, industrial, or political world. Chaperons are a thing of the past. Woman enters every occupation from digging ditches to practicing law or medicine. In politics, she may hold any position she can win; the whole field is open to her. If our daughters, entering into this rough commingling with men, go in purity and strength of mind and body; in dignity and self-control; and in the old sweetness and modesty of womanhood—if they thus enter, they will purify and glorify every place they enter; they will lift with tireless strength and Godlike patience, until there shall dawn that golden age of which Frances Willard dreamed, when 'Men and women, hand in hand, shall stand on equal heights of purity and

peace.' But if they lower their standard, if this new freedom causes them to adopt the vices of men, race degenera-
tion and, eventually, race extinction must follow. Twentieth
century science says: 'The smallest dose of alcohol lowers
the moral tone and weakens self-control just in proportion
to the amount of alcohol ingested, and every succeeding
dose increases the disaster.' Oh, for the leaping fire of a
great conviction which, in view of these facts, will send us
to our knees in honest, earnest, believing prayer! Then up
from our knees to go out 'with faith illumined and high
heart of grace,' and so preach the gospel of purity and total
abstinence that we may arouse every indifferent woman and
persuade her to enlist in the ranks of the Woman's Christian Temperance Union. Only by baptizing all work with
prayer and following all prayer with work, can we attain
our end."

The announcer says: "During fifty years, white ribboners have been singing their way into the hearts of the
electorate. No department of music was created, but in
nearly every state, campaigners have composed hymns which
song leaders have used to swing into line hundreds of
apathetic listeners. Who can forget the thrilling effect
caused by the repetition of the victorious refrains! Many
have aided with instrumental music. In state annals these
leaders have received honorable mention. Other white ribboners such as are now chronicled are known throughout
the nation and some of them have written hymns which
have found their way into the series of white ribbon song-
books gratuitously prepared for the W .C. T. U. and the
L. T. L. by Anna A. Gordon. These women have been
generous with their musical gifts: Frances E. Willard,
Anna A. Gordon, Mrs. Alice Osborne Harris, Mrs. F. A.
Bent (of the golden cornet), Frances W. Graham (National
Musical Director), Mary A. Lathbury, Mary T. Lathrap,
Lide Meriwether, Antoinette A. Hawley, Mabel Dufford,
Katharine Lent Stevenson, Rose Bower (Cornetist). Mrs.
Frances B. Damon, Mrs. William Jennings Bryan, Mrs.
Katherine Call Simonds."

249

"Listeners in" again are invited to "stand by," for the resourceful treasurer of the National W. C. T. U., Mrs. Margaret C. Munns, will tell her invisible audience how the Jubilee dollars have aided many of these departments. Listen to Mrs. Munns: "The financing of the several departments budgeted under the Jubilee Fund, has made it possible to secure the services of experts to lead these departmnts, and as never before, the broad scope of the W. C. T. U. has been recognized. It is the day of the specialist and an organization that would serve the present generation must have trained leadership. Very fortunate is the organization that can secure for a modest emolument, the services of such leaders. It is the same self-sacrificing spirit that has actuated the workers from the beginning, though volunteer service cannot always be given.

"The Americanization department, conducted training schools in Chautauqua, New York, New York City, and Chicago for two years in which a number of talented young women were trained. Of these, six became field secretaries and several others are located in Americanization Centers, where they are doing excellent work. With the hope of reaching many more than could attend a training school, a correspondence course was established which is proving helpful to those interested in learning the best methods of reaching their foreign-born neighbors. Americanization Centers were aided for one year in Bridgeport, Connecticut; St. Louis and Kansas City, Missouri; for two years in Pittsburgh; Seattle; Baltimore; Passaic, New Jersey; San Francisco; Flint, Michigan; Indianapolis; Cleveland and Omaha, Nebraska. Small appropriations have been given the Centers in Carlsbad, New Mexico, and Emporia, Kansas. The immigrant station at Ellis Island is supplied with a white-ribbon missionary who meets the immigrant with welcoming hand and sympathetic heart.

"The department of Child Welfare has fostered Mother-Child Centers which have proved blessings to the hundreds of mothers and children who have come under their influ-

ence. For over a year the department maintained such a
Center in Detroit and for more than another year partial
support was given. Help was also extended to a Mother-
Child Center in Toledo and among the colored people in
Washington, D. C. The largest contribution, $50,000, has
been made to the Child Welfare Research department of
the University of Iowa, the first to establish a Research
department for an extensive study of the normal child. Our
Loyal Temperance Legion work has been supported under
the Child Welfare division of the budget.

"The work of the fundamental department of Scientific
Temperance Instruction has won the plaudits of the world.
The very necessary maintenance of the high standard of
this scientific phase of anti-alcohol education has been made
possible by the Jubilee Fund. Scientific research, which
includes the invaluable findings of the New York investigations, lectures before schools, colleges and teachers' associations, the promotion of essay and poster contests and
the exhibits at great educational meetings, may not be spectacular, but they are very essential in reaching the coming
generation with the truth.

"Without publicity, the world at large would never
know the W. C. T. U. existed, except as false reports are
furnished by its opponents. Our Publicity director can show
many thousands of items clipped from local papers all over
the country which have been furnished by her, concerning
the work of the organization and the results of prohibition.
A correspondence course has proved a valuable aid to local
press workers.

"Social Morality is one of the crying needs of the day
and the department, through the spoken and written word,
has made a valuable contribution to a constructive policy
for a higher moral plane for our country. Especially helpful has been the direct contact with the young people of the
public schools and work-shops through lectures of the department. Because they believe prevention is better than

cure, the New Mexico white-ribboners founded a school for Spanish-American girls who need home care. The Jubilee Fund has contributed $10,000 to this school started by a small band of workers in a missionary state.

"The department of Health, also financed by this fund, has been active and persistent in its constructive policy. The W. C. T. U., through this department, made the first contribution to the Woman's Foundation for Health. For a year and a half the department of Christian Citizenship was financed by the Jubilee Fund. Mrs. Deborah Knox Livingston's valuable contribution to our great program of citizenship is well known and the department has been a force for righteousness. Women who work for a wage comprise a large proportion of the adult woman population. To win these women to sympathetic interest in prohibition, to assist in securing industrial justice, is the object of the department of Women in Industry. By literature and by personal and visual presentation, the department is helping the wage earning woman to a new vision of responsibility.

"With a number of department field workers busy here and there, it was found difficult to route them from several headquarters without loss of time. The routing was done with great success by an executive secretary of field service, and was financed by the Jubilee Fund. When the Jubilee Fund was raised, there were many notable gifts, the largest amount, $5,000, being given by Mrs. Caroline McDowell."

In recounting the Jubilee activities and gifts, the generosity of Frances E. Beauchamp is gratefully remembered. Mrs. Beauchamp, for twenty years the honored and beloved president of the Kentucky W. C. T. U., was the first to respond to the national president's special appeal for gifts of $1,000 to the Jubilee Fund. At the time the proclamation for National Constitutional Prohibition was issued, the District of Columbia W. C. T. U. gave a banquet to visiting white-ribboners. Miss Gordon displayed the pen, one of quite a number used by acting Secretary of State Polk in signing the proclamation. It chanced to be the first pen taken up by Secretary Polk, and with it he wrote his given name "Frank." Miss Gordon promised to use this pen to write a letter of thanks to any and all givers of $1,000 to the Jubilee Fund. Mrs. Beauchamp, with characteristic generosity, immediately sent to the platform her personal check for $1,000. The liquor traffic had no foe more determined and relentless than was Frances E. Beauchamp. For a decade Mrs. Beauchamp was a general officer of the National W. C. T. U. Her rugged zeal for state and national prohibition has not been surpassed by any of her fellow toilers. For many years she was a member of the National Prohibition Party Committee. Mrs. Beauchamp was not only a prohibition warrior, but a great-souled philanthropist and an indefatigable social-welfare enthusiast. Hundreds of young lives in the mountain schools of Kentucky were blessed and brightened by Frances E. Beauchamp. Her home and her heart alike were big and hospitable.

A handsomely bound Book of Remembrance containing hundreds of names of well-known white-ribboners and friends is kept at National W. C. T. U. headquarters. On a beautifully illuminated page is this inscription: "Each name in this Book of Remembrance represents one hundred dollars given to the Jubillee Fund, the one million dollar thank offering of the Woman's Christian Temperance Union in celebration of its fiftieth anniversary."

The national treasurer states that during the fifty years a number of bequests have been received. Among the outstanding bequests have been those of John and Emilie Martin which together amounted to $25,272. Other bequests received were from the estates of Mrs. S. I. Chenoweth, Ransom N. Chaddock, Daniel L. F. Chase, Loren J. Austin, Samuel Simpson, George Woodford, Mrs. Buell, C. E. Rumsey, Mrs. H. B. Hudson, Ellen Mitchell, F. A. Pritchard, Sarah Douther, M. J. Kenney, Louise Butler, Rev. Joseph Thomas, H. and K. Hunt, Riley Memorial, Belva M. Herron, Mary E. Dodds, Alberta Pogue, Eliza Warren, Mary C.

Sturdy, Louise C. Purington, Elizabeth A. Russel, Agnes Stebbens, A. Nesta, Lucia F. Masslich, Maryetta A. Older, Clara Austin Shrigley, Elizabeth W. Greenwood, and Sarah L. Adams. In addition to these, two bequests have been received for the Frances E. Willard Memorial Organizing Fund from the estates of Martha Mairs Turner and Jennie Mitchell.

Willard Fountain, Lincoln Park, Chicago, Illinois (above).
W. C. T. U. Float, Waterbury, Conn.

CHAPTER X

A Golden History: A Golden Prophecy

"To be alive in such an age
With every year a lightning page
Turned in the world's great wonderbook.
When every breath of common air
Throbs a tremendous prophecy
Of things that are to be.
When steel and stone and rail and rod,
Become the avenues of God, ·
A trump to sound His wonder through
And crown the work that man may do.

"O age of strife! O age of Life!
When progress rides her chariot high
And 'neath the borders of the sky
The signals of the centuries
Proclaim the things that are to be.
The rise of woman to her place,
The coming of a nobler race.

"To be alive in such an age!
To live in it, to give to it!
Rise, soul, from thy despairing knees,
Give thanks with all thy flaming heart.
Crave but to have in it a part,
Give thanks and claim thy heritage,
To be alive in such an age."
—Angela Morgan

THE national W. C. T. U. president gives these reasons why the white-ribbon should be worn: "It is a blessed bond of fellowship among our members; it is a privilege of which we are proud; it is a plea for purity of life; it is a pledge of total abstinence; it preaches the international prohibition of the liquor traffic; it proclaims the gospel of peace and a world-wide family of nations; it is a prayer for home protection; it predicts a safe path for children's feet; it is an emblem of patriotism; it is a protest against the drink habit and the liquor traffic; it is a promise of hope to the tempted and help to the suffering; it prophesies the coming of Christ's brotherhood in all hearts, all homes and all governments."

On motion of Miss Margaret Winslow of New York, the National W. C. T. U. convention of 1887 adopted a white-ribbon bow as the official badge of the organization. Of this symbol Katharine Lent Stevenson has said: "It is particularly appropriate for our organization—its white the inclusiveness—no color, because combining all colors." Mrs. J. K. Barney told many a sin-sick soul that it meant penitence, purity and consecration. The badge is recognized and respected the world over as an emblem of peace, purity, total abstinence and prohibition. In 1905, one of the trips made by Mrs. L. M. N. Stevens and Anna Gordon covered nine weeks of travel and about ten thousand miles. The ninety yards of white-ribbon tied into little bows and placed upon new members by Miss Gordon, indicate the number who joined during this trip.

A prominent educator and author, Louise Manning Hodgkins, founder of the Department of English Literature and for years a professor in Wellesley College, who is most heartily in sympathy with the W. C. T. U., has the good fashion, when traveling, of wearing the white-ribbon. Recently, she said to the writer: "Merely wearing the white-ribbon may achieve something for our cause. On one occasion, I was crossing the Atlantic and chanced to be seated with the officers at the captain's table. Among the passengers was a liquor dealer going to Africa on the ignoble errand of receiving at a West African port a load of New England rum. Always over-dressed with diamond studs and ring, even at breakfast, he ostentatiously made a wine-party and invited many more folk than came. Next morning someone asked the officer sitting opposite to me, 'Did you go to the party?' 'No,' he answered promptly, 'I was afraid to face that white-ribbon this morning'—and yet the white-ribboner had not mentioned the subject."

For a number of years, the National Woman's Christian Temperance Union, at its annual conventions, endorsed three affiliated interests over which it had no financial control but to which it gave cordial, sympathetic co-operation: "The Woman's Temperance Publishing Association of Illinois," "The Frances E. Willard National Temperance Hospital of Chicago," and "The Temple Building Association of Chicago." The Woman's Temperance Publishing Association of Illinois, a stock company organized by Mrs. Mathilda B. Carse of Chicago, in 1880, owned and published a large supply of excellent temperance literature and *The Union Signal*, the official organ of the National W. C. T. U. The W. C. T. U., however, had editorial control of its official paper. In 1903, the Publishing Association dissolved and the National W. C. T. U. purchased its official paper, generous friends contributing to a fund raised for this purpose, by Anna A. Gordon. Since 1909, the National W. C. T. U. has created and conducted a publishing house of its own. The Frances E. Willard National Temperance Hospital of Chicago, which today continues successfully to demonstrate the principle that alcohol is not needed as a medicine, withdrew early in 1900, as an affiliated interest.

The Temple Building Association of Chicago, a stock company with Mr. Marshall Field, president of the board of trustees, owned The Temple, the third of the affiliated interests of the National W. C. T. U. This handsome office building at the corner of Monroe and La Salle Streets, Chicago, was erected at a cost of $1,200,000 on ground leased to the Association by Mr. Field. The heavy yearly ground rental—$40,000—was each year the first financial obligation to be met from Temple rental receipts. Mrs. Matilda B. Carse, a member of the board of trustees and president of the Central W. C. T. U. of Chicago, was the chief promoter of plans for its ownership by the W. C. T. U. The untiring but vain endeavor of the National W. C. T. U. towards such ownership covered a period of eleven years. Willard Hall, was the soul of the Temple Building. The strength of its appeal to Frances E. Willard and the active workers of that decade cannot be overestimated. Daily, it was the scene of a noontide gospel temperance meeting, which perpetuated the old Farwell Hall daily prayer service of the early years of the Chicago W. C. T. U.

Following the passing onward of Frances E. Willard in February, 1898, her successor to the presidency of the National W. C. T. U., Mrs. Lillian M. N. Stevens, with her co-officers and members of the Official Board made every possible effort to carry to successful completion certain plans adopted at the Buffalo, New York, convention in 1897. This program featured an endeavor to raise $300,000 to pay off the purchasers of Temple Trust Bonds, issued by Mrs. Carse "as an individual for and on behalf of the National W. C. T. U."

It became necessary to call a meeting of the National Executive Committee to discuss the Temple situation. This meeting was held in Chicago, July 15, 1898. After two days of careful, prayerful discussion, a resolution to be recommended to the national convention was adopted, providing that all effort on the part of the National W. C. T. U. to own the Temple Building should be discontinued. "While not legally bound," the resolution stated, "we regard it as a sacred trust to purchase before the next convention the $300,000 worth of Temple Trust Bonds issued by the promoters of The Temple enterprise." At the National W. C. T. U. convention in St. Paul, Minnesota, a few months later, after prolonged and dispassionate discussion, these recommendations were adopted by a yea and nay vote— 285 for, to 71 against; and The Temple as an affiliated interest was discontinued. Many of the Temple Trust Bonds held by needy individuals were retired, but, much to the regret of the committee in charge, it proved impossible to raise the entire amount of $300,000.

Historic Rest Cottage   The Willard

National W. C. T. U. Administration Building

A visit to the National W. C. T. U. headquarters in Evanston, Illinois, which includes the Publishing House, is well worth while. Rarely does any national woman's organization possess so commodious and handsome a building and such suitable, attractively furnished offices. The budget of $40,545, appropriated from the Jubilee Fund, made it possible for the National W. C. T. U. for the first time to erect and own an adequate building and an up-to-date equipment for its national and international service.

This administrative building in brick, erected in 1921-1922, was joined to the Publishing House constructed in 1910. An expansion of the literature department was thus made possible and greatly increased its efficiency by providing sufficient room for the growing business. In 1919, a new policy had been adopted which resulted in all department literature being printed at National W. C. T. U. headquarters. Concentration of the stock of departmental as well as general literature proved an advance step. The amount of stock now on hand all paid for, inventories about $17,000. The change in the situation created by the passing of the Eighteenth Amendment necessitated a complete revision of literature and the abandonment of much that was in stock. That loss has been overcome, and the literature department has been able to pay expenses. A catalog of sixty-eight pages gives particulars regarding the stock of leaflets, books, pledge cards, music, pictures, medals, posters, slides and badges carried by the Publishing House. Millions of pages of literature are annually sent out from this plant, not only to every section of our own country, but to foreign lands as well. Miss Jeannette E. Nichols is the present business manager of the literature department, with a staff of assistants. Mrs. Margaret B. Platt is the gifted editor. The national general officers constitute the publishing board, of which the National W. C. T. U. treasurer, Mrs. Margaret C. Munns, is the chairman.

It will be recalled that one of the outstanding events of the National W. C. T. U. convention held in Seattle, Washington, in 1915, was the discovery of the eminent ability of Mrs. Margaret C. Munns, of Seattle, and her election as National W. C. T. U. Treasurer. Since that time her devotion and resourcefulness as one of the three resident General Officers who administer National W. C. T. U. activities at headquarters, have been especially evinced in the expert care of the Jubilee Fund and in her success in carrying responsibilities connected with the erection of the Administration Building.

The development of the literature department is noteworthy. It was under the management for some years of an affiliated interest not now existing, and later the literature stock was purchased by Miss Ruby I. Gilbert, who was assisted by Miss Addie A. Austin. In 1908, a committee was appointed to consider the feasibility of establishing a literature plant in connection with National W. C. T. U. headquarters. This was under the management of the national corresponding secretary, Mrs. Parks.

In 1910, the National W. C. T. U. purchased the entire stock. Under the wise leadership of Mrs. Lillian M. N. Stevens, a building fund was raised in 1909-1910. Without a dollar's indebtedness, and with every detail planned by Mrs. Stevens and her co-officers at Evanston this building was dedicated December 10, 1910, "to the cause of temperance, the cause of total abstinence and prohibition, and the cause of humanity." Skilled workers were soon at their several posts of duty in office and shipping room, and the literature Publishing House of the National W. C. T. U. was launched. Every year has shown a substantial growth of the business.

The memorial W. C. T. U. convention held in St. Paul, Minnesota, 1898, the first to meet without Miss Willard's visible presence, was the twenty-fifth annual meeting since the days of the Crusade. An hour was given to "Crusade Memories," when fifty-two original Crusaders were on the platform and conducted a service of great spiritual force and fervor. Miss Anna Gordon was asked to close the hour. Expressing her regret not to be able to share the honor of having been an original Crusader, she suggested the creation of a Frances E. Willard Memorial Organizing Fund for the extension and perpetuation of the work to which Miss Willard gave her life. Miss Gordon considered it a personal privilege to make Mrs. Judge Thompson, leader of the Hillsboro, Ohio, Crusade, a life member of the National W. C. T. U., and expressed the wish that life members received at this convention and during the convention year might be contributors to a Frances E. Willard Memorial Organizing Fund. This proved to be the spark that re-ignited the enthusiasm of the convention, and fifty-four life and memorial members at twenty-five dollars each were quickly given.

At the post-executive Committee Meeting, on motion of Mrs. Katharine Lent Stevenson, the seventeenth of February was designated as Frances E. Willard Memorial Day and every union was requested to hold a special service and to send two dollars or more to the Memorial Organizing Fund. This fund in memory of the supreme W. C. T. U. organizer builds in her name a living memorial. The story of the offerings sent in yearly by local unions is one of fascinating interest. The Frances Willard Memorial Fund has made possible the missionary work of the W. C. T. U. Isolated places have been reached, new unions organized and weak unions strengthened. National representatives in the outlying "mission stations"—Alaska, Porto Rico, and the Philippines—have been assisted. "Open house" has been maintained during the season at National W. C. T. U. headquarters in Chautauqua, New York. The Memorial Fund has been applied to aid work among negroes, provide free literature for libraries, students, organizations and individuals; posters, maps and charts for exhibit purposes. This fund helped to win prohibition and ratification campaigns. During the five-year Jubilee membership campaign, under the able management of the national corresponding secretary, this fund helped win thousands of new members to support the Constitution and aid law observance and law enforcement; 19,618,000 pages of Jubilee membership appeal literature have been distributed by states, aided on the fifty-fifty basis in the purchase of this literature from the National W. C. T. U. Field service has been greatly extended by means of this Jubilee Fund, and it has played a most important part in the program of activities for the Jubilee Year. There have been received for the Frances E. Willard Memorial Organizing Fund since 1898 (receipts for 1924 being estimated) $206,825.

January sixteenth will ever be to the Woman's Christian Temperance Union a Red Letter Day. It was on that date, in 1920, that the legalized liquor traffic in the United States passed out of existence. "It is fitting," says the national treasurer, "that this day should be called the Lillian Stevens Legislative Fund Day. The splendid service she gave in unstinted measure always will be remembered and her name perpetuated through coming generations. Those who were privileged to listen to the marvelous address of Mrs. Stevens in 1911, in which she pledged the National W. C. T. U. to highest service for constitutional prohibition and declared that 'the God who hath led our hosts still leads and by the sign of the Cross we shall conquer,' can never forget the thrill of that moment, nor the absolute accord with which the vast audience rose and consecrated its powers to the accomplishment of the high purpose for which the dauntless leader plead. Though Mrs. Stevens was not permitted to see with human vision the victory day, none can doubt that her spirit is with us rejoicing at the onward march of the cause she loved so well, and her name will be ever indissolubly linked with national constitutional prohibition.

"This splendid work is supported solely by the contributions to the Lillian Stevens Legislative Fund. What nobler tribute could be paid to that great-souled stateswoman, Lillian M. N. Stevens, than to perpetuate her memory in a fund recruited yearly to fortify and protect prohibition

EDITORS OF THE UNION SIGNAL

Harriet B. Kells   Mary Bannister Willard   Julia A. Ames
Julia F. Deane   Margaret Suddeth   Mary Allen West
Clara C. Chapin   Cornelia T. Hatcher

legislation? Who that ever heard that deep, impassioned voice plead for national constitutional prohibition can doubt that she would feel honored to have every local union in the country, as well as individual friends, contribute to this fund. Keep the legislative machinery moving.

"The Legislative Fund provides for the maintenance of National W. C. T. U. legislative headquarters in Washington, D. C., in order that the organization may be a force in securing Federal legislation and promote many lines of public welfare of special interest to women and children and the homes of our country. This fund is the only one that provides for legislative work. Each local W. C. T. U. has the privilege of contributing at least one dollar a year to maintain it, in memory of the fearless leader who so mightily inspired the temperance hosts of our country to move forward to the supreme and successful battle for national constitutional prohibition."

The Lillian Stevens Campaign Fund (later changed to the Lillian Stevens Legislative Fund) established in 1914, has brought into the treasury (receipts for 1924 being estimated) $61,040.

In the national president's home office in Rest Cottage, for many years a "prohibition map" of the United States has hung. Visitors from everywhere have watched that historic map grow from "black" to "white." The original map had only three "white" states—Maine, Kansas, North Dakota. When the Eighteenth Amendment was secured, thirty-two states had their own prohibition laws, Kentucky soon falling into line, and the remaining "black" states, most of which had large "white" areas, by Federal enactment became "white."

Already references have been made to benefits conferred by the prohibitory laws of Maine and Kansas. North Dakota has the unique distinction of being the first state to enter the Union with prohibition of the liquor traffic in its constitution, and to hold it, until prohibition became the law of the land. In the long, bitter fight to keep and enforce the prohibition law, the state W. C. T. U. has led. The honored state president, Mrs. Elizabeth Preston Anderson, for more than thirty years has been present at every session of the legislature and the pressure she has been able to bring to bear upon the members, through the local unions in their respective districts, again and again, has saved the day.

When prohibition was established and well enforced, Governor John Burke (afterwards Treasurer of the United States) received from the North Dakota W. C. T. U. a life size portrait in oil of their beloved state president, Elizabeth Preston Anderson, and in recognition of her services for prohibition and other moral laws, it was hung in the rotunda of the State Capitol. Mrs Anderson was the author of the Presidential and Municipal Suffrage Law which passed in 1917.

The voice of *The Union Signal*, the popular progressive weekly organ of the National W. C. T. U., is heard around the world. It is a pithy persuasive, powerful voice. *The Union Signal* gives incontrovertible facts regarding the success of the Eighteenth Amendment, the Volstead Code and all progressive lines of work. The present editorial staff consists of Miss Julia Freeman Deane, managing editor; Miss Windsor Grow, who is also editor of *The Young Crusader*, and an assistant editor, Miss Dorothy McAllister. Miss Deane has rare facility as an editorial writer and in the line of research and securing valuable contributions. In 1920-21, during Miss Deane's extended absence in Europe and South America, Miss Vida Thompson faithfully served as associate editor of the official organ. The national president is editor-in-chief. Mrs. Della F. Withers, at the head of the Circulation department, is enthusiastic in her endeavor to increase the circulation of *The Union Signal* so that the valuable news it contains may reach around the world.

The National W. C. T. U. official organ has an interesting fifty-year old story. In 1874, a committee to consider the establishment of a National W. C. T. U. paper was appointed. In June, 1875, *The Woman's Temperance Union* appeared as a monthly paper, and at the second national convention, was endorsed as the official organ. The managing editor from 1875 to 1876 was Mrs. Jennie Fowler-Willing. Miss Margaret Winslow served in this capacity from 1876 to 1883. In 1877, the promising literary child received the name of *Our Union,* and in 1878 was pronounced free from debt. In January, 1883, *The Union Signal,* with Mrs. Mary Bannister Willard as its brainy, managing editor, made its first appearance. It was a consolidation of *Our Union* and *The Signal,* which, in the west, for three years had represented the growing W. C. T. U. work. In a "lead pencil letter," written while "en route in Virginia," in January, 1883, Frances Willard sent to *The Union Signal* editor this letter of congratulation: "My heart is thankful as I write the new name of our organ for the first time. It is as if two armies of allies had affected a junction and in united phalanx were marching on the foe. It means the brains of the west plus the brains of the east. It means progressive and conservative: old plus new; mother plus daughter. It is a strong move and conducts to a strategic position. Launch the good *Union Signal* ship, and 'Give her to the God of storms, the tempest and the gale.' Nor ship nor character is worth much if it cannot make its forceful way through storm to sunshine— across the foaming waves into the restful haven." Mrs. Mary Bannister Willard served as editor from 1883-1886. Between 1886 and 1889 the official organ was edited by Mary Allen West, Julia A. Ames, Elizabeth Wheeler Andrew, Frances E. Willard, Lady Henry Somerset, Margaret Sudduth, Mrs. Harriet B. Kells, Jane A. Stewart, Mrs. Katharine Lent Stevenson, Mrs. Susanna M. D. Fry, Mrs. Clara C. Chapin, Ada M. Melville, and Mrs. Isabella Webb Parks. In 1899, Mrs. Clara C. Chapin was appointed managing editor, a change from the earlier plan of a staff of four, five or six editors. Miss Margaret Sudduth served as managing editor from 1902-1903. Mrs. Cornelia T.

Jewett, from 1903-1911. During this period Miss Julia H. Thayer and Miss Alice M. Krimbill rendered valuable editorial service. In 1910, Julia F. Deane was elected managing editor.

The Union Signal in fact is a world missionary. A distinguished statesman, living in one of the larger cities of Europe, thus expresses his appreciation of the paper: "Recently I gave a public lecture on the social and economic effects of prohibition in the United States of America, in which I availed myself of the rich and valuable information which I have derived from the regular reading of *The Union Signal*. I cannot tell you, by the way, how deeply I am indebted to you for receiving this paper of yours which has enabled me to form a right opinion of the significance of the Eighteenth Amendment. For many of my hearers, I dare say for most of them, the facts which I laid before them were quite a revelation; for our newspapers, which are generally speaking under the influence of liquordom, are unfortunately making great and successful efforts to withhold the truth about prohibition from their readers, or to give them only a distorted view of it. Some of the smaller papers of our city were represented at my lecture by correspondents, but the most influential and most widely spread of our papers was conspicuous by absence of any representative, although to it had been formally extended an invitation to be present. The liquor people of all countries are fully aware of the immense importance of the legislative reform you have achieved in America and are doing therefore their utmost to conceal the truth from the public."

The Union Signal publishes all the telling things the W. C. T. U. is doing in many lines, including child welfare, scientific temperance instruction, Americanization, legislation, citizenship, social morality, publicity, women in industry and young people's and Loyal Temperance Legion work.

The Young Crusader is a charming, illustrated paper for the boys and girls. The gifted editor, Miss Windsor Grow, features citizenship talks, programs, funnies, puzzles, scientific temperance instruction and anti-cigaret material, articles by the General Secretary, and sugar-coated stories that have educational value. The paper is a help to grade and Sunday-school teachers and is popular among the boys and girls. Beginning with 1887, the editors have been Alice M. Guernsey, Ada Melville Shaw, Margaret Wintringer, Mildred Auten Spencer, Ella W. Brown, Susanna M. D. Fry and Windsor Grow.

The W. C. T. U. for two decades has co-operated with the Chautauquas. In Kellogg Hall, Chautauqua, New York, built by James Kellogg of Rochester, New York, in honor of his mother, Mrs. Annie Kellogg, one of the first graduates of the Chautauqua Literary and Scientific School, and a pioneer white-ribboner, a permanent place was provided by the donor for the use of the National W. C. T. U.

August 15, 1889, these rooms were dedicated in an impressive celebration of the fifteenth anniversary of the date on which the first steps were taken in the organization of the National W. C. T. U.

Bishop Vincent presided.

In the following letter of presentation, Mr. Kellogg appreciatively recognizes the influence of the National W. C. T. U. at the "Mother Chautauqua":

"Cherishing, as I do, the most profound respect for the splendid leadership and the sublimely splendid following which have made your society the most potent woman's alliance in the world, I consider it both an honor and a privilege to provide a place in this building, sacred to the memory of my sainted mother, for the use of your representatives. Organized, as you are, on these grounds, it is befitting that here a choice and central spot should be the place from which the sweet influences of your noble work should go out in blessing to multitudes throughout the earth. I know that my beloved mother, always imbued with the grace of hospitality, would as quickly open door and hand and heart to your beloved organization as to her best friend. While the sun of your glory was flooding the sky of the morning, her sun was sinking into twilight shadows, but she knew of your successes, she sympathized with your lofty aims, and esteemed it an honor, a jewel in the crown of her old age, to be recognized as your friend.

"It is a credit to Chautauqua, famed for far-reaching projects, that your grand association is recognized in its halls and on its platform. I would say to those who gather amid the leafy groves of this 'fair point,' stand by the noble women who, in God's name, care so truly and tenderly for 'Home and Native Land.' May your widening influence increase until not a spot shall fail to be illumined by the warm rays of your careful thought and holy sympathy. May your successes be extended until the white-ribbon shall flutter in every breeze, the world-adopted ensign of an all-conquering host. May your allegiance to the truth be an incentive to all Christian men to bind themselves in an invincible phalanx for righteousness. Under your wise teachings may a generation arise, anchored in the principles of sobriety, to stand as adamant against the hatefulness of strong drink, and for all that can make for goodness, purity and truth." On behalf of the organization, Mrs. Caroline B. Buell, national corresponding secretary, graciously accepted Mr. Kellogg's gift.

The Frances E. Willard memorial window, in Kellogg Hall, generously presented to the National W. C. T. U. by Mr. and Mrs. John C. Martin, was dedicated July 22, 1904. In 1908, a fountain was placed in the grass plot in front of the memorial window. This was a tribute from many friends. For ten years, the courtesy of the use of the Hall of Philosophy for the four o'clock hour on Saturday afternoons throughout the session, has been extended. Attractive programs have been presented by the W. C. T. U. hostesses, Mrs. C. F. Lindsay, Mrs. M. B. Wilson, Mrs. Maude B. Perkins and Mrs. Jennie M. Kemp. Group and evening meetings have been held at Kellogg Hall. Beginning with 1898, the hostesses at Kellogg Hall have been: Mrs. Addie Northam Fields, Mrs. Helen L. Bullock, Mrs.

S. M. D. Fry, Mrs. Mary B. Wilson, Mrs. Caroline B. Buell, Mrs. Emma S. Shelton, Mrs. C. F. Lindsay, Mrs. Maude B. Perkins, Miss Helen G. H. Estelle, and Mrs. Jennie M. Kemp. Mrs. Frances W. Graham, national musical director, acted as hostess at Kellogg Hall, Chautauqua W. C. T. U. headquarters during the Jubilee week of August 11-16.

Scores of white-ribboners, presidents and members of adjacent county and local unions, and many W. C. T. U. women, residents on Chautauqua grounds, have freely aided, in countless ways, the official leaders. Prominent among these gracious helpers were Mrs. Emily Huntington Miller, Mrs. Caroline McDowell, Mrs. Frances W. Graham, Miss Florence Bullock, Mrs. Dorothy Wilson Rue, Mrs. Caroline Leech and her daughter Carolyn, Miss Mary Mather, Miss Mary McDowell, Miss Jessica Morgan and Miss Elizabeth P. Gordon.

As the National W. C. T. U. work at Chautauqua has been one of the beneficiaries of the Frances E. Willard Memorial Fund, the national corresponding secretary, Mrs. Frances P. Parks, has had the supervision of Chautauqua arrangements. She has rendered untiring and successful service. Exhibits, at considerable expense, have been sent and installed. For many years W. C. T. U. Day has contributed an annual, attractive feature to the general Chautauqua program. As guests of the Chautauqua Woman's Club under the administration of Mrs. Emily Huntington Miller, 1888-1895, Mrs. B. T. Vincent, 1896-1916, and later of Mrs. Percy V. Pennybacker, W. C. T. U. speakers always have been welcomed.

The fiftieth anniversary of the initial steps in the organization of the W. C. T. U. was celebrated August 16, 1924, heralded as W. C. T. U. Day at Chautauqua. Here in the summer of 1874, Crusaders attending the first Sunday School Assembly, decided to call an organizing convention to meet in Cleveland, Ohio, the following November. In honor of this triumphant event a large audience assembled in the amphitheater both morning and afternoon. Dr.

Arthur E. Bestor, president of the Chautauqua Institution, which also in 1924 is celebrating its semi-centennial, expressed his pleasure in the co-operation of Chautauqua and the W. C. T. U. in this commemorative occasion. The historic background as it contributed to the future progress of the W. C. T. U. was the theme of the morning exercises when the story of the calling of the first W. C. T. U. convention by the valiant Crusaders assembled fifty years ago at Chautauqua was inspiringly told. The National W. C. T. U. president, Anna A. Gordon, the national vice-president, Mrs. Ella A. Boole and Dr. Arthur E. Bestor, president of the Chautauqua Institution, made the principal addresses. By invitation of the National W. C. T. U. the afternoon program embodied the law enforcement activities of the Council of Women for Home Missions, the Federation of Woman's Boards of Foreign Missions of North America, and the Woman's National Committee for Law Enforcement. Mrs. D. E. Waid represented the Council of Women for Home Missions, Miss Elizabeth Bain, the Woman's National Committee for Law Enforcement, and the chief speaker of the afternoon was Mrs. Helen Barrett Montgomery, the noted Baptist missionary leader, traveler and author. The National W. C. T. U. president presided, and presented the high points of the World's and National W. C. T. U. program in connection with the passage of the Eighteenth Amendment and the new campaign for law observance and law enforcement. Representatives of the seventeen states on the roll of honor, as having sent delegates to the Cleveland organizing convention were given seats on the platform. These seventeen states were: Maine, Vermont, Massachusetts, New York, Pennsylvania, Alabama, Ohio, Colorado, Iowa, California, Illinois, Indiana, Kansas, Michigan, New Hampshire, West Virginia and Wisconsin. Profound interest centered in a group of original Crusaders who were presented to the great audience and received tumultous applause. Three of these, Mrs. Arminda A. Shaw of New York, Mrs. Martha Beaujeau, and Mrs. Sarah H. Mossman.

Mary B. Ervin

*The Loyal Temper-
ance Legion is a
human garden in
which are planted
our pure principles.*

A. A. G.

attended the tent meeting at Chautauqua fifty years ago, where, after prayer, song and discussion, these brave souls "buckled on their armor for a long campaign."

It was foreordained that the National W. C. T. U., the organization of "mother love," should early declare for peace. "The great peace movement," said Frances Willard, in 1884, "seeking as its final outcome a Court of International Arbitration, as a substitute for war, promises more momentum to our home cause than any other; for, as the chief cornerstone of the peaceful state is the hearthstone—so, the chief pulverizer of that hearthstone is war."

When the Peace department of the National W. C. T. U. was created in 1889, that great-hearted Friend, Mrs. Hannah J. Bailey of Maine, was placed at its head. The principles of peace and arbitration continued to be taught far and wide, and through the generosity of the national superintendent and many state superintendents, children in the public schools received prizes for the best essays on some practical phase of the subject of peace.

At a Peace and Arbitration Congress held in 1907 in New York City, delegates, including white ribboners from all parts of the United States, from France and Great Britain, were present, all with hearts moved by the same high purpose. President Mary E. Woolley of Mount Holyoke College, asserted that "the fundamental principles of the peace movement enter into the most common experience, for they govern all just and pure living." Jane Addams' suggestion was that an attempt should be made to solve the difficult problem by investing the peaceful arts and peace movement itself with something of the glamour and attractiveness that attaches to war. Later, Mrs. William Jennings Bryan gave valuable plans in the same line. She states definite steps that should be taken, in order to place in the schools, histories that shall emphasize the achievements of peace rather than those of war.

At the present time *The Westminster Gazette* of England voices the opinion of a large part of the British Government when it says, "The value of common sense given and taken between great nations is demonstrated by the signature of the Anglo-American liquor convention. It presents a notable instance of how apparently insurmountable international difficulties may be overcome by the exercise of patience and good will."

The peaceful relations which ever have existed between the United States and Canada are symbolized by a magnificent arch dedicated to everlasting friendship between the two nations. The arch is sixty-six feet high, built of plain solid concrete with portals twenty-five feet wide—and a great space between them. It spans the Grand Pacific highway in British Columbia in commemoration of the one hundred years of peace between the United States and Canada. Across the top, on the United States side is engraved, "Children of a common mother," and on the Canadian side, "Brethren dwelling together in unity." On the summit of the high peak of the Andes mountains stands a majestic statue—the Christ of the Andes. The benignant figure of the Christ, with uplifted cross, was placed on its commanding pedestal to forever signalize the peace pact between the two republics of Argentina and Chile. The inscription on the base of the statue reads, "Sooner shall these mountains crumble into dust than Argentines and Chileans break the peace that they have sworn at the feet of Christ, the Redeemer, to maintain." In the address of dedication, Bishop Jard said, "Not alone to Argentina and Chile do we dedicate this monument, but to the world, that from this it may learn its lesson of universal peace."

The active white-ribboner of today is as interested in the daily news from Europe and the Orient as was the early woman Crusader in her immediate home area. At the present writing, W. C. T. U. women are deeply concerned while watching America's connection through the Dawes' reparation plan in the peaceful settlement of Europe's financial difficulties. In his famous report, Brigadier General Dawes says the diplomats on the committee are seek-

272

ing to cultivate a "universal conscience." This appeal to statesmen to "rise above the small things over which the small so often stumble" may well be taken to heart.

Rev. Ernest F. Tittle, D. D., of Evanston, Illinois, declared recently: "It isn't enough to work for a World Court. We must actively engage to make war an outlaw. It was thought once that slavery could not be abolished. Is it not possible for us to create public opinion against war, so that all differences of opinion may be solved by nations going to a court, even as individuals solve their problems in that way? We can have a family of nations. It is a possibility."

"National defense," asserted President Coolidge on July 4, 1924, "is a necessity and a virtue, but peace with honor is the normal, natural condition of mankind, and must be made the chief end to be sought in human relationship." In regard to the participation of the United States in the world court, President Coolidge has well said, "I am one of those who believe we would be safer and that we would be meeting our duties better by supporting the World Court and making every possible use of it. I feel confident that such action would make a greater America; that it would be productive of a higher and finer national spirit, and of a more complete national life." In a message to the Associated Advertising Clubs of the World, President Coolidge recently said: "As truth is essential between buyers and sellers, so in a larger sense, it is essential in the wider relationship between nation and nation."

All the national leading religious denominations have made recently strong pronunciamentos in favor of "uniting their energies in a great movement for a war-free world." The expression quoted is from the report of the committee on war of the recent Methodist Quadrennial Conference. It is typical of others passed in church assemblies of all denominations. The same opinion is held by prominent white-ribboners, notably Judge Florence Allen of Ohio, and the distinguished Assistant United States Attorney General,

273

Mrs. Mabel. Walker Willebrandt of Washington, D. C., and by an ever-increasing number of influential people in business and professional life. Melville E. Stone of the Associated Press awakened a patriotic keynote when he said, "I do hope that there will be a time when some other people will feel as I do that we have little respect for a man who boasts that he is one hundred per cent American and not a one hundred per cent international man. This country cannot isolate itself. We have got to participate in world activities."

In 1921, the National W. C. T. U. was the means of arousing public interest in the great Conference on the Limitation of Armaments held in Washington, D. C. A mammoth peace petition to the President of the United States was presented on behalf of the National W. C. T. U. November 21, by the president, Anna Gordon. This petition expressed the gratitude of these women to President Harding for calling the Conference on the Limitation of Armaments and the prayer that its fundamental purpose might be achieved. The petition, impressive in size, the whole tied with white ribbon, the insignia of the W. C. T. U., was more than one mile in length. It was circulated, signed, forwarded to Washington, and prepared for presentation to Secretary Hughes within one month. Miss Gordon, in presenting the appeal to Mr. Hughes in his capacity as chairman of the American delegation to the Conference, said:

"This petition of 199,531 names, each signed individually, and including appeals from national women's organizations representing a combined membership of 2,256,684, expresses the gratitude of these women to the President for calling the Conference on Limitation of Armaments. It embodies the hopes and prayers of the women of the United States, of all organizations and of all faiths, that such conclusions shall be reached by the Conference as will mean success for its fundamental purpose. The magnificent program given to the Conference by you on November 12,

1921, has met with the loud acclaim of the entire world. We pray that this keynote may be approved by the Conference in harmony with the prayers of those whose petitions we bring you today, and of hundreds of millions of other women the world over for Peace on Earth and Good Will to Men." With Miss Gordon when she presented the petition were Mrs. Lenna Lowe Yost, Washington, D. C., Legislative representative; Mrs. Emma S. Shelton, Miss Claire Lusby, and several other members of the District of Columbia W. C. T. U. As a part of the petition went also the signatures, in their official capacities, of national presidents of women's organizations. As a result of this Conference, a United States Treaty, insuring for a decade a beneficent peace, was consummated with all the nations bordering on the Pacific. The question, "What does mankind most need?" is answered by Rev. Ira Landrith, well-known to the prohibition and peace forces of the United States. He says, "The greatest need is 'pure religion, undefiled.' President Harding died with the words on his lips. Woodrow Wilson once came back from the brink of his own grave to write almost these same words. The idealism of the great Peace Maker must be substituted for fiddling partisanship and unholy greed. There are fifteen million graves on battlefields, nearly every one of them the grave of youth that was denied the inherent right of youth to live for his country—while we fiddle over whether we shall stop war or start another."

"War has had the first call on the flag long enough," believes the W. C. T. U., and "war does not need to be made more alluring, but less. Old Glory should be used more to glorify the victories of peace."

"When the women of Christendom resolve that war shall cease, it will cease," declared Ruskin. Today, millions of women are saying that war must cease, and the World's W. C. T. U. president voices their thought in her utterance, "When Christ's Golden Rule triumphs in custom and in law we shall have reached the goal of international good-will." The permanent lighting of the Statue of Liberty in New York Harbor is significant of the fact that peace can come to the world only with the illumination of education, justice and friendliness. Dante said, "Give light, and the people will find their own way." The Woman's Christian Temperance Union steadily sends forth the light that shall help bring the day prophesied by Tennyson, "when universal peace shall lie like a shaft of light across the land and like a line of beams across the sea."

The National W. C. T. U. from its earliest history has received whole-hearted support from the Friends—that church denomination which ever is foremost in advocating the Christian principles of prohibition, purity, and peace. John G. Whittier, the poet and apostle of the Friends, always warmly supported the W. C. T. U. One of the general officers of the National W. C. T. U., Mrs. Sara H. Hoge, president also of the Virginia W. C. T. U., is a minister in the Friends Church. Her long-time statesmanlike service for Virginia and the nation has been freely given.

Rev. Charles M. Sheldon, in his description of the "ideal city" pictures, it is hoped, the new era upon which the National W. C. T. U. is entering:

> "This is a city that shall stand,
> A Light upon a nation's hill;
> A Voice that evil cannot still,
> A source of blessing to the land;
> Its strength, not brick, nor stone, nor wood,
> But Justice, Love, and Brotherhood."

In the year, 1915, Harvard University conferred on Bela Lyon Pratt, one of Boston's eminent sculptors, an honorary degree because "he taught bronze and marble to whisper his secrets of beauty and power." White-ribboners always have been carving on the immortal souls of boys and girls the truth regarding total abstinence, in order that they may be living statues that radiate purity and power.

The importance of the study of child welfare was emphasized in the speech of a profound thinker when he said: "The voices that spoke to me as a child are speaking through me to the world." Herbert Hoover says: 'If we could grapple with the whole child situation, for one generation, our public health, our economic efficiency, the moral character, sanity, and stability of our people would advance three generations in one—every child delinquent in body, education, or character is a charge upon the community."

Looking forward to the work of the next fifty years, Anna Gordon says: "We should invest whole-heartedly time, prayer and holy endeavor to rally the children of the public schools, the Sunday schools and our Loyal Temperance Legion. We should enlist the boys and girls as workers for our cause today and as its Torch-Bearers of Tomorrow in the new America that is to lead the nations of the world into the kingdom of a safe sobriety and a righteous peace."

A leading educator has declared: "The business of the modern woman is to prepare her children for the world." The modern woman believes that it is her business also to make the street over against her home, the town over against her home, the nation over against her home, and the world over against her home, safe for her children. Today there are no narrow limits to the boundaries of the home. Each child has a world inheritance.

Mrs. Ellen Dayton Blair, of Los Angeles, California, who has worked so successfully in the Loyal Temperance Legion, is the only original Crusader who is still in active W. C. T. U. work. Mrs. Blair, although an octogenarian, still works for the boys and girls—holding a state and national office in the W. C. T. U. and has given service for a life time. While pushing well to the front the youth and those in the prime of life, the W. C. T. U. leaders never forget that "Age is opportunity, no less than youth itself, though in another dress; and as the evening twilight fades away, the sky is filled with stars invisible by day."

277

Another invaluable asset of a nation is its youth—the high school boys and girls. They are the "Golden Prophecy." The Woman's Christian Temperance Union is visualizing the improved conditions which await the youth of the future who, unhampered by the devastating effects of alcoholic liquors, will enter upon their high and holy duties. To the W. C. T. U., "the Youth Movement" is, in its essence, no new emergence. As early as 1874, this society began its work with the youth. Organized, the Crusade meant the consecration of 30,000 young women in the Young Woman's Christian Temperance Union to the service of God and humanity. By their side stood thousands of their brothers.

Today, in the United States, enthusiastic groups of pledged young women and young men are making many a meaningful gesture toward the goal of a social standard that will popularize a punch bowl filled only with delicious fruit juice.

A number of the religious denominations today rejoice in church papers, which in substance say: "The Youth Movement is absolutely opposed to alcoholism in every form. The millions of boys and girls enlisted disapprove the drinking habits of their parents and want to scrap alcoholism along with militarism and materialism." Hearty applause greeted the three young men who expressed these convictions at the recent Methodist General Conference that represented a world-wide membership of fifteen millions. There are different classifications of the young men and young women who are dissatisfied with the present and are declaring for a change. The W. C. T. U. is sponsoring those who are giving to the world the basic principles of Christianity—a Christianity that in trade, civic and social contact "worketh no ill to his neighbor."

"The oncoming generation," says Dr. John R. Mott, "is out on a quest for reality. There is a seething ferment in heart and brain. The reality that the oncoming generation is seeking is to be found in such a Christian organization as the W. C. T. U." "Youth Holds the Key!" is today the watchword that indicates the spirit of the young people of America and of many other nations. A young American woman wearing the white-ribbon calls to young men and young women everywhere in these appealing words: "Let us keep the door locked fast against the liquor traffic and cry to the enemies of prohibition, 'They shall not pass.' A more sacred, more challenging trust has never been offered since the world began. The Woman's Christian Temperance Union, fifty years ago, unmindful of creeds, dogmas, or political differences, banded themselves together in Christian love and in spite of ridicule and contempt, went out to fight in defense of all who were oppressed by the curse of liquor. They cry to the Christian young women of America: 'To you from falling hands we throw the torch: Be yours to hold it high. The youth of America have one supreme task— to prove to the world that a nation can voluntarily destroy the liquor traffic within its borders. What account shall young women of America render to the youth of the next generation?"

Another progressive member of the young people's organization, herself a teacher, sends out this compelling call to those who are members of her profession: "Our temperance task is not yet finished. Enemies of the social order for personal gain, seek to break down the prohibitory law. Patriotic Americans are rallying for the protection of the home. To this end, we of the W. C. T. U. send out a clarion call to the teachers of America for their renewed assistance in this fight. How can you, as teachers, have a part in this momentous campaign ? First, by emphasizing through the study of biology and hygiene, the effects of alcohol upon the human system; second, by computing in mathematics classes, the enormous cost in dollars and cents, of the liquor traffic; and by showing through the study of graphs, the statistical reports of health boards in regard to the ratio of deaths due to various diseases in the three years before prohibition and the three years succeeding; third, by preparing lessons—plans in history and civics in which the immediate or ultimate aim is the disclosing of political losses due to drink; fourth, by work in sociology and economics, whereby the students can ascertain the part played by strong drink in causing and promoting poverty, crime, and disease; fifth, by joining the Woman's Christian Temperance Union, thereby allying yourselves with the greatest organized force of women banded together for the protection of the home, the church, and the school. We need your help; you need ours."

At a great convention an intensely earnest young man, seeking knowledge on the questions of the day, said respectfully to those older than himself, "It seems to me these resolutions are so general that they don't mean anything. What is the use of talking if we are afraid people will understand what we say? We young people, for instance, would like the question of war brought out into the open—and no side-stepping."

One of the white-ribbon young women leaders enthusiastically declares, "With the 'I hope' of Tennyson, the 'I know' of Browning and the 'I can' of God, we'll yet completely overthrow the enemy." "Trust the youth," says Dr. W. H. Foulkes, a noted contributor to *The Christian Endeavor World.* "It is the spirit of youth that is always the hope of the world. Let us be thankful for the resurgence of youth." It will be recalled that a mighty slogan of the prohibition campaign that brought the Federal victory—"A saloonless nation by 1920"—originated with a Christian Endeavor leader. The young people made it resound throughout the hills and valleys of the nation.

In an address given at Washington, D. C., under the auspices of the Intercollegiate Prohibition Association, Admiral William S. Sims brought the issue very close to his hearers in the following words: "It is rather a singular thing for a naval officer to speak on prohibition. In my youth, the teetotaler was a milk-sop; he was not considered a good sport nor a companionable man. The drinking of the young men caused the forming of clubs for those who did not frequent saloons.

"I believe prohibition is here to stay. Do you young men present here, tonight, want to join the class of cynical violators of the law? If you do, the wets will supply you with plenty of arguments. If you pay a man to get you a bottle of whiskey, or a drink, you are paying for the services of the bootlegger who smuggles it in—you are, in reality, a bootlegger. The influence of our young men on the future of the United States will be great. In a few years, you will be the controlling force in the nation. The future—our and perhaps the world's future—will be determined by your mental equipment, your moral principles, your clean flesh, your physical stamina, and your ideals of private and national life. It is up to you to do some serious things—to form the habit of thinking straight. It is my belief that if college students should decide to obey the law in confidence, and if their example should be followed by the great mass of students in all the colleges and schools, the moral influence would eventually be such as to sweep out of office every corrupt official, and to create that respect for law without which no democracy can succeed. No nation can resist the determined moral conviction of its young men. The future is in the hands of you young men and young women. More than to any other class of citizens, it is up to you."

"The fellowship of youth is for peace," declares one of the American young men. "It is up to the youth of this generation to solve the war problem—before it is too late. The Youth Movements among the European nations are sounding the one note of hope for a peaceful solution of Europe's tangle of distrust."

A piece of statuary by Rodin, the great French sculptor, in the Metropolitan Museum of Art in New York City, is inspiring to all those who are working for the welfare of the youth of the world. The rough outline of a strong hand is carved out of a small block of marble. The figures

of a man and a woman are being shaped by the fingers of
the hand. Rodin, it is stated, calls this piece of sculpture,
"The Hand of God." White-ribboners see in it a great hope
for the new Youth Movement which is spreading in all
lands. Does the statue not prophesy that "the chaos of a
mighty world is rounding into form?"

In many nations even restlessness and revolt among
students and other youth, indicate progress. A significant
incident is related in the *International Record*, of a juvenile
group of the national socialist party in Vienna, Austria,
seeking a room for its meeting. One was found in a public
house and the landlord, himself a socialist, agreed to let
it on conditions that liquor should be absolutely prohibited
on the evening of the meeting. The result was that all
similar juvenile groups have adopted prohibition of liquors
at their gatherings.

Sui Ling Wang, of China (brother of Mrs. Frances
Willard Wang Liu), for three years has been a student
in Syracuse University, New York. In a leading paper of
that city, he gives an intimate picture of conditions in his
home land. He says, "When the Youth Movement came
to play its part it undertook the tremendous task of revolu-
tionizing our people's thought. It was the custom for venerable pedagogues to gather at tea houses to compose rhymes
and to discuss rather lightly the Buddhist doctrines. Young
students generally followed the currents of thought, yet
there were some young men of will-power who saw the
light and glimpsed the meaning of human life. In her
future development, as in her past awakening, China will
continue to look to her youth for guidance." Sui Wang will
some day be a force in China, assisting his sister, Frances
Willard Wang Liu of Shanghai, and her husband, Herman
C. E. Liu (one of the leaders in the Chinese Y. M. C. A.)
in their educational and temperance campaigns among the
students and people of the Orient.

In a recent eloquent baccalaureate address, Bishop
Thomas Nicholson called attention to the many problems

the young graduates would find as they journeyed along in the wilderness of doubt and faced many bewildering situations. He said their commission was "to bring the moral and spiritual life of today up to the level of the commercial, and to invest their lives in great causes."

"Be true to the dreams of your youth. Hold fast to the high ideals that flash upon your vision in hours of exaltation," many years ago said that patriot and seer, Frances Willard. Today, Anna Gordon, the president of the World's and National W. C. T. U., sends this cheering message to the young people: "If a singing army is a victorious one, the young people of the Woman's Christian Temperance Union are bound to win. Their prize song that rings out triumphantly in many a convention, is a challenge to all American youth:

" 'Though poppies are blooming in Flanders,
    Hiding the Crosses bare,
The Spirit of Youth still is living
    Ready to do and to dare.

Out o'er the world Youth is marching
    With emblem a Ribbon White,
Till it enfolds all the nations
    In purity, peace and light.' "

Many and varied are the memorials to Frances E. Willard. Stately school buildings in cosmopolitan cities, and modest structures in small towns perpetuate her distinguished name. The Frances E. Willard Settlement in Boston has made articulate and most successful one of her cherished ideals. Handsome windows in church edifices symbolize her character and her humanitarian work. Children, horses and dogs drink at fountains erected to her honor. Hundreds of local unions bear her name, and Frances Willard's namesakes are legion.

On February 17, 1905, for the first time in history the legislative wheels of the Federal government were stilled for a time to pay tribute to a woman's memory. On this notable day, Congress accepted from the state of Illinois, in accordance with the practically unanimous vote of its legislature, the statue of Frances E. Willard, placing it in Statuary Hall under the dome of the National Capitol. This action forever commemorates the life work of one who is acknowledged to be the most beloved character of her day, and the foremost woman of the nineteenth century. Manhood was ennobled, womanhood uplifted, childhood blessed through the lessons of that day. Strong, manly, eloquent addresses were given in both Senate and House by the statesmen who eulogized Frances E. Willard, and many other men reverently paused before the statue, speaking of Miss Willard as teacher, philanthropist, reformer, benefactor and friend. Among the hundreds of visitors there were some, no doubt, who could not easily adapt their views to correspond with the new order, but if this were so, they were silent, and only words of praise and admiration were heard.

This beautiful marble portrait, designed by Helen Farnsworth Mears of Wisconsin, a pupil of St. Gaudens, blessed the women who stood so silently before it, some with tears in their eyes but with a smile upon their lips as they were impressively reminded of the true meaning of womanliness, spirituality and Christianity. It blessed the children who made up the unique and inspiring procession, the like of which was never before seen at the Capitol, as thousands of little hands placed flowers at the foot of the statue and bore away with them a visible reminder of Frances E. Willard which will be an educator in many a home—the statue medal presented to each child by Miss Anna A. Gordon, chairman of the Frances E. Willard Statue Commission, appointed by the governor of Illinois. These blessings were by no means confined to the large number of people who were privileged to be present in the Capitol, but they radiated throughout the entire world.

Someone writing of the reception of the statue has aptly said that "The heroes and statesmen in this Valhalla looked on in astonishment, and when someone asked if Miss

Willard had signed the Declaration of Independence, James A. Garfield replied that she had, and was worthy to stand among the immortals of all time, for he had heard her voice and knew of her labor for the freedom of her people; freedom from the combination of vice and drunkenness."

On the pedestal are Frances Willard's own words: "Ah! it is women who have given the costliest hostages to fortune! Out into the battle of life they have sent their best beloved with fearful odds against them. Oh, by the dangers they have dared; by the hours of patient watching over beds where helpless children lay; by the incense of ten thousand prayers wafted from their gentle lips to heaven, I charge you give them power to protect along life's treacherous highway those whom they have so loved."

At the large evening gathering, presided over by the national president, Mrs. Lillian M. N. Stevens, women from all over the country participated in the program. Katharine Lent Stevenson's inspirational poem was read, two stanzas of which follow:

"How great she stands!
A mountain-peak, her soul;
An ocean wide; a river sweeping on with full, free tide;
A sacred shrine where holiest things abide;
How great she stands!

"Stand, radiant soul!
Here, in the center of our nation's heart;
Forever of its best life thou'rt a part;
Here thou shalt draw thy land to what thou art;
Stand, radiant soul!"

In commenting on this statue, Margaret Ellis said, "It makes this historic hall seem homelike and peaceful. It points the way for women, not only to stand amid the statues of the great and powerful of our country, but to sit in council as well in national legislative halls. Many times, when in perplexity, I have visited the statue and received

285

the strength I needed. Members of Congress of like mind with us say that they have had similar experiences."

Another commemoration of Frances Willard, occurring many years later, also is of lasting interest and influence. At the opening of the twentieth century in the city of New York, there was established by New York University, a Hall of Fame for the preservation and exaltation of the names of the great of our country. A board composed of 110 electors decides once in five years what names shall be added. In 1910, ten distinguished men and women were elected. Included in that honored list was the illustrious name of Frances E. Willard.

In the summer of 1921, a handsome bronze tablet, to the memory of Frances Willard, was unveiled in the Hall of Fame, New York University. A most impressive ceremony took place in the colonnade. Many others were honored by memorial tablets. Each new tablet was covered by an American flag which was lifted to the roll of a drum and the sound of a trumpet. Mrs. L. M. De Silva, corresponding secretary of New York state W. C. T. U., drew aside the Stars and Stripes from Miss Willard's tablet, while Mrs. Ella A. Boole, vice-president-at-large of the National W. C. T. U. and president of the New York W. C. T. U., said feelingly: "As a representative of the National Woman's Christian Temperance Union, I have the great honor to unveil the tablet inscribed with the name of Frances Elizabeth Willard, which has been chosen by the electors for perpetual commemoration in the Hall of Fame for Great Americans, and which bears the following inscription: 'Were I asked to define in a sentence the thought and purpose of the Woman's Christian Temperance Union, I would reply, "it is to make the whole world homelike!" ' "

In 1923, when in the Hall of Fame the bust of Frances Willard, designed by Lorado Taft, was unveiled, the commemorative address was made by Anna Gordon. Mrs. Boole made the presentation announcement, and Mr: Oliver A. Willard, a relative, unveiled the portrait bust.

Frances J. Barnes   Maude B. Perkins
Grace Leigh Scott   Charlotte B. Fraser

Young People's Branch Field Day in New York.

Impressively, Miss Gordon said: " 'Blessed are the inclusive, for they shall be included'—a beatitude original with Frances Willard, characterizes this distinguished woman of rare, radiant personality. Today, this Hall of Fame where, through the gracious generosity of New York University, mighty memories are to be kept alive, is honored in receiving the portrait bust of Frances Elizabeth Willard.

"Frances Willard passionately loved humanity.

"Next to her belief in God, she believed in humanity. She was a profound student and eloquent advocate of all great humanitarian and social reforms. 'God bless the crowd,' ever prayed her yearning, sympathetic, unselfish soul. She scouted the old adage, 'Each for himself and the devil take the hindmost.' She heralded the coming day for which she valiantly toiled—the day when the spirit of a new adage based on New Testament ethics, 'Each for the other that there may be no hindmost for the devil to take,' shall usher in as a gloriously established fact, the brotherhood of man, the federation of the world. 'Only the Golden Rule of Christ can bring the Golden Age of Man,' declared this prophetic genius—this spiritual seer.

"Frances Willard was a pioneer.

"She came of pioneer New England stock, a direct descendant of Major Simon Willard, the first Willard to come from the old England to the new, and who was one of the founders of Concord, Massachusetts. Another paternal ancestor was pastor of the Old South Church in Boston and president of Harvard University. Still another was the architect of Bunker Hill monument. Born in New York State of intellectual, adventurous parents, Frances Willard became a pioneer in fields of philanthropy and reform. Here her wide vision, her patriotic fervor, her true womanliness, her daring faith, and her invincible courage helped blaze through the jungles of apathy, ignorance, prejudice and opposition, a trail that American womanhood today safely and victoriously is following.

"Frances Willard was a brilliant student and a renowned educator.

287

"In her young womanhood as teacher, preceptress and dean of women, she held many influential positions. She was president of the first college for women entirely under the management of women. At Evanston, Illinois, her long time home, she was Dean of Women and Professor of Aesthetics in her alma mater, Northwestern University. Thousands of young men and women pupils came under the charm of her unique class-room methods and were indelibly impressed with high and noble ideals of life and service.

"Frances Willard was a persuasive, magnetic orator.

"In the hearts of the people throughout the nation and the world she kindled a conscience on the temperance question. She was the most remarkable woman organizer of her century. She was one of the first internationalists among women. Thirty-nine years ago she founded the World's Woman's Christian Temperance Union and sent out the first world-wide clarion call for the protection of the home, for the outlawing of the liquor traffic, for the enfranchisement of women, for courts of international arbitration, for an equal standard of purity for men and women, for justice as opposed to greed and gain, and for the triumph of Christ's golden rule in custom and in law. Our Quaker poet, John G. Whittier, who wrote an introduction to Miss Willard's first literary venture, said of her as in later years, she launched her constructive program of world activities: 'She knew the power of banded ill, but felt that love was stronger still; and organized for doing good, the world's united womanhood.'

"Frances E. Willard helped make the world wider for women and more homelike for humanity. 'She had the will to serve and bear,—The will to love and dare.' Thus shall history's verdict immortalize America's patriot, philanthropist, author, orator, educator, lover of humanity—Frances Elizabeth Willard."

The writer has given only glimpses of the high points of the past. If she could portray a composite picture of the W. C. T. U., it would be the portrait of a youthful mother, a rarely endowed woman looking hopefully into the foreground of an unknown future. Again the W. C. T. U. is a pioneer, a forerunner in a new crusade and she points the way to a forward, moral and spiritual movement.

While trying to keep up the swift pace required of a prohibition patriot, white-ribbon women have been reminded of Lewis Carroll's story of "Alice in Wonderland." The Queen, it will be recalled, took Alice by the hand and together they started to run a race. At last Alice, in a breathless condition, said to her companion, "We do not seem to get anywhere. In my country by this time we surely would be somewhere." "In this country," replied the Queen, "it takes all the running you can do even to keep in the same place!"

In the early years of organization work, the women when confronted with the legally protected liquor traffic persistently declared, "The liquor traffic must go!" Since the victory of Federal prohibition, and the reaction of the World War, faced with the difficulties and dangers from nullifiers of the prohibition law, an apathetic electorate, groups of self-centered politicians, mercenary propagandists of war and a spirit of international hate, the white-ribboners are righteously determined that, "The nullifiers of prohibition and the war-makers must go." The same high principles and progressive program adopted at the first convention of the National W. C. T. U. are the identical ideals being pressed today by the organization, and are in reality the basis of action for all the allied temperance and philanthropic forces. This practical, progressive program will be carried over into the new era—the coming fifty-year crusade.

Recently while talking with Dr. Sarah F. Whiting, long professor of astronomy at Wellesley College, about the slow but sure progress of reforms, Dr. Whiting taught the writer a moral and scientific lesson when she exclaimed: "It is like the precession of the equinoxes, in that the sun and the moon work together to draw the equatorial belt into their own plane; but the equatorial belt cannot move without dragging with it the whole inert mass of the earth. The motion is slow but continuous, but give it time enough and the whole heavens are changed." Dr. Whiting, an ardent white-ribboner, well understands how to reach the human inert mass, and many young lives have responded to her temperance appeal.

Carlisle, in writing the epitaph of a great woman, used one of the finest phrases in literature when he said she had about her "a soft invincibility." Beginning with the Crusaders who not only prayed, but used hatchets, the host of heroic W. C. T. U. leaders who made possible the vast victories of fifty years have at times, in a womanly way, displayed "a soft invincibility"—as forceful and explosive as nitro-glycerine. When the word of the Lord came to Moses he numbered the Israelites—especially the men of war. When the word of the Lord, through the National W. C. T. U., came to "Elizabeth"—the historian, she tried to number the women of war—the peaceful war of the W. C. T. U.! Since 1873, the day of the marching mothers of the Crusade, an innumerable host have said, "We are well able to overcome the enemy and to possess the promised land."

The gratitude of thousands of white-ribboners is most heartily extended to the brotherly men of America—the best in the world—who have rendered in so many ways invaluable aid in securing W. C. T. U. victories. These men, it will be noted, are in a different class from the politicians who fittingly have received the term of the "masculinity superiority complex."

Those still facing the problems of the earthly life take courage each morning as they think, "Every day is a new beginning. Every day is the world made new." How beautiful has been the experience of each one who has awakened some new morning to the life abundant. These inspired lines strengthen our faith in immortality:

> "On any morning think of
> Stepping on shore and finding it Heaven,

Of taking hold of a hand and
Finding it God's Hand,
Of breathing of new air and
Finding it celestial air,
Of feeling invigorated and
Finding it immortality,
Of passing from storm and tempest
To an unknown calm,
Of waking up and finding it Home."

"The joy of life and of sacrificial service was theirs in fullest measure—these 'comrades of yesterday now saints of God,'" reverently and reminiscently says the national president. "Their beloved names are forever enshrined in our hearts. These warrior-souled comrades have left their indelible impression upon our national work. Men, women and children of this generation and for years to come will rise up and call them blessed. Their faith and courage triumphed over all fears. We hopefully take up the tasks that they have laid down. The memory of their devoted lives will incite us to pray with their faith and work with their courage, and so in the new crusade bring our organization to even greater heights of power and influence."

There is a new map of the world. It is stated by geographical experts that "fifty new political and territorial divisions have arisen, aggregating one-fifth of the land area and one-fifth of the population of the globe." Twenty republics are located in portions of the area that constituted Russia. Others are in the territory once occupied by Germany, Austria, Hungary, and Turkey, and still others are scattered in various parts of the world—as colonies, protectorates or dependencies. How to live together in harmony, is the vital question. The United States Secretary of State, Charles Evans Hughes, president of the American Bar Association, speaking recently in Europe, said: "We worship with you in an invisible temple of justice, whose votaries know no distinction of race, country or condition." Did not this eminent statesman point the way toward a higher civilization? It is not enough for America to have first honors in the recent Olympic Games. Should not the United States furnish the leadership for the democracies of the world? The program of the Woman's Christian Temperance Union for the opening of the next fifty years will make more articulate and visible this "temple of justice" built by those who know "no distinction of race, country or condition."

Guido's wonderful picture, "The Archangel Michael and Fiend Lucifer in Deadly Struggle" typifies our conflict with Alcohol. The angel, "strong, serene and sunny-haired," as Frances Willard used to say, is represented with his foot upon the head of his already prostrate foe. "With one hand he is tightening about the monster's body a chain of moral suasion, and in the other he holds the swift downgliding sword of law, while in constant motion are his outspread wings of faith and prayer."

"At first the Woman's Christian Temperance Union was but a beam in the darkness, then a torch held up in the gloom, then a 'light in the window for thee, brother,' then a beacon flaming grandly out upon the most dangerous headland of the republic's coast, but steadily it grows and gathers light, until at last it shall climb the zenith like another sun and shed the healing radiance of its beams into the darkest heart and most desolate home. Let us never be discouraged. It is God's great beacon-light, not ours."

"Hold high the torch! You did not light its glow:
'Twas given you from other hands you know.
'Tis only yours to keep it burning bright,
Yours to pass on when you no more need light.
For there are little feet that you must guide,
And little forms go marching by your side;
Their eyes are watching every tear and smile,
And efforts that you think are not worth while,
May sometimes be the very helps they need,
Actions to which their souls would give most heed,

292

Statue of Frances E. Willard in Statutary Hall,
Washington, D. C.

So that in turn they'll lift it high and say,
'I watched my mother carry it this way.'"

It is hoped that history's verdict upon the women torch-bearers shall be, "By God's blessing they helped to make the world wider for women and more homelike for humanity."

APPENDIX

Woman's Christian Temperance Union
History of Fifty Years

CHRONOLOGICAL SUMMARY
1874-1924

Woman's Temperance Crusade
1873-1874

National Woman's Christian Temperance Union
The First Decade: 1874-1884

1874 Woman's Temperance Crusade continued from 1873.

1874 August 16: Crusaders at Chautauqua issue call for organizing convention.

1874 November 18-20: National Woman's Christian Temperance Union organized in Cleveland, Ohio—Officers elected: President, Mrs. Annie Wittenmyer; corresponding secretary, Frances E. Willard; recording secretary, Mrs. Mary C. Johnson; assistant recording secretary, Mrs. Mary T. Burt; treasurer, Mrs. W. A. Ingham.

1876 Huge W. C. T. U. petition for Constitutional Prohibition presented to Congress by Senator Henry W. Blair of New Hampshire. Frances Willard addressed the Judiciary Committee on its behalf.

1879 Frances E. Willard elected president at Indianapolis convention.

1880 The term, "Superintendent of Department," substituted for "Standing Committee." Nearly all departments now existing were adopted in this decade —many of them under different names. Some of the early departments have been merged into those of today.

1882 Secured enactment in Vermont of Scientific Temperance Education Law—the first in all the world. In twenty years every state and the Congress had passed similar laws.

1883 Nation-wide organization tour of Frances Willard and Anna Gordon; many southern and western states organized.

1883 The official organ *Our Union* consolidated with *The Signal* of Illinois. *The Union Signal* made its first appearance on January 4.

1883 National convention in Detroit, Michigan; departments of work classified under heads of Organization, Preventive, Educational, Evangelistic, Social and Legal.

1883 World's W. C. T. U. organized.

The high points of the first decade were: Organization of the W. C. T. U.; "Declaration of Principles" written by Frances Willard; "Do Everything Policy" resulting in department work; Scientific Temperance Instruction in the public schools developed by Mary Hanchett Hunt, national superintendent; first memorial to the International Sunday School Association, asking for a quarterly temperance lesson; petitions introduced into Congress.

The Second Decade: 1884-1894

1884 Petition addressed to all the governments of the world, called the "Polyglot," written and sent out by Frances Willard. It asked for the prohibition of the manufacture and sale of alcoholic liquors, opium, and legalized vice.

1885 W. C. T. U. constitutional amendment adopted requiring ten cents per member dues from state auxiliaries.

1886 An affiliated interest—the National Temperance Hospital and Training School for Nurses—established; Mrs. J. B. Hobbs, Mrs. L. H. Plumb and Dr. Mary Weeks Burnett, managers.

1889 An affiliated interest—the Woman's Temperance Publishing Association founded; President, Mrs. Matilda B. Carse; editor, Miss Alice M. Guernsey; advisory committee, National W. C. T. U. president, National W. C. T. U. secretary.

1889 W. C. T. U. Lecture Bureau established.

1889 *The Oak and Ivy Leaf,* organ of the Young Woman's Christian Temperance Union founded; editors, Miss Margaret A. Sudduth, Miss Jennie A. Stewart.

1890 The International Sunday School Convention held at Pittsburgh, Pennsylvania, granted a Quarterly Temperance Lesson, distinct and uncomplicated with any other subject.

1891 First World's W. C. T. U. convention held in Faneuil Hall, Boston, Massachusetts.

1893 World's and National W. C. T. U. conventions held in Chicago, Illinois, in connection with the Columbian Exposition.

In this second decade there was marked development in department plans and programs. For convenience, the data about all departments up to 1924 is included. The date the department was adopted is first given, and the list is alphabetically arranged.

Anti-Narcotics: (1884) Superintendents: Mrs. Mary Bynon Reese; (1886—Changed to Department of Narcotics) Mrs. J. H. Harris, Mrs. E. B. Ingalls; (1898—Changed to Anti-Narcotics) Mrs. Alta Bohren, Miss Helen G. H. Estelle.

Child Welfare: (1907) (Juvenile Courts, Industrial Education, and Anti-Child Labor). Superintendent: Mrs. Minnie U. Rutherford. Associate: To prevent employment of young children, Mrs. Harriet B. Kells. (1917—Department name changed to Child Welfare). Superintendents: Mrs. Minnie U. Rutherford, Mrs. Elizabeth A. Perkins.

Christian Citizenship: (1896) Superintendents: Mrs. Anna F. Beiler, Miss Lucy Page Gaston, Mrs. Margaret Dye Ellis, Mrs. C. B. Buell, Mrs. Mary Jewett Telford, Mrs.

Helen D. Harford, Mrs. Emma L. Starrett, Mrs. Deborah Knox Livingston, Mrs. Ida B. Wise Smith.

Evangelistic: (1883) Superintendents: Mrs. Hannah Whitall Smith, Mrs. Annie Palmer, Mrs. S. M. I. Henry, Miss Helen L. Hood, Miss Elizabeth W. Greenwood, Rev. Mary E. Kuhl, Rev. Helen Hyde Carlson, Mrs. Mary Harris Armor.

(1898) Almshouse Work was added to this department.

Fairs and Open Air Meetings: (1880) (State and County Fairs) Superintendents: Mrs. G. A. Moody, Mrs. Mary A. Leavitt, Mrs. Josephine R. Nichols, Mrs. M. C. Campfield, Mrs. Clara V. Weaver, Mrs. Rebecca B. Chambers, Mrs. Hannah T. Guild; (1902—Name changed to Fairs and Open Air Meetings) Mrs. Julia D. Phelps, Mrs. Carolyn P. Lindsay. (1920—Name changed to Exhibits and Fairs).

Flower Mission: (1883) Superintendents: Miss Jennie Casseday, Miss Gertrude Ferguson, Miss Alice Sudduth, Mrs. Angie F. Newman, Miss Ethel Austin Shrigley, Miss Lella M. Sewall, Miss Etta F. Lockwood, Miss Lella M. Sewall.

Franchise: (1881) Committee: Frances E. Willard, Mary A. Livermore, J. Ellen Foster. Superintendents: Mrs. Mary G. C. Leavitt, Mrs. Zerelda G. Wallace, Rev. Anna H. Shaw, Mrs. Theresa A. Jenkins, Dr. Louise C. Purington, Miss Marie C. Brehm, Mrs. Ella Stewart, Dr. Maude McIlvaine Sanders, Rev. Mecca Marie Varney, Mrs. Sophie L. Clark, Mrs. Deborah Knox Livingston. (1918—Department name changed to Suffrage) (1920—Mrs. Livingston carried on the work in the department of Christian Citizenship).

Health and Heredity: (1881) (Heredity) Superintendents: Dr. Sarah Hackett Stevenson, Mrs. M. L. Griffith, Mrs. J. H. Kellogg, Dr. Mary Weeks Burnett, Dr. Orpha Baldwin, Mrs. R. A. Armstrong, Dr. Annette J. Shaw; (Health) Dr. Bessie Cushman, Miss Mary H. Mather, Dr. Orpha Baldwin, Dr. Annette J. Shaw, Miss Julia

Colman. (1894—Departments combined under the name of Health and Heredity) Miss Julia Colman, Dr. Louise C. Purington; (1914—Health and Heredity and Physical Education combined under Health) Mrs. Frances Waite Leiter, Dr. P. S. Bourdeau-Sisco.

Institutes: (1889) (School of Methods) Superintendents: Miss Mary Allen West, Mrs. Narcissa White Kinney. (1894—School of Methods and Parliamentary Usage) Mrs. Anna S. Benjamin. (1900—Changed to W. C. T. U. Institutes) Mrs. Mary Hadley Hall, Mrs. Margaret C. Munns, Mrs. Lettie Hill May, Mrs. Anna Marden De Yo.

Kindergarten: (1884) Superintendents: Mrs. E. G. Greene, Miss Lily Reynolds, Miss Mary McDowell, Miss Mary Bannister Willard, Miss Jennie M. Williamson, Miss Martha Crombie Wood, Miss Clara Wheeler.

Legislation: (1874) Standing Committee: Mrs. Annie Wittenmyer, Mrs. Mary A. Woodbridge, Mrs. J. Ellen Foster. (1880) Superintendents: Mrs. J. Ellen Foster, Mrs. Mary A. Woodbridge, Mrs. Ada M. Bittenbender, Mrs. Catharine Waugh McCulloch, Mrs. Frances Belford, Mrs. Mary Towne Burt, Mrs. Margaret Dye Ellis, Mrs. Lenna Lowe Yost.

Loyal Temperance Legion: (1874) (Juvenile Work) Committees: (1880) Superintendents: Miss Elizabeth W. Greenwood, Mrs. Nellie H. Bayley, Mrs. Anna M. Hammer, Mrs. Helen G. Rice, Miss Margaret Wintringer. (1890—Department changed from Juvenile Work to Loyal Temperance Legion) (1895—Changed from a department to a branch) Mrs. Culla J. Vayhinger, Miss Edna Rowan, Miss Mary B. Ervin.

Literature: (1877) Superintendents: Miss Julia Colman, Mrs. F. H. Rastall, Mrs. Katharine Lent Stevenson, Mrs. Esther T. Housh, Miss Helen L. Hood, Miss Ellen D. Morris, Mrs. Mae A. Davis, Mrs. Susanna M. D. Fry, Miss Addie A. Austin. Literature carried by National W. C. T. U. Publishing House. (1915—National department discontinued.)

Medal Contests: (1896) Superintendents: Mrs. A. E. Carman. (1897) (W. C. T. U. and Demorest Contests Systems united) Mrs. Maude Carman Cathcart.

Medical Temperance: (1883) Superintendents: Miss Jennie P. Duty, Mrs. J. Butler, Mrs. Caroline A. Leech; In 1895, Mrs. Martha M. Allen.

Mercy: (1890) Superintendent, Mrs. Mary F. Lovell; (1916 —Transferred to Loyal Temperance Legion Branch).

Purity: (1875) (Suppression of Social Evil) (1880) Mrs. Dr. J. H. Kellogg; (1886—Name changed to Social Purity) Frances E. Willard; (1888—Changed to Department of White Cross and White Shield) (1890—Promotion of Social Purity) (1892—Department of Purity) Dr. Mary Wood Allen, Mrs. Helen L. Bullock; (1907—Moral Education) (1908—Purity) Mrs. Rose Wood Allen Chapman; (1908—Mothers Meetings and White Ribbon Recruits) Mrs. Helen L. Bullock (1911—Curfew) Miss Mary E. Brown; (1912—Purity) Mrs. Leona T. Field; (1913—Curfew and Policewomen) Miss Mary E. Brown; (1914—Mothers' Meetings, White Ribbon Recruits and Purity) Mrs. Helen L. Bullock; (1916—Moral Education and Race Betterment) Miss Mary E. Brown; (1917— Mothers' Meetings and White Ribbon Recruits) Mrs. Frances B. Heald; Mrs. Susan McWhirter Ostrom; (1920—Social Morality) Mrs. Gertrude S. Martin, Dr. Valeria H. Parker.

Parliamentary Usage: (1887) Superintendents: until 1917 —thirty consecutive years—Mrs. Anna S. Benjamin; Mrs. I. W. Gleason.

Peace and International Arbitration: (1888) Superintendents: Mrs. Hannah J. Bailey, Mrs. William J. Bryan, Mrs. Ida De Garmo, Miss Alice L. Kercher, Mrs. Effie Danforth McAfee.

Penal and Reformatory Work: (1877) Standing Committee: Mrs. W. K. Denny, chairman. (1878-1890) Superintendent: Mrs. J. K. Barney. (1891) Department divided into three parts: Mrs. Mary Teats, superintendent

of *Prison and Jail Work;* Miss C. E. Coffin, of *Police
Station Work;* Miss M. A. Morrison, of *Almshouse Work.*
(1892) Mrs. Jane M. Kinney, superintendent of *Penal
Work.* Mrs. Emma L. Starrett, Mrs. Minnie B. Horning.
(1898) *Almshouse Work* given to *Evangelistic Department.* (1915) Department changed to *Prison Reform.*

The Press: (1874) Chairmen of Standing Committees:
Mrs. L. M. N. Stevens, Mrs. A. C. Hillyer. (1880)
Superintendents: Miss Mary C. Bancroft, Miss Laura
Moore, Mrs. Caroline B. Buell, Mrs. Esther T. Housh,
Miss Mary Henry, Miss Julia A. Ames, Miss Alice E.
Briggs, Mrs. Harriet B. Kells, Miss Lodie Reed, Mrs.
Katharine Lent Stevenson, Mrs. Minnie B. Horning, Miss
Eva Kilbreth Foster, Mrs. Jennie M. Kemp, Mrs. Mildred
A Spencer, Mrs. Susan McWhirter Ostrom, Mrs. Mar-
garet B. Platt; (1919—Publicity) Mrs. Clara C. Chapin,
Mrs. Anna P. George, Miss Bertha Bowman, Mrs. Rosa-
lind Scott Dunkin.

Purity in Literature and Art: (Suppression of Impure
Literature) (1884) Superintendents: Miss Lucy J.
Holmes, Mrs. Naomi Tomlinson, Mrs. Deborah Leeds,
Mrs. Samuel Clements. (1890) under the title of Purity
in Literature and Art this department became a sub-
division of the department of Purity with Mrs. Emilie
D. Martin as superintendent; Mrs. Harriet Pritchard.

Sabbath Observance: (1884) (Suppression of Sabbath
Desecration) Superintendents: Mrs. Josephine Bateham,
Mrs. Varila F. Cox, Mrs. Kathryn Wert Holler, Mrs.
Susan McWhirter Ostrom, Mrs. Kate C. Heidel, Mrs.
L. E. Hudson, Mrs. Emma L. Starrett.

Scientific Temperance Instruction: (1874) Teaching in public schools and Sunday Schools outlined in Plan of Work.
Inaugurated under committee on *Juvenile Work,* Frances
Willard, chairman. (1878) Mrs. S. J. Steele, chairman
of Committee on Colleges, Seminaries and Public Schools.
(1880) Superintendents: Mrs. Mary H. Hunt, Mrs. Edith

Smith Davis, Mrs. Elizabeth O. Middleton, Miss Cora Frances Stoddard.

School Savings Banks: (1891) Superintendent: Mrs. Sara Louise Oberholtzer (1916) transferred to Loyal Temperance Legion Branch.

Social Meetings and Red Letter Days: (1880) Drawing Room Meetings) Superintendents: Mrs. Mary C. Johnson, Mrs. Margaret Bottome, Mrs. Harriet B. Kells, Mrs. Anna M. Hammer, Mrs. Mary D. Tomlinson. (1900) Department changed to *Social Meetings and Red Letter Days.* Mrs. Mary D. Tomlinson.

Sunday School: (1874) Committee: Chairman, Mrs. E. J. Hackett, Miss Lucia E. F. Kimball. (1880) Superintendents: Miss Lucia E. F. Kimball, Mrs. Julia Bidwell, Mrs. Stella B. Irvine.

Temperance and Labor: (1881) Superintendents: Mrs. M. C. Nobles, Mrs. W. S. Woods, Mrs. C. S. Jackson, Mrs. Augusta Cooper, Mrs. Anna Sneed Cairns, Mrs. S. E. V. Emery, Mrs. Mary G. Stuckenberg, Mrs. Mae M. Whitman, Mrs. Lucia H. F. Additon. (1921—Department changed to *Women in Industry*) Mrs. Laura Parks Miller.

Temperance and Missions: (1907) Superintendents: Miss Ella Gilbert Ives, Dr. Louise C. Purington, Mrs. Caroline McDowell.

The Bible in the Public Schools: (1911) Superintendents: Mrs. Jean B. Wylie, Mrs. Lettie Hill May.

Work Among Colored People: (1880) Sub-divisions. (1881) Superintendents: Mrs. Jane M. Kinney, Mrs. Frances E. Harper, Mrs. J. E. Ray, Mrs. Lucy Thurman, Mrs. E. E. Peterson, Mrs. Marvin Williams.

Work Among Foreigners: (1880) Superintendent: Miss Sarah P. Morrison. (1881) Different divisions of the department headed by Mrs. Henrietta Skelton, Mrs. Mary Stapler, Mrs. R. A. Hull, Miss Saugstad, Mrs. Jane M. Kinney. (1883-1899) Mrs. Sophie F. Grubb, Mrs. Anna J. Darley, Mrs. Cornelia B. Forbes, Mrs. Mary B. Wilson, Mrs. Ella B. Black. (1918—Department of American-

ization) Mrs. Katharine Lent Stevenson, Mrs. Mary
Clark Barnes, Mrs. Culla J. Vayhinger.

Work Among Indians: (1884) Superintendents: Mrs. H. C.
McCabe, Mrs. Dorothy J. Cleveland, Mrs. Dorcas J.
Spencer. (1916) Transferred to Christian Citizenship
Department.

Work Among Lumbermen and Miners: (1883) Superintend-
ents: Mrs. R. G. Peters, Mrs. Emma Obenauer, Mrs.
Mary C. Upham, Mrs. Winnie F. English, Mrs. Emma
Shores, Mrs. W. A. Loyne, Mrs. Mary E. Kuhl, Mrs.
Anna A. Walker. (1916) Transferred to Christian Cit-
izenship department.

Work Among Railroad Employes: (1881) Superintendents:
Miss Jennie Smith, Mrs. Caroline M. Woodward, Mrs.
Evalyn N. Graham. Railroad Evangelist, Miss Jennie
Smith. (1916) Transferred to Christian Citizenship
Department.

Work Among Soldiers and Sailors: (1881) Superintendents:
Mrs. Sarah A. McClees, Mrs. Ella Hoover Thacher, Mrs.
Richmond Pearson Hobson, Mrs. Louise F. Chez, Miss
Rebecca Naomi Rhoads.

Young Women's Unions: (1877) Committees: Miss Jennie
F. Duty, Mrs. Frances W. Leiter, Miss Fanny McCart-
ney. (1879) Superintendents: Mrs. Frances J. Barnes.
(1883) Name changed to Young Woman's Temperance
Work. (1890) Name changed to Young Woman's Work.
(1892) Name changed to Young Woman's Branch, Gen-
eral Secretary, Mrs. Frances J. Barnes, Mrs. Ella A.
Boole, Miss Clara Parrish, Mrs. Cora E. Seberry, Miss
Rhena E. G. Mosher. (1910) Name changed to Young
People's Branch, Mrs. Ross Hayes Schachner, Mrs. Mary
Anderson Crawford, Mrs. Maude B. Perkins.

> High points of second decade: Progress in educa-
> tional lines in the public schools and in the Sunday
> Schools. Increase in membership resulting from
> larger number of organizers, lecturers and state presi-

dents in the field. An intersphering with white ribbon leaders of other lands.

Third Decade: 1894-1904

1895 National W. C. T. U. opened headquarters at Washington, D. C. Mrs. Margaret Dye Ellis appointed resident National Legislative representative.

1896 Great relief measures for American refugees, instituted by Frances E. Willard and Lady Henry Somerset; generously responded to by many states.

1896 Twenty organizers and eight lecturers listed under the department of Organization.

1897 World's W. C. T. U. convention held in Toronto, Canada; followed by National W. C. T. U. convention in Buffalo, New York—the last convention over which Frances Willard presided. Distinguished foreign guests present.

1898 Passing onward of Frances E. Willard, February 17. Mrs. Lillian M. N. Stevens assumed presidential duties.

1898 Lillian M. N. Stevens elected president at National W. C. T. U. convention, at St. Paul, Minnesota.

1898 Frances E. Willard Memorial Fund established for the purpose of organizing and extending National W. C. T. U. activities.

1899 Silver Anniversary convention of National W. C. T. U. held in Seattle, Washington.

1899 Hon. John D. Long, Secretary of Navy, issued orders prohibiting the use by enlisted men of alcoholic liquors.

1900 Removal of National W. C. T. U. Headquarters from Chicago to Evanston.

1900 National W. C. T. U. convention held in Washington, D. C. Large influence on pending bills in Congress exerted at hearings by W. C. T. U. leaders. Sentiment made for the Anti-Canteen bill.

1901 Anti-Canteen bill passed by Congress .

1901   National W. C. T. U. Educational Exhibit at Buffalo, New York, Exposition.

1902   National W. C. T. U. Exhibit at Charleston, South Carolina, Exposition.

1903   Agitation by National W. C. T. U. for an Anti-Polygamy amendment to the Constitution of the United States. Gain of 7,000 in membership.

1903   Bill passed by Congress prohibiting the sale of liquor in the two Capitol Building restaurants.

1903   Large number of delegates attended the World's W. C. T. U. convention held in Geneva, Switzerland.

1903   *The Union Signal* and *Young Crusader* owned by National W. C. T. U.; edited and published at National W. C. T. U. Headquarters.

High points of third decade: Marked increase in influence on Congress. W. C. T. U. a large factor in passage of important bills. Plans and programs for the enlistment of children and youth. Growth of international spirit.

Fourth Decade: 1904-1914

1904   National W. C. T. U. exhibit at St. Louis Exposition received medal.

1905   Statue of Frances E. Willard unveiled in Statuary Hall, in Capitol, Washington, D. C. Appropriate ceremonies held in Senate and House, by Congress.

1905   National W. C. T. U. Exhibit, at Portland, Oregon, received prize medal.

1906   World's W. C. T. U. convention held in Boston, Massachusetts.

1906   At National W. C. T. U. convention, treasurer reported 13,000 new members.

1909   Estimated by national president, Mrs. Stevens, that one-half the people live in saloonless territory. Great National Prohibition program broadcasted.

1910   World's W. C. T. U. Convention held in Glasgow, Scotland.

1910 National W. C. T. U. Literature Building erected in Evanston, Illinois.

1911 W. C. T. U. delegates appointed by government to attend Anti-Alcoholic Congress at The Hague, Holland.

1911 Resubmission campaign in Maine. Prohibition retained in state constitution.

1911 Proclamation by Mrs. Lillian M. N. Stevens for National Constitutional Prohibition.

1911 Bill for National Constitutional Prohibition introduced into Congress by Captain Richmond Pearson Hobson.

1913. World's W. C. T. U. convention held in Brooklyn, New York, followed by National W. C. T. U. convention at Asbury Park, New Jersey.

High points of the fourth decade: Increase in membership; progress in department work; the sending out of twelve white-ribbon missionaries; and the larger financial returns received from life and memorial memberships in the World's W. C. T. U.

Fifth Decade: 1914-1924

1914 Passing of Lillian M. N. Stevens on April 6. Anna A. Gordon assumed duties of president.

1914 Anna A. Gordon elected president National W. C. T. U., at convention held in Atlanta, Georgia.

1914 Lillian Stevens Legislative Fund established.

1914 Definite plans and programs for a campaign for National Constitutional Prohibition adopted.

1914 Huge W. C. T. U. petition for National Constitutional Prohibition, presented to Congress. Large petition for National Constitutional Prohibition, representing Sunday School scholars of all grades, sent by the national Sunday School superintendent, Mrs. Stella B. Irvine, to Congress.

1915 Grand gold medal awarded National W. C. T. U. for its exhibit at Panama-Pacific Exposition, in San Francisco.

1915   National president at Seattle convention proposed appointment of committee to inaugurate plans for a suitable celebration of the fiftieth anniversary of the National W. C. T. U. in 1924.

1916   State and Interstate conferences held. Anti-Alcohol exhibits featured.

1917   Organization of the National W. C. T. U. War Work Committee. National W. C. T. U. at the front in expenditure and activities for the safeguarding, comfort and mothering of soldiers and sailors. Three thousand French war orphans adopted. National W. C. T. U. superintendent received medal from French government—for distinguished service.

1917   Hon. Josephus Daniels, Secretary of the Navy, issued orders prohibiting the use of alcoholic liquors by officers of the navy.

1917   September 8, Prohibition in the District of Columbia went into effect. National and District W. C. T. U. led in the campaigns that secured this victory.

1917   Anti-Advertising and Bone Dry law passed the Congress. For years the National W. C. T. U. worked for this law.

1917   Congress prohibited the use of foods for malt and vinous liquors.

1917   Submission to the states of the Eighteenth Amendment. Leaders of the W. C. T. U. were present December 17, 1917, in the House of Representatives, when the resolution providing for National Constitutional Prohibition passed by a more than two-thirds majority—the vote being 282 for and 126 against. The Senate concurred.

1918   War Prohibition Act passed. Became effective July 1, 1919.

1918   Mrs. Margaret Dye Ellis having resigned after twenty-four years of service, Mrs. Lenna Lowe Yost was elected National W. C. T. U. Legislative representative. At the headquarters in Washington,

D. C., there are filing cabinets containing cards on which, by Congressional Districts, the name of each W. C. T. U. member is enrolled.

1918 W. C. T. U. memorial to the President, asking for food conservation, prohibiting the use of foodstuffs in the manufacture of alcoholic liquors, signed by 6,000,000 women, including other women's organizations; assembled by National W. C. T. U. Legislative representative.

1918 November 11, World War Armistice. Third proclamation for world prohibition issued.

1918 National W. C. T. U. maintained resident hospital mothers in reconstruction hospitals. Generous gifts for the wounded boys and the National W. C. T. U. hospital reception room received from state and local unions.

1918 (In chapter on Patriotism and War Prohibition, see summary of war activities and war funds.)

1919 January 16, the thirty-sixth state ratified the bill for National Constitutional Prohibition.

1919 January 29, proclamation declaring the ratification of the Prohibition Amendment to the Federal Constitution. The pen first used in signing the proclamation presented by Acting Secretary Polk to the president of the National W. C. T. U.

1919 Plan of national president for five-year intensive campaign in preparation for the celebration of Jubilee year, 1924, adopted at St. Louis convention.

1920 January 16, National Prohibition became operative. Lillian Stevens Legislative Fund Day created.

1920 The Congress proclaimed adoption of the Nineteenth Amendment to the Constitution of the United States, giving the ballot to women.

1920 W. C. T. U. department of Franchise merged into Christian Citizenship.

1920 First World's W. C. T. U. convention following war held in London in April. At the close of the convention the National W. C. T. U. president, Anna A. Gordon, commissioned by the National W. C. T. U., accompanied by Miss Julia F. Deane, editor *The Union Signal*, made a European survey for the establishment of work already organized, and the extension in other lands of the W. C. T. U.

1921 National W. C. T. U. sent out a proclamation to women of America, inviting every woman to join and co-operate in the broad-gauged program of the W. C. T. U.

1921 Series of regional conferences held in ten cities: New York, Pittsburg, Chattanooga, Chicago, Omaha, Boise, Seattle, Los Angeles, Denver, Kansas City (Missouri).

1921 National W. C. T. U. president, accompanied by Miss Julia F. Deane, made W. C. T. U. survey in South America.

1921 Conference for Disarmament held in Washington, D. C. Madame Yajima of Japan presented by the president of the National W. C. T. U. to President Harding at the White House. Madame Yajima brought a Peace Petition signed by thousands of Japanese women.

1921-1922 National W. C. T. U. Publishing House greatly enlarged, furnishing well-equipped, commodious headquarters for the administrative, editorial, literature and business offices of the National W. C. T. U.

1922 National W. C. T. U. president made survey of work in Mexico, and strengthened existing organizations.

1922 World's and National W. C. T. U. convention held in Philadelphia, Pennsylvania. Co-operation with church and allied temperance forces for the enforcement of the Volstead Code, and allegiance to the Constitution.

1923 Co-operation with governmental and other great associations.

1923 In Columbus, Ohio, at national convention, Jubilee celebration of Woman's Crusade. Motto: Allegiance to the Constitution.

1923 Jubilee celebration of Woman's Crusade. Motto: Allegiance to the Constitution.

1923 Anniversary celebration at Cleveland, Ohio, under National W. C. T. U. auspices, of November 18, 1874, date of organization of National W. C. T. U.

1924 Large increase in membership and Jubilee Fund.

1924 National W. C. T. U. held Jubilee celebrations in fifty cities; states held similar victorious demonstrations.

1924 National W. C. T. U. held celebration December 23, at Hillsboro, Ohio, in honor of Crusaders.

1924 National W. C. T. U. Day at Chautauqua, New York, August 16; Jubilee anniversary celebrated in Amphitheater.

1924 Jubilee convention held in Chicago, Illinois. Large reception held at National W. C. T. U. Headquarters in Evanston, Ill.

High points of fifth decade: National W. C. T. U. War Work Committee organized. W. C. T. U. exerted great influence for prohibition, patriotism and peace, and protection and benefit of soldiers and sailors.

Victory for National Prohibition by the enactment of the Eighteenth Amendment to the Federal Constitution. Passage of the Nineteenth Amendment giving women the ballot.

Jubilee celebrations of Crusade in Hillsboro, Cleveland and Columbus, and a large number of Jubilee historic W. C. T. U. celebrations by National W. C. T. U. and state unions. Jubilee convention in Chicago and Jubilee reception at National W. C. T. U. Headquarters in Evanston, Illinois.

NATIONAL W. C. T. U. GENERAL OFFICERS
(1874-1924)

The following notable list of National W. C. T. U. General Officers is of historic interest:

President: Annie Wittenmyer, 1874-1879; Frances E. Willard, 1879-1898; Lillian M. N. Stevens, 1898-1914; Anna A. Gordon, 1914—.

Vice-President: Lillian M. N. Stevens, 1895-1898; Anna A. Gordon, 1898-1914; Ella A. Boole, 1914—.

Corresponding Secretaries: Frances E. Willard, 1874-1877; Mary T. Burt, 1877-1880; Caroline B. Buell, 1880-1894; Mary A. Woodbridge, 1894-1895; Katharine Lent Stevenson, 1895-1898; Susanna M. D. Fry, 1898-1908; Frances P. Parks, 1908—.

Assistant Corresponding Secretaries: Sarah K. Bolton, 1876-1877; Louise S. Rounds, 1877-1878.

Recording Secretaries: Mary C. Johnson, 1874-1878; Mary A. Woodbridge, 1878-1894; Clara C. Hoffman, 1894-1907; Elizabeth Preston Anderson, 1907—.

Assistant Recording Secretaries: Mary T. Burt, 1875-1877; Mary A. Woodbridge, 1877-1878; Caroline B. Buell, 1878-1880; Lillian M. N. Stevens, 1882-1895; Frances E. Beauchamp, 1895-1905; Elizabeth Preston Anderson, 1905-1907; Sara H. Hoge, 1907—.

Treasurers: Mary B. Ingham, 1874-1875; Abbie F. Leavitt, 1875-1878; Esther Pugh, 1878-1894; Helen M. Barker, 1894-1905; Harriet W. Brand, 1905-1909; Elizabeth P. Hutchinson, 1908-1915; Margaret C. Munns, 1915—.

STATE W. C. T. U. PRESIDENTS
(1924)

The State Presidents are ex-officio vice-presidents of the National W. C. T. U. A list of those in office in 1924, follows: Alabama, Mrs. Mary T. Jeffries; Alaska, Mrs. Cornelia T. Hatcher; Arizona, Mrs. Leora L. Brewer; Arkansas, Mrs. Minnie U. Rutherford-Fuller; California (North), Mrs. Addie Garwood Estes; California (South),

310

Mrs. Eva C. Wheeler; Colorado, Mrs. Adrianna Hunger-
ford; Connecticut, Mrs. Mary B. Wilson; Delaware, Mrs.
Georgia G. Pierce; District of Columbia, Mrs. Emma San-
ford Shelton; District of Columbia, No. 2, Mrs. Alma J.
Scott; Florida, Miss Minnie E. Neal; Georgia, Mrs. Lella
A. Dillard; Idaho (North), Mrs. Jennie Cross; Idaho
(South), Dr. Emma F. A. Drake; Illinois, Miss Helen L.
Hood; Indiana, Mrs. Elizabeth T. Stanley; Iowa, Mrs.
Ida B. Wise Smith; Kansas, Mrs. Lillian M. Mitchner;
Kentucky, Mrs. J. H. Spilman; Louisiana, Mrs. Alice C.
McKinney; Maine, Mrs. Althea G. Quimby; Maryland,
Mrs. Mary R. Haslup; Maryland, No. 2, Mrs. Margaret
Peck Hill; Massachusetts, Mrs. Alice G. Ropes; Michigan,
Mrs. E. L. Calkins; Minnesota, Mrs. Josephine E. Sizer;
Mississippi, Mrs. W. E. Sigler, Missouri, Mrs. Nelle G.
Burger; Montana, Mrs. W. C. Dawes; Nebraska, Mrs. Lela
G. Dyar; Nevada, Mrs. Maude C. Edwards; New Hamp-
shire, Mrs. Charline M. Abbott; New Jersey, Mrs. Eva E.
Gebhardt; New Mexico, Mrs. Anna W. Strumquist; New
York, Mrs. Ella A. Boole; North Carolina, Mrs. T. Adelaide
Goodno; North Dakota, Mrs. Elizabeth Preston Anderson;
Ohio, Mrs. Florence D. Richard; Oklahoma, Mrs. Josephine
M. Buhl; Oregon, Mrs. Mary L. Mallett; Pennsylvania,
Mrs. Ella M. George; Philippines, National W. C. T. U.
representative, Miss Marguerite Hewson; Porto Rico, Mrs.
Edith Irvine Rivera; Rhode Island, Mrs. Ethelyn H. Rob-
erts; South Carolina, Mrs. Joseph Sprott; South Caro-
lina, No. 2, Mrs. L. A. J. Moorer; South Dakota, Mrs. Flora
A. Mitchell; Tennessee, Mrs. Minnie Allison Welch; Texas,
Mrs. Claude De Van Watts; Utah, Mrs. D. W. Jenkins;
Vermont, Mrs. Elsie Pease Barney; Virginia, Mrs. Sara
H. Hoge; Washington (East), Miss Edith G. Whiting;
Washington (West), Mrs. Lillian M. Vincent; West Vir-
ginia, Mrs. Olive C. Barnes; Wisconsin, Mrs. Annie W.
Warren; Wyoming, Rev. Minnie Fenwick.

W. C. T. U. TERRITORIAL SERVICE

In the new territorial possessions of the United States, W. C. T. U. women have done valiant service. Their names are well known. For many years Mrs. Cornelia Templeton Hatcher has been the president and strong staff of the Alaska territorial union. In the Philippines, the National W. C. T. U. representative is Miss Marguerite Hewson. Miss Consuela Valdez is the youthful W. C. T. U. organizer. Porto Rico is well officered. The president is Mrs. Edith Irvine Rivera. Mrs. Abbie B. Hillerman has made the W. C. T. U. well known in the Canal Zone. Mrs. Mary S Whitney's gracious hospitality to early World's W. C. T. U. travelers, as they journeyed by way of Honolulu, commands the sincere gratitude of the World's and National W. C. T. U. membership. For many years Mrs. Whitney was president of the Hawaii W. C. T. U. when it was an auxiliary of the world's union. In later years she has been an active promoter of the temperance cause in these beautiful islands of the Pacific.

EDITORS OF STATE PAPERS

Inestimable help has been rendered through the state W. C. T. U. official papers. The list of editors (1924) is as follows: Mrs. M. W. Alderson (Montana), Mrs. Olive C. Barnes (West Virginia), Mrs. Leora L. Brewer (Arizona), Mrs. Nelle G. Burger (Missouri), Mrs. August Burghard (Georgia), Mrs. Effie B. Clement (Virginia), Mrs. Elizabeth D. Collins (Tennessee), Mrs. Mary M. Coman (California S.), Mrs. E. B. Dickenson (New Jersey), Mrs. Maria J. Earle (Rhode Island), Mrs. Minnie Fenwick (Wyoming), Miss Edith P. Flanders (New Hampshire), Mrs. Ada B. Frisbee (Massachusetts), Mrs. Ida S. Gage (Washington East), Mrs. Alice R. Gossage (South Dakota), Miss A. V. Grosh (Pennsylvania), Mrs. Emma W. Grover (Kansas), Miss Rozette Hendrix (Minnesota), Mrs. Claudia Hightower (Texas), Miss Helen L. Hood (Illinois), Mrs. Adrianna Hungerford (Colorado), Mrs.

D. J. Huse (Vermont), Miss Julia Hutchinson (Wisconsin), Mrs. Mary Jeffries (Alabama), Mrs. Gertrude Stevens Leavitt (Maine), Mrs. Mary L. Mallett (Oregon), Miss Mary Helen McLean (California North), Mrs. Luella F. McWhirter (Indiana), Miss Rebecca T. Miller (Maryland), Mrs. J. L. Mims (South Carolina), Mrs. Norma F. Mudge (Michigan), Mrs. W. L. Nicholson (North Carolina), Mrs. Mabel Perkins-Dean (Florida), Mrs. Ludie Day Pickett (Kentucky), Mrs. Jennie Carr Pittman (Arkansas), Mrs. R. M. Pollock (North Dakota), Miss Margaret Sloat (New York), Mrs. Mary Isabella Smith (Iowa), Mrs. Mae Thompson (Oklahoma), Miss Consuelo Valdez (Philippines), Mrs. Lucy E. Van Kirk (Ohio), Mrs. Harriet Vance (Nebraska), Mrs. Lillian M. Vincent (Washington West), Mrs. Mary E. Welles (Connecticut).

MEMBERS EMERITUS OF THE NATIONAL W. C. T. U.

Mrs. A. S. Benjamin, Michigan; Mrs. Caroline B. Buell, Connecticut; Mrs. Helen L. Bullock, New York; Mrs. Margaret Dye Ellis, New Jersey; Mrs. Maude L. Greene, New Mexico; Mrs. Elizabeth M. Haughton, Texas; Mrs. Mary F. Lovell, Pennsylvania; Rev. Eugenia St. John Mann, California; Mrs. M. W. Newton, Virginia; Mrs. S. L. Oberholtzer, Pennsylvania; Mrs. Helen G. Rice, California; Miss Annie Robbins, Florida; Miss May Russell, Mississippi; Mrs. Anna R. Simmons, South Dakota; Miss Jennie E. Smith, District of Columbia; Mrs. Lurenda B. Smith, Kansas; Mrs. Marcia A. B. Smith, Wisconsin; Mrs. Dorcas J. Spencer, California; Mrs. Ella Hoover Thacher, New Jersey; Mrs. Mary D. Tomlinson, New Jersey; Mrs. Sena Hartzell Wallace, Kansas; Mrs. Mary J. Weaver, New York; Rev. Emily C. Woodruff, New York; Mrs. Mae Laverell Woods, Missouri.

ORGANIZERS AND FIELD WORKERS
(1874-1924)
(Alphabetically Arranged)

During four decades not only elected organizers and lecturers, national and state, awakened public sentiment against the use of alcoholic liquor, but many other W. C. T. U. officials, including the state presidents, were much of the time in the field. On Sundays, in union church services, they reached hundreds of thousands of people. The following partial list of state presidents, organizers, lecturers and evangelists, while gathered from incomplete records, forms an Honor Roll of which the Woman's Christian Temperance Union is justly proud:

Mrs. S. C. Acheson, Mrs. McVean Adams, Miss Emma Alexander, Mrs. M. J. Aldrich, Dr. Mary Wood Allen, Mrs. J. B. Ammerman, Mrs. Anna Angier, Miss Lucy E. Anthony, Mrs Mary Harris Armor, Mrs. Florence E. Atkins, Mrs. Mary A. Babcock, Mrs. Nelly H. Bailey, Mrs. L. E. Bailey, Mrs. Ruth Baker, Mrs. M. E. Balch, Mrs. Summerfield Baldwin, Madame Layyah Barakat, Miss Mary E. Barbour, Rev. Alice S. N. Barnes, Mrs. Carrie Barr, Mrs. W. D. Barnett, Mrs. Josephine C. Bateham, Mrs. Marion B. Baxter, Mrs. Daisy E. Beaty, Mrs. L. M. Beck, Mrs. H. E. Beckley, Mrs. Helen Coffin Beedy, Mrs. Anna S. Benjamin, Miss Margaret Bilz, Mrs. Sarah H. Black, Miss Alice Stone Blackwell, Mrs. Suessa Blaine, Mrs. Ellen A. Dayton Blair, Mrs. Lucy S. Blanchard, Mrs. E. F. Blanks, Miss Mary A. Blood, Mrs. E. C. Bodwell, Rev. Edith Hill Booker, Mrs. Sarah Knowles Bolton, Rev. May J. Borden, Mrs. Emma Bourne, Mrs. A. S. Bowen, Miss Rose Bower, Mrs. Elizabeth Boynton, Mrs. John C. Brady, Miss Marie C. Brehm, Miss Ella Broomell, Mrs. Alice C. Brown, Mrs. Ella W. Brown, Mrs. Henrietta Brown, Mrs. Sterling N. Brown, Mrs. Sue Uhl Brown, Mrs. Wilhelmina Brown, Mrs. Caroline B. Buell, Mrs. A. B. Buckley, Mrs. Helen L. Bullock, Mrs. Emily U. Burgess, Miss C. S. Burnett, Mrs. E. S. Burlingame, Mrs. Mary T. Burt, Miss Anna Buswell,

Mrs. N. P. J. Button, Mrs. Minnie Byrd, Mrs. A. A. W. Cadwallader, Mrs. Anna Sneed Cairns, Mrs. E. L. Calkins, Mrs. Vie H. Campbell, Mrs. L. D. Carhart, Mrs. Adelia E. Carman, Mrs. Carrie Lee Carter, Mrs. Emma Cash, Miss Caroline Caswell, Mrs. Emma E. Caulk, Mrs. Fannie D. B. Chase, Mrs. Lydia M. Chase, Mrs. Rebecca B. Chambers, Mrs. Sallie F. Chapin, Mrs. Rose Wood Allen Chapman, Mrs Nettie R. Chipp, Mrs. Fannie L. Chunn, Mrs. Abbie F. B. Church, Mrs. Annie W. Clark, Mrs. Fannie Clark, Mrs. Dorothy J. Cleveland, Miss Ida Clothier, Dr. Eliza Cook, Mrs. E. M. J. Cooley, Mrs. Mary E. Cartland, Mrs. Della C. H. Cox, Mrs. Varila Cox, Mrs. Mary Grant Cramer, Mrs. C. E. Craven, Mrs. E. D. Crawford, Mrs. Mary Frances Willard Anderson Crawford, Mrs. Frances Crooks, Mrs. M. L. Cummings, Mrs. Mary H. Curlee, Mrs. Nannie Webb Curtis, Mrs. William E. Currah, Mrs. Annie G. Darley, Mrs. Gratia E. Davidson, Miss Rose A. Davison, Mrs. E. M. J. Decker, Mrs. Ellen K. Denney, Mrs. William Jennings Demorest, Mrs. Lyversa M. De Silva, Mrs. Emma G. Dietrick, Miss Eula Dixon, Miss Cornelia M. Dow, Mrs. Sarah J. Dorr, Mrs. Mildred A. Dorsey, Miss Clara M. Doughty, Miss Anna Downey, Mrs. J. C. Downs, Dr. Emma F. A. Drake, Mrs. Fannie A. Drummond, Mrs. Marion H. Dunham, Mrs. Lucy Van Deventer, Mrs. L. B. Dyer, Mrs. S. J. H. Early, Mrs. Charleton Edholm, Miss Esther H. Elfreth, Mrs. R. A. Emmons, Mrs. E. L. Evans, Mrs. F. S. Evans, Mrs. Emma P. Ewing, Mrs. Carrie C. Faxon, Mrs. Catharine E. Ferguson, Mrs. Susan S. Fessenden, Mrs. Cornelia B. Forbes, Frances H. Ensign Fuller, Mrs. A. A. Garlock, Dr. Carolyn Geisel, Mrs. Annette A. Gibson, Rev. M. Cammack Gibson, Mrs. Lem Gilreath, Dr. Myra A. Gillette, Mrs. Lulu Thomas Gleason, Mrs. M. E. A. Gleason, Mary Read Goodale, Elizabeth H. Goodwin, Elizabeth P. Gordon, Mrs. Evalyn Graham, Frances W. Graham, Mrs. Mattie Graves, Mrs. E. G. Greene, Maude L. Greene, Miss E. W. Greenwood, Mrs. Elizabeth Grice, Miss Frances E. Griffin, Mrs. Hester T. Griffith, Minnie Johnson Grinstead,

Mrs. Caroline F. Grow, Mrs. Sophie F. Grubb, Miss Alice
M. Guernsey, Mrs. Harriet D. Hall, Mrs. Mary Hadley
Hall, Mrs. Anna M. Hammer, Mrs. Cora D. Hammett, Mrs.
Helen D. Harford, Mrs. F. E. W. Harper, Mrs. Laura E.
Harsha, Mrs. Edna Rowan Harvey, Mrs. Mary Haslup,
Mrs. E. M. Haughton, Miss Mollie G. Hay, Mrs. Bettie
Pace Hayes, Mrs. Alice C. Hays, Mrs. J. H. Haynes, Mrs.
A. A. Hawley, Mrs. F. B. Heald, Miss Harriet Henderson,
Miss Rozette Hendrix, Mrs. S. M. I. Henry, Rev. Lida M.
Herrick, Mrs. Nettie P. Hershiser, Mrs. Nina W. Higby,
Mrs. Eva Higgins, Abbie B. Hillerman, Margaret T. Hillis,
Jessie Brown Hilton, Mrs. M. A. Hitchcock, Rev. Alice B.
Hoag, Mrs. H. A. Hobart, Clara C. Hoffman, Mrs. Mary
E. Haggart, Mrs. Susan Holbrook, Mrs. H. E. Hollings-
head, Silena Moore Holman, Miss Louise E. Hollister, Mrs.
Rhena Mosher Holyoke, Miss Helen L. Hood, Mrs. Mary
E. Hopper, Miss Auretta Hoyt, Esther T. Housh, Mrs. Cal-
lie E. Howe, Mrs. Mary Seymour Howell, Mrs. Emma H.
Howland, Mrs. Laura E. Howey, Mrs. George S. Hunt,
Mrs. C. E. Hunt, Mrs. Dora Hull, Mrs. Etta B. Hurford,
Mrs. Allie Updyke Hutchinson, Mrs. Jean McArthur Hyde,
Mrs. E. B. Ingalls, Mrs. Neal B. Inman, Miss Ella G.
Ives, Mrs. Azuba Jones, Miss Emma Jones, Miss Winona
R. Jewell, Mrs. Jane A. Johnson, Mrs. Frances A. Jones,
Mrs. Mary H. Jones, Mrs. R. H. Jones, Mrs. Frances A.
Joseph, Miss Belle Kearney, Mrs. Dr. J. H. Kellogg, Mrs.
Jennie M. Kemp, Mrs. Mary A. Kenney, Mrs. M. L. Ken-
yon, Mrs. Belle C. Kimball, Miss Addie M. Kinnear, Mrs.
Jane M. Kinney, Mrs. Georgia Swift King, Narcissa White
Kinney, Mrs. J. H. Knox, Mrs. E. J. Knowles, Mrs. Ella
Kroft, Rev. Mary E. Kuhl, Mrs. Imogene F. LaChance,
Mrs. Sarah D. LaFetra, Mrs. Isabel Wing Lake, Mrs. Effie
M. Lambert Lawrence, Mrs. E. Norrine Law, Mrs. W. A.
Lawson, Mrs. Caroline A. Leech, Miss Carolyn Leech, Mrs.
Frances W. Leiter, Mrs. Lilah D. Lindsey, Mrs. Nora P.
Linville, Mrs. Mary F. Lovell, Mrs. W. A. Loyne, Mrs.
Lora S. La Mance, Miss Permelia C. Mahan, Rev. Eugenia

F. St. John Mann,, Mrs. Jeannette H. Mann, Miss Elizabeth March, Mrs. Lulu A. Markwell, Mrs. B. Emma Marshall, Miss Mary H. Mather, Mrs. Emilie D. Martin, Mrs. G. W. Martin, Miss Mary C. McClees, Mrs. G. H. McLeod, Mrs. Mabel I. McCrea, Mrs. A. P. McDonald, Mrs. Emily McLaughlin, Mrs. Luella F. McWhirter, Mrs. Amelia Mentz, Mrs. Lide Meriwether, Mrs. Caroline E. Merrick, Mrs. J. C. Mitchell, Mrs. R. Mitchell, Mrs. Sarah Mitchell, Mrs. Henrietta L. Monroe, Mrs. M. L. Montgomery, Miss Alice H. Moore, Miss E. C. Moore, Miss Henrietta G. Moore, Mrs. Lila Carlin Moore, Mrs. Vina D. Moore, Mrs. Cornelia Moots, Rev. Mary L. Moreland, Miss Jessica Morgan, Miss Ellen D. Morris, Mrs. N. R. C. Morrow, Mrs. Amy Kellogg Morse, Mrs. L. S. Mount, Mrs. Nannie Munell, Mrs. Margaret C. Munns, Mrs. K. Ellett Murrow, Mrs. Kate F. Newton, Mrs. M. W. Newton, Miss E. P. Nichols, Mrs. J. R. Nichols, Mrs. L. A. Northrup, Mrs. S. C. Nutter, Mrs. Ora Oakes, Mrs. S. L. Oberholtzer, Mrs. M. J. O'Connell, Miss Lillie O'Daniel, Mrs. J. S. Ogden, Mrs. Otis, Mrs. Annie M. Palmer, Rev. Alice R. Palmer, Miss Emma Page, Miss Mary S. Page, Mrs. Julia R. Parish, Mrs. Frances P. Parks, Mrs. Katharine B. Patterson, Mrs. Matilda E. Patterson, Mrs. T. E. Patterson, Mrs. S. A. Pearson, Mrs. F. T. Pederson, Mrs. B. Sturtevant Peet, Mrs. Sarah M. Perkins, Mrs. E. N. Peters, Mrs. Amanda Peterson, Mrs. E. E. Peterson, Mrs. Margaret B. Platt, Mrs. F. C. Potter, Mrs. Esther T. Pritchard, Miss Esther Pugh, Mrs. E. Elma Pyle, Mrs. Luella A. Ramsey, Mrs. Fannie H. Rastall, Mrs. Eva Ratcliffe, Mrs. Ida H. Read, Miss Lodie E. Reed, Mrs. M. B. Reese, Mrs. Ellen R. Richardson, Mrs. Kate Roach, Miss Annie A. Robbins, Mrs. Viola D. Romans, Mrs. Kara Smart Root, Mrs. Louise S. Rounds, Miss May Russell, Dr. Maude M. Sanders, Mrs. M. A. Schaffer, Mrs. A. A. Scott, Mrs. O. W. Scott, Mrs. Alma J. Scott, Mrs. E. T. Scott, Mrs. Cora E. Seberry, Mrs. Bessie Laythe Scovell, Miss Roena E. Shaner, Rev. Etta S. Shaw, Mrs. Lulu L. Shepard, Mrs. Lilian A. Shepherd, Mrs. Mary F. Shields, Miss Eva M. Shontz, Mrs. S. E. Shorthill, Miss Ethel Austin Shrigley, Rev. Mary Sibbitt, Mrs. Jennie Hart Sibley, Mrs. W. C. Sibley, Mrs. Jackson Silbaugh, Mrs. Anna R. Simmons, Mrs. C. M. Simpson, Mrs. S. Wright Simpson, Mrs. Henrietta Skelton, Miss Cassie Smith, Mrs. Clinton Smith, Mrs. Frances C. Smith, Mrs. I. N. Smith, Miss Jennie E. Smith, Mrs. L. B. Smith, Miss Lois Smith, Mrs. Marcia A. B. Smith, Mrs. K. E. Smithers, Miss M. Madeline Southard, Mrs. Martha L. Spencer, Mrs. Joseph Sprott, Mrs. Ingham Stanton, Mrs. L. Jane Stapler, Mrs. Susan J. Steele, Mrs. Emily Pitt Stevens, Mrs. Kate P. Stewart, Miss Gabrella T. Stickney, Mrs. Helen M. Stoddard, Mrs. Carrie Lee Carter Stokes, Miss Ellen M. Stone, Mrs. Katherine Stone, Mrs. J. C. Stone, Mrs. M. L. Stratford, Mrs. Lella O. Stratton, Mrs. Mary G. Stuckenberg, Mrs. Lucy A. Switzer, Mrs. Mary E. Teats, Mrs. Mary Jewett Telford, Mrs. Ellen L. Tenney, Miss A. Elizabeth Thomas, Mrs. Julia Thomas, Mrs. C. D. H. Thompson, Mrs. Lucy Thurman, Miss Christine I. Tinling, Miss Elizabeth S. Tobey, Mrs. Harriet T. Todd, Mrs. Sue V. Tomlinson, Mrs. Mae G. Tongier, Rev. Frances E. Townsley, Mrs. R. J. Trego, Mrs. Cora L. Trippett, Mrs. Mattie R. Turner, Mrs. Lucie B. Tyng, Mrs. Ada Wallace Unruh, Mrs. Mary C. Upham, Mrs. Ida D. Van Valkenburgh, Miss Mary A. Wadsworth, Mrs. Anna A. Walker, Mrs. H. D. Walker, Miss May C. Walker, Mrs. S. M. Walker, Mrs. Sena Hartzell Wallace, Rev. B. C. H. Washburn, Mrs. Booker T. Washington, Mrs. Lucy H. Washington, Mrs. Kate H. Watrous, Mrs. Mary J. Weaver, Mrs. Martha E. L. Webb, Mrs. S. H. Webb, Mrs. Maria C. Weed, Mrs. Annie K. Weisel, Mrs. M. L. Welles, Mrs. M. J. Wells, Miss C. R. Wendell, Dr. Ellen J. Wetlaufer, Miss Clara Wheeler, Mrs. Dora V. Wheelock, Miss Margaret Whitechurch, Mrs. Mary S. Whitney, Mrs. Kate E. Wilkins, Mrs. Jennie Fowler Willing, Mrs. Eunice P. Wilson, Miss Margaret Wintringer, Mrs. H. B. Wisner, Miss Lillian Wood, Mrs. Mary B. Wood, Rev. Emily C. Woodruff, Mrs. Mae L. Woods, Mrs. Caroline M. Woodward, Mrs. Mary C. Woody, Mrs. Clara Parrish Wright, Mrs. Mary A. Wylie, Miss Elizabeth U. Yates, Mrs. A. C. Zehner, Mrs. Jane Eggleston Zimmerman.

National W. C. T. U. Annual Meetings or Annual Executive Sessions
(1874-1924)

Cleveland, Ohio, 1874; Cincinnati, Ohio, 1875; Newark, New Jersey, 1876; Chicago, Illinois, 1877; Baltimore, Maryland, 1878; Indianapolis, Indiana, 1879; Boston, Massachusetts, 1880; Washington, D. C., 1881; Louisville, Kentucky, 1882; Detroit, Michigan, 1883; St. Louis, Missouri, 1884; Philadelphia, Pennsylvania, 1885; Minneapolis, Minnesota, 1886; Nashville, Tennessee, 1887; New York, New York, 1888; Chicago, Illinois, 1889; Atlanta, Georgia, 1890; Boston, Massachusetts, 1891; Denver, Colorado, 1892; Chicago, Illinois, 1893; Cleveland, Ohio, 1894; Baltimore, Maryland, 1895; St. Louis, Missouri, 1896; Buffalo, New York, 1897; St. Paul, Minnesota, 1898; Seattle, Washington, 1899; Washington, D. C., 1900; Fort Worth, Texas, 1901; Portland, Maine, 1902; Cincinnati, Ohio, 1903; Philadelphia, Pennsylvania, 1904; Los Angeles, California, 1905; Hartford, Connecticut, 1906; Nashville, Tennessee, 1907; Denver, Colorado, 1908; Omaha, Nebraska, 1909; Baltimore, Maryland, 1910; Milwaukee, Wisconsin, 1911; Portland, Oregon, 1912; Asbury Park, New Jersey, 1913; Atlanta, Georgia, 1914; Seattle, Washington, 1915; Indianapolis, Indiana, 1916; Washington, D. C., 1917; Chicago, Illinois, Executive Committee, 1918; St. Louis, Mo., 1919; Washington, D. C., Executive Committee, 1920; San Francisco, California, 1921; Philadelphia, Pennsylvania, 1922; Columbus, Ohio, 1923.

LEGISLATION

In addition to important Congressional legislation noted in this Appendix, all important legislative measures the W.

C. T. U. has aided in securing are found in the chapter, "Legislative Achievements." A detailed list of Congressional enactments from 1901-1924 is a marvelous showing of the rapid growth, during that period, of prohibition sentiment.

HANDBOOK

The National W. C. T. U. issues, each year, a Handbook, which contains a list of officers, department directors and superintendents, and other absolutely essential information.

OUR OFFICIAL ORGANS AND LITERATURE

THE UNION SIGNAL, *The Young Crusader* and a complete supply of books, booklets and leaflets on the many phases of our activities can be obtained at The National W. C. T. U. Publishing House, 1730 Chicago Ave., Evanston, Illinois.

Printed in the United States
41943LVS00003B/115-132